FINISHING and MOUNTING

YOUR

NEEDLEPOINT PIECES

FINISHING and MOUNTING YOUR NEEDLEPOINT PIECES

Katharine Ireys

THOMAS Y. CROWELL COMPANY

New York   Established 1834

BY THE AUTHOR

The Encyclopedia of Canvas Embroidery Stitch Patterns

Finishing and Mounting Your Needlepoint Pieces

PHOTOGRAPHS BY HARRY S. COUGHANOUR

Copyright © 1973 by Katharine Ireys

DESIGNED BY ABIGAIL MOSELEY

Manufactured in the United States of America

ISBN 0-690-00085-5

2 3 4 5 6 7 8 9 10

Library of Congress Cataloging in Publication Data

Ireys, Katharine.
 Finishing and mounting your needlepoint pieces.

 1. Canvas embroidery.   I. Title.
TT778.C3174 1973   746.4'4   73-12154
ISBN 0-690-00085-5

Many of these items, and much of the practical information, I owe to my long-time friend and mentor, Elcy McGrew. I want to thank her for her help and advice.

Contents

Octagonal boxed pillow designed, worked, and mounted by the author, all canvas work.

Hanging designed, worked, and mounted by Marilyn Clark.

Tote bag designed, worked, and mounted by the author.

Director's Chair designed by Sally Schreiber, worked and mounted by Barbara Goodson.

Cylindrical pillow designed, worked, and mounted by Sally Schreiber.

Glasses Case designed, worked, and mounted by the author.

Church banner adapted for canvas embroidery by the author.

Coat of Arms designed, worked, and mounted by the author.

GENERAL DIRECTIONS

Importance of Finishing

Careful finishing is very important. A beautifully embroidered piece can be spoiled by sloppy, unimaginative or inappropriate mounting. The following directions are for home finishing only. Having pieces professionally finished can be costly, and sometimes it is not as carefully done as you might do it yourself. Seams might be sewed on a sewing machine that would look much better sewed by hand.

When a piece of needlework has been professionally finished, it may look fine, but you don't know what is under the surface, what sort of interlining, or other materials have been used, how well it is finished inside where you can't see. You can't tell if the piece can be washed, or even dry cleaned. When you do your own finishing you can select all the extra materials that go into finishing your piece, so you will know how to take care of it. You can add strengthening stitches where you know strain will come, something the professionals probably wouldn't bother to do. You just need to know how to go about it, and this book will tell you.

These directions are very detailed, so even an inexperienced person should be able to follow them.

Handling Canvas

Many people don't realize that canvas can't be handled like other materials. It is stiff and bulky. Because single mesh canvas is so loosely woven, it frays easily. For instance, you can't just sew the canvas to the lining material, right sides together, and then turn them right side out. The canvas will bunch and warp, especially at corners. So it is necessary to hem back the canvas and miter the corners before turning pieces right side out, or finish the edges without turning at all.

You may feel you haven't the patience to work with fine canvas, 14 threads to the inch or finer, but if you do use it you will be glad when you get to the finishing. Fine canvas is so much easier to handle. Not only is the actual needlework less bulky, but the canvas will bend, and fold, and tuck under much more easily. It can be handled almost like a piece of material. Only when your needlework is to receive hard wear, such as in a rug or foot stool, do we recommend the coarser weaves.

Buying Foresight

It is a good idea to buy lining material, ribbons, etc., before selecting the yarn to work the embroidery, because the choice of colors and appropriate materials is limited. This may save you from going from store to store trying to match a color that could be hard to find.

Interlining

After blocking, many pieces seem stiff enough so they don't seem to need interlining, but this stiffness will not last. Handling and use will soon make the canvas soft. So if you want your piece to be stiff, it is best to use an interlining. There are many types of material available. Some are quite stiff, some only moderately so; some are waterproof, some dry clean proof. If the piece you wish to interline will need washing or dry cleaning at intervals, be sure to use material that is washable or can be dry cleaned. There is one type of interlining that can be ironed onto the material. Or you can iron this onto the lining, if you wish. This will stiffen the lining as well as provide your work with the additional body needed. Interlining materials are available in drapery and yard goods departments and stores. The sales people should be able to advise you as to the best type for your purposes.

Lining

Materials for lining should be closely woven and smooth, with enough body to stand wear. Felt can be used for some things, but it is not washable. When you are planning a piece it is a good idea to choose the material for the lining before selecting the yarn because of the limited color choice. A neutral or dark color is practical, as it won't show dirt so soon.

Zippers

Many people want zippers put on practically everything. Zippers are very useful devices, but their use is overdone. If an opening is to be used frequently, the zipper is very convenient, but where an opening is to be used only once in a while, it isn't needed. For instance, a zipper on a piece of embroidery, such as a pillow, is unnecessary. It is bulky, scratchy, hard to install, and far from beautiful. The cover of a pillow is seldom removed, if ever. A seam of hand sewing can be almost invisible, and, if necessary, can be opened with very little effort. Use zippers for slip covers, if you like, but don't mar the appearance of beautiful embroidery with the ubiquitous zipper.

Protection from Soiling

The commercial sprays to protect fabric from soiling can be used on canvas. Be sure all paint or ink is waterproof, however. It is risky to spray work that has been bought in kit form unless you have blocked safely first so you know the paint won't run. If you are not sure what kind of paint was used, spray the yarn surface very lightly, not enough to wet the underlying canvas.

Measuring Tools

You may not realize it but many measuring devices are very inaccurate, particularly the home type cloth tape. Compare yours with a reliable ruler, and you will see. So use steel measuring tapes or rigid rulers.

Blocking

Before starting to work a piece of canvas embroidery, make a note of the outside measurements of the canvas. Also make a paper pattern of the area to be embroidered. The piece of canvas should be rectangular, even if the worked area is another shape. It makes blocking much easier (Figs. 1, 2).

If you have bought a painted piece, test the paint to see if it is waterproof. If it is not waterproof, choose stitch patterns that produce little or no distortion so a minimum of moisture is needed to block it into its original shape.

When you have completed the embroidery, get out the measurements and the paper pattern you made before beginning. Cover a board with a

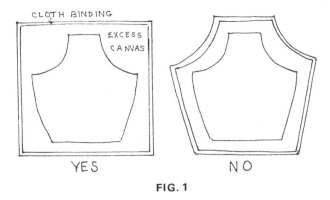

CLOTH BINDING

EXCESS CANVAS

YES   NO

FIG. 1

PAPER PATTERN

FIG. 2

piece of sheet, fastening it securely. Draw a pencil outline of the measurements on the sheet, making sure the corners are square.

Sometimes people buy pieces of canvas with the design painted on. Some of these have been painted by artists of little or no experience with canvas embroidery, and the paint is not waterproof. If you should wet this type of paint, the results would be disastrous. Even though you have used washable yarn, the underlying paint will run through everything, creating an awful mess. So, unless you are sure of your materials, it is best to pull your piece back into shape dry as much as you can, and steam press it.

Steam-pressing method

Using the sheet-covered board with the penciled outline on it, pull and tack the corners in place, face up. Wet a piece of cheesecloth and wring it out. Using a steam iron, if you have one, press and pull the edges straight, starting in the corners, and tacking them along the line. Check the shape of the worked area with the paper pattern as you go along. If the piece is badly out of shape, it may be necessary to pull the edges of the canvas beyond the pencil line in some places or it may be necessary to remove and reset some of the tacks. The shape of the worked area must match the pattern. This is the final check (Figs. 3, 4).

Don't let the full weight of the iron rest on the work or you will crush the stitches flat. The steam will dampen the piece slightly, softening it enough so it can be pulled into shape. There will

probably be peaks along the edges caused by the tacks, but these will be in the excess canvas that is to be cut off or turned under. You can put the tacks in the binding or into the canvas near it. The binding will prevent the canvas threads from being stripped off. Put in as many tacks as necessary to make the edges of the worked area match the

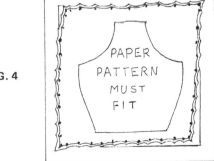

SHEET COVERED BOARD

PENCIL LINE ON SHEET

FIG. 3

PAPER PATTERN MUST FIT

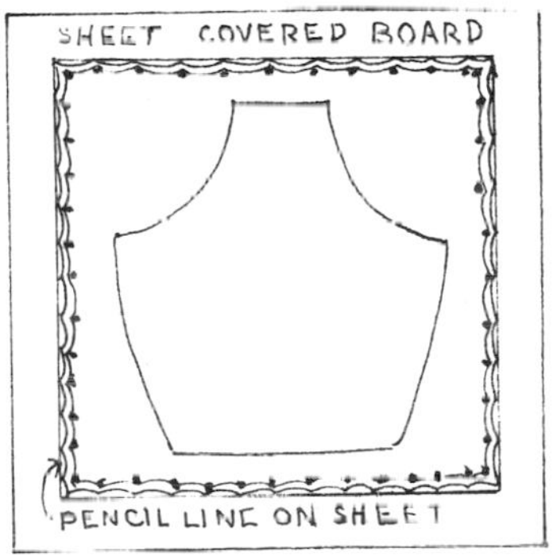

FIG. 4

pattern. Don't drive them in all the way; just far enough to hold firmly. Ordinary tacks will do if the excess canvas is wide enough so that the binding and some of the excess canvas will be cut off when the piece is made up. If there are any rusty marks they will be cut off with the binding. Don't use thumb tacks; they will pop out when the canvas is pulled tight.

Allow the piece to dry thoroughly before removing it for finishing.

Washing method

If you are sure that all materials and paint, if any, are waterproof and colorfast, it is best to wash the piece gently, even though it doesn't seem to be soiled. Wash it as you would any fine wool product. The special detergents for wool will do a good job. Don't rub or squeeze; this would roughen up the stitches. Use tepid water throughout. Press the piece down into the water as flat as possible. Slosh it up and down, pat or pinch any soiled areas. Rinse thoroughly in tepid water. Even if they are colorfast some yarns will have loose dye that may color the wash or rinse water slightly. Repeated rinsing will remove this. Roll the piece in a towel to remove excess moisture; don't wring.

Starting with the corners, tack the piece to the sheet-covered board, making the bound edges conform with the pencil lines. Check the shape of the worked area with your paper pattern as you go along. See "Steam Pressing Method" for further tacking directions.

Be sure to allow the piece to dry thoroughly before removing it from the board for finishing.

Hemming Canvas

On most pieces—coasters, glasses, cases, etc.—you will have to turn the excess canvas under and hem it down as a first step. Use a sewing needle and fairly heavy sewing thread. Make large hemming stitches. Pierce the canvas threads that are perpendicular to the edge, rather than using the holes in the canvas to avoid stripping off the threads

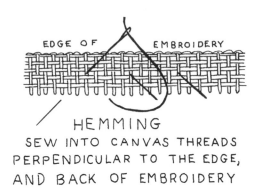

HEMMING
SEW INTO CANVAS THREADS
PERPENDICULAR TO THE EDGE,
AND BACK OF EMBROIDERY

FIG. 5

that are parallel to the edge (Fig. 5). The binding is usually cut off to reduce bulk. If you cut off the binding, do so a little at a time, as you come to it. This will prevent fraying of the canvas while you are handling it.

Mitered Corners

Mitering produces sharp square corners. Cut off the binding, leaving at least ¾ inch. Fold the corner diagonally so you can just see the corner stitch (Fig. 6). It is not necessary to cut off the tip of the corner. As you work the hemming stitches up to the corner, fold first one side of the corner

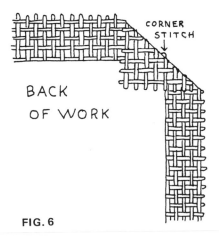

FIG. 6

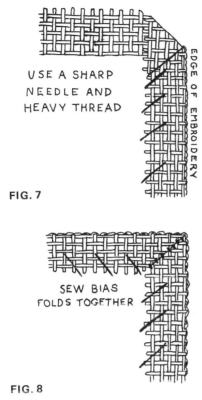

USE A SHARP
NEEDLE AND
HEAVY THREAD

EDGE OF EMBROIDERY

FIG. 7

SEW BIAS
FOLDS TOGETHER

FIG. 8

and then the other (Fig. 7). Sew the 2 bias folds together (Fig. 8). Handle the edges carefully, especially on the folds, to prevent fraying.

Joining Pieces of Canvas

Seaming

The excess canvas left around the edges of two completed and blocked pieces can be turned under, the corners mitered, and the two pieces seamed on the right side with heavy carpet thread if the pieces are large and the canvas coarse. Use finer thread for smaller pieces and fine canvas. You may trim off the binding or leave it on, as you wish.

It would be a natural motion to pass the needle horizontally across under matching threads, and then move down and do it again (Fig. 9). But if you do this, the right side would slide up, evening the angles of the stitches. There are two ways to keep the two sides of the seam in place. You can zigzag along with even angles in the stitches (Fig. 10) or you can take an extra horizontal stitch over the first horizontal stitch (Fig. 11). This method makes a strong seam.

After the seam has been completed with the sewing thread, it can be covered with yarn to match or contrast with the adjacent sides, making it almost invisible (Fig. 12).

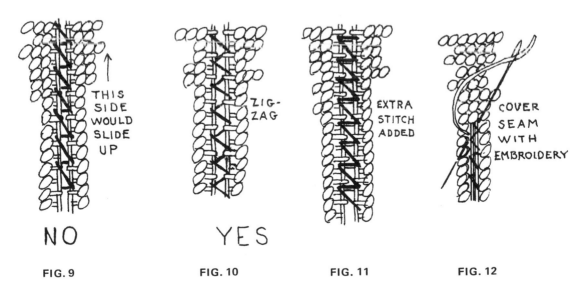

THIS SIDE WOULD SLIDE UP

NO

ZIG-ZAG

YES

EXTRA STITCH ADDED

COVER SEAM WITH EMBROIDERY

FIG. 9   **FIG. 10**   **FIG. 11**   **FIG. 12**

Splicing

A strong and almost invisible joining is achieved by splicing. This must be done as you are working the stitchery when you are within about an inch of the edge to be spliced. Remove all the threads of the excess canvas on one piece that are parallel with the edge up to the line where the stitchery will end. This will leave a fringe (Fig. 13). Lay the fringed piece on top of the second, unworked piece, so areas to be worked are next to each other. Carefully pull each piece of fringed edge through to the back of the second piece, matching thread for thread. Baste the pieces securely together. As you work the stitchery up to the excess canvas of the second piece, which will be under the first, do the stitchery through both pieces. It will be necessary to use a plucking technique; that is, taking the needle through to the back and out to the front again in separate motions. Work across the joint and onto the second piece (Fig. 14). Lastly, cut away the binding of the second piece so a smooth joining is achieved.

There will be a slight difference in appearance over the splice if Tent stitch is used. With other stitch patterns the joint is practically invisible. Certainly this makes the strongest joining possible.

Finishing Canvas on a Curve

Convex

Unless curved edges are very large, as in an oval or round rug, it is best to use fine canvas. It makes finishing them easier. After the piece is blocked, make 2 rows of machine stitching, one on top of the other, around the curve, ¼ inch out from the worked area (Fig. 15). On a rug put the machine stitching 1 inch out. Run a gathering thread through this stitching before trimming off the excess canvas ¾ inch out from the worked area, 2

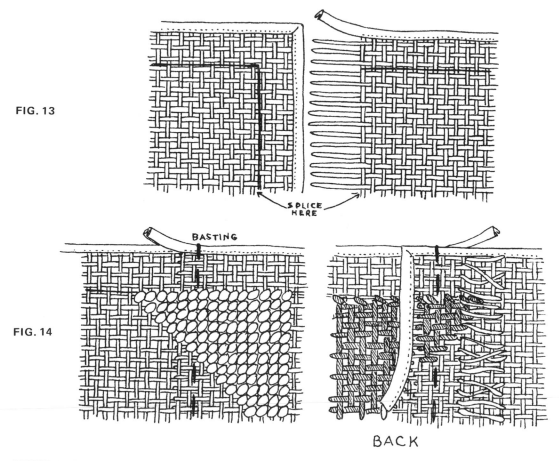

FIG. 13

FIG. 14

BACK

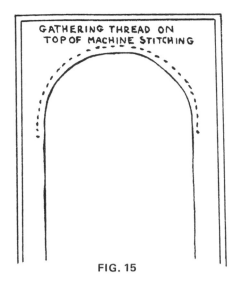

GATHERING THREAD ON
TOP OF MACHINE STITCHING

FIG. 15

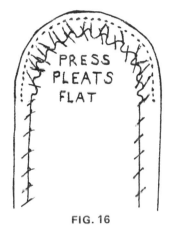

PRESS
PLEATS
FLAT

FIG. 16

stitches (Fig. 17). Slash at intervals through the excess canvas and the facing, up to the stitching. Be careful you don't cut the machine stitching. Turn the facing to the inside, spreading the slashed edges. Lay the piece on a flat surface with the facing flat, the slashed edges spread open, and the canvas bunched up. Handle these slashed edges very carefully so as not to fray the canvas. Baste the slashed seam allowance to the facing in their spread-out position, and stitch about ⅛ inch from the first line of stitching, through the slashed seam allowance, and the facing (Fig. 18). Smooth the canvas down over the facing. The facing should lie flat (Fig. 19). When lining the piece, bring the lining up to the curve, slash a slightly larger curve, and hem the lining to the facing (Fig. 20).

inches on a rug. Draw up the gathering thread until the excess canvas turns in, and the worked area lies flat (Fig. 16). Press the resulting pleats and hem in place, sewing into the back of the stitchery, and the gathering thread, and the line of machine stitching (Fig. 16).

Concave

Use fine canvas if you can. This curve is treated much the same way as it would be treated on any loose weave material. Cut a facing of lining material 2 inches wide, plus ¾ inch seam allowance around the curve. Baste it in place, right sides together. Trim away the excess canvas, leaving ¾ inch along the curve. On the canvas side, stitch on the machine next to the embroidery. Use small

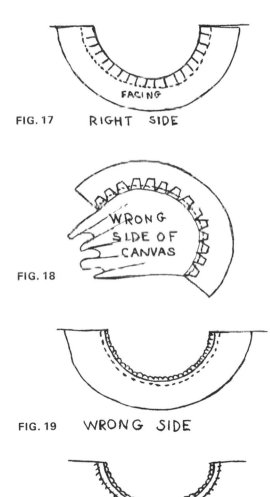

FIG. 17   RIGHT SIDE

FIG. 18

FACING

WRONG SIDE OF CANVAS

FIG. 19   WRONG SIDE

FIG. 20   LINING

HOUSE FURNISHINGS

Mounting Canvas for Framing

There are many ways to frame your work. A visit to a stitchery exhibit will give you some ideas that are new and different. Your work can be covered with glass or left exposed. If it is covered, the glass can be set out a little way, so as not to crush the stitchery. Consult a professional framer for suggestions. Simple frames are best. Many moldings can be used to make rectangular frames at home, using a miter box to cut and fit the corners. Cover the back with cloth or paper.

Rectangular

Before blocking a piece of canvas embroidery that is to be framed, make sure the cloth binding is sewed on securely, especially if the canvas is fairly coarse monocanvas. Use a sewing machine and small stitches. The binding should cover at least 3 canvas threads along all edges, except a selvage, which need not be bound. There should be at least 1 inch of excess canvas around the edges, 1½ inches is even better (Fig. 1).

Block the piece with accurate, square 90° corners (Fig. 1). It should be mounted on a thin rigid piece of board, cut to fit the worked area, ⅛ inch composition board is good. You can use the type with perforations that is sold for inserting hooks to hang things on. A piece of corrugated board can be used if it is very stiff. Be careful you don't crush the corners.

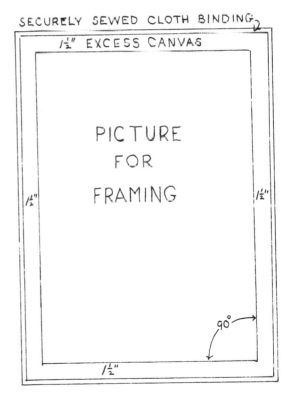

SECURELY SEWED CLOTH BINDING

1½" EXCESS CANVAS

PICTURE FOR FRAMING

1½"

1½"

90°

1½"

FIG. 1

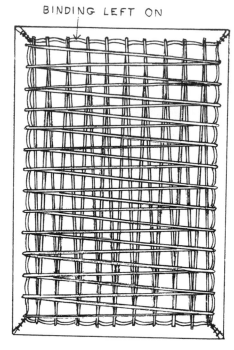

BINDING LEFT ON

FIG. 2

around the inside opening on a piece of paper to use when blocking. Plan the embroidery on a rectangular piece of canvas large enough to allow 1½ inches excess canvas at the top, bottom, and sides (Fig. 3). Fold the paper pattern both ways so as to get accurate centers at the top, bottom, and sides. Line up the folds with the canvas threads, open up the pattern, and trace its outline on the canvas.

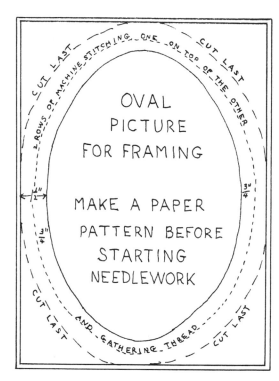

OVAL PICTURE FOR FRAMING

MAKE A PAPER PATTERN BEFORE STARTING NEEDLEWORK

CUT LAST · 2 ROWS OF MACHINE STITCHING ONE ON TOP OF THE OTHER · CUT LAST

CUT LAST · AND · GATHERING · THREAD · CUT LAST

FIG. 3

Leave the binding on the canvas. Fold the excess canvas over onto the back of the board, and lace it tightly with string, going back and forth from end to end, and from side to side (Fig. 2). Thread the long piece of string into a sharp needle. If you need to piece the string, you can knot a new piece onto the old. Sew into the binding, if it is stitched on securely enough, or sew into the canvas next to the binding. The binding will keep the canvas threads from stripping off. Fold the corners as nearly as you can like mitering, and sew the bias folds across the corners. Don't worry if the worked area doesn't extend over the edge of the board. The frame will cover these edges.

Large pieces can be tacked to artist's stretchers, used for painting. They can be obtained at an artist's supply store.

Oval (elliptical)

Unless you are using an oval frame that you already have, buy one before planning the needlework. Ovals vary in proportion. Draw a line

Bind the canvas, work the embroidery, and block, using the paper pattern as a guide. Put 2 rows of machine stitching, one on top of the other, ¾ inch out into the excess canvas. Run a gathering thread through the stitching (Fig. 3). See "General Directions: Finishing Canvas on a Curve."

Cut a piece of ⅛ inch stiff board the size of the pattern. See above for the type of board suggested. Hem a piece of heavy muslin in the shape of the oval, but about 2 inches smaller each way (Fig. 4). Now cut away the binding and the corners of the canvas, leaving at least 1 inch excess canvas all around (Fig. 3). Place the board against

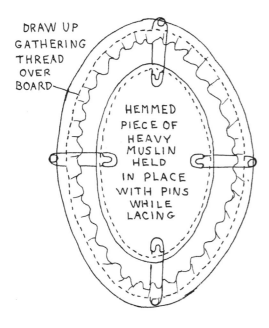

DRAW UP GATHERING THREAD OVER BOARD

HEMMED PIECE OF HEAVY MUSLIN HELD IN PLACE WITH PINS WHILE LACING

FIG. 4

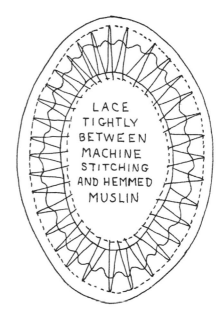

LACE TIGHTLY BETWEEN MACHINE STITCHING AND HEMMED MUSLIN

FIG. 5

the back of the embroidery, and draw up the gathering thread, turning the excess canvas in. Place the piece of muslin in the center, and put large safety pins in at the top, bottom, and sides to hold it in place (Fig. 4). With heavy thread or string sew back and forth between the machine stitching and the hemmed muslin, lacing the two tightly together (Fig. 5).

A circular piece can be mounted the same way.

Coasters and Table Mats

Materials Needed

Piece of canvas to accommodate one or several coasters.
   Be sure to have 1¼ inches excess around the edges.
Heavy aluminum foil to equal the worked area
Outing flannel to equal the worked area
Washable lining material to equal the worked area, plus ½
   inch seam allowance around each piece
Yarn of your choice

Coasters

Square. Coasters are usually made 4 inches square. Prepare a 6 inch square piece of canvas, bind, embroider, and block (Fig. 1). Remove the binding and hem the excess canvas to the back of

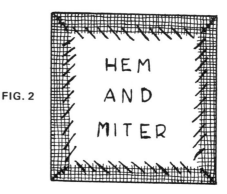

FIG. 2

FIG. 3

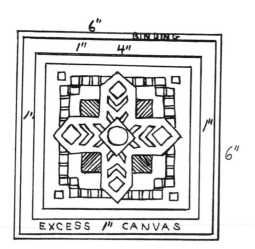

FIG. 1

your stitchery. See hemming and mitering directions, page 4. (Fig. 2.)

Coasters should be waterproof, washable, and pressable, so the best interlining is a piece of aluminum foil. Use the heavy grade, it's a little stiffer. Cut a square that comes up to but does not overlap the turned under canvas (Fig. 3). It will stay in place without any fastening. Next, sew on a piece of outing flannel up to ¼ inch of outside edges (Fig. 4). Don't turn under the edges of the flannel. Now line with something washable, mitering the corners (Fig. 5). The seam can be covered with binding stitch or a fine cord, sewed on invisibly (Fig. 6). Steam press lightly.

trimming off the excess canvas. Run a gathering thread through the machine stitching. Now trim away the binding and the excess canvas, leaving about ¾ inch of canvas. Draw up the gathering thread until the excess canvas turns in, and the worked area lies flat (Fig. 8). Press the resulting pleats before hemming the excess canvas to the back of the stitching. Trim off the corners of the foil so the piece will fit, but don't try to cut a

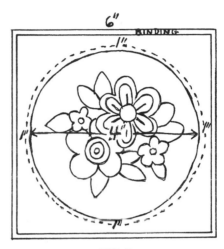

FIG. 4 OUTING FLANNEL

FIG. 5 LINING

FIG. 6

FIG. 7

GATHER, HEM, AND PRESS

FIG. 8

Round. If fine canvas is used, you can make coasters circular. Work with a square 2 inches larger than the circle's diameter (Fig. 7). To turn canvas under in a smooth curve, make 2 rows of machine stitching, one on top of the other, about ¼ inch out from the worked area. Do this before

PIECE OF ALUMINUM FOIL

FIG. 9

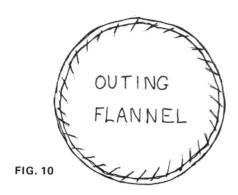

FIG. 10

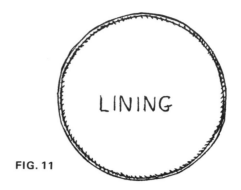

FIG. 11

circular piece (Fig. 9). Use the last 3 steps for square coasters, omitting the mitered corners (Figs. 10, 11, 12).

Table mats

The above directions can be enlarged to any size for table mats. If the waterproof quality is not needed, omit the foil. You can substitute an extra layer of outing flannel if you feel the mat isn't thick enough.

FIG. 12

Napkin Rings

Since we are all digging out our linen napkins to help reduce the amount of paper trash, how about individual napkin rings? They are so simple to make.

Materials needed

A piece of canvas 6½ inches by 2½ inches
A piece of interlining 4¾ inches to 5 inches by ⅞ inch
A piece of lining material 6 inches by 2 inches
Yarn of your choice

Embroider a strip of canvas about 5 inches by 1 inch wide. Allow ¾ inch excess canvas around the edges (Fig. 1). If you plan a design to cover the entire length, try to match it across the seam. Count the number of threads. You may have to add or subtract a few threads to make the design fit perfectly (Fig. 2).

MATCH THE DESIGN ACROSS THE SEAM

FIG. 2

Bind the canvas, work the embroidery, and block. Cut off the binding, and enough excess canvas so the edges will just meet when they are turned in. Hem the canvas, mitering the corners (Fig. 3). Sew on the interlining, and hem the lining all around (Fig. 4). Bring the end together and

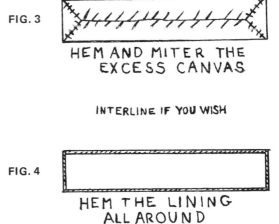

FIG. 3

HEM AND MITER THE EXCESS CANVAS

INTERLINE IF YOU WISH

FIG. 4

HEM THE LINING ALL AROUND

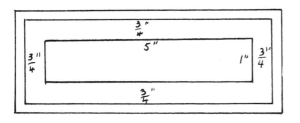

FIG. 1

HEM THE ENDS
TOGETHER INVISIBLY

FIG. 5

hem on the right side as invisibly as possible (Fig. 5). Work a decorative edging along the sides (Fig. 6).

FINISH WITH A
DECORATIVE EDGING

FIG. 6

Pillows

Pillows can be made in many shapes and sizes. The traditional square pillow can be boxed or left plain. Pillows can be round, cylindrical, heart shaped. They can be made with fabric backing and boxing, cording added, or left plain. They can have box-pleated corners, or small pleats can be made around the edge of a round pillow. Both sides can be worked in canvas embroidery, which, by the way, simplifies the finishing process. Also, it is not necessary to find an appropriate backing material.

The following patterns for fifteen styles of pillows will give you a good variety to choose from.

Style A. Rectangular (Square), 1 side canvas

PLAIN-ONE SIDE FABRIC

Materials needed

1 piece of canvas in the desired size and proportions, plus 1¼ inch excess canvas all around (Fig. 1)

1 piece of backing material equal in dimensions to the worked area, plus ¾ inch seam allowance

Muslin enough to make a pillow 1 inch larger each way than the dimensions of the pillow; the muslin form is made larger so as to be sure the pillow is packed firmly

Stuffing, flaked foam rubber, kapok, feathers, down, polyester fiber, etc.

Yarn of your choice

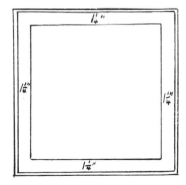

FIG. 1

Bind the canvas, work the embroidery, and block. Prepare the muslin pillow, stuff it quite firm, and close all seams. Right sides together, and backing side up, baste the backing to the canvas on

3 sides, including all 4 corners. Turn over to the canvas side, and machine stitch as close to the embroidery as possible (Fig. 2). Trim off the binding and hem the excess canvas to the back of the embroidery, mitering the corners (Fig. 3). Turn the casing right side out, put in the pillow, and close the opening as invisibly as possible (Fig. 4). Cover the seams with yarn cording, or Binding stitch. Add tassels, if you like.

FIG. 2

FIG. 3

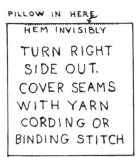

FIG. 4

Style B. Rectangular, 1 side canvas, fabric covered, or commercial cording added

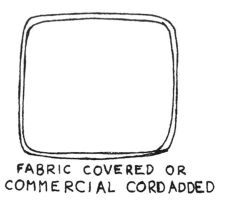

FABRIC COVERED OR COMMERCIAL CORD ADDED

Materials needed

Same as pillow A, plus 1 piece of cording 3 inches longer than the perimeter of the pillow. If you buy commercial cording, get the kind with a flange along one side Fabric cording is made of 2 inch wide bias strips covering white cotton cording made for the purpose. You can get it in a drapery department.

Fold the bias strip over the white cord, and machine stitch close to the cord. Piece the strip on the bias, if necessary. Baste the cording, unfinished, or flanged edge out, to the right side of the edge of the canvas worked area. Overlap the ends at a corner, bringing the ends to the outside. You will have to round the corners slightly. Turn over to the wrong side, and stitch as close to the embroidery as possible (Fig. 5). Turn back to the right side, and baste the backing over the cording on 3 sides, including all 4 corners. Turn over again

FIG. 5

to the canvas side, and stitch exactly on top of your first line of stitching on the 3 sides (Fig. 6). Trim off the binding, and hem the excess canvas, making modified mitered corners as in Figure 3. Turn right side out, insert the previously made pillow, and hem the edge of the backing to the stitching of the cording as invisibly as possible (Fig. 7).

FIG. 6

FIG. 7

Style C. Rectangular, boxed, 1 side canvas, fabric boxing, fabric or commercial cording

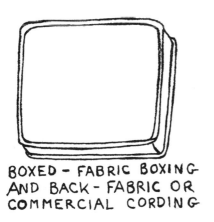

BOXED - FABRIC BOXING
AND BACK - FABRIC OR
COMMERCIAL CORDING

Materials needed

Same as B, plus a second piece of cording, and fabric enough for a boxing 2½ inches wide by the perimeter of the pillow, plus 3 inches

Muslin enough to make a boxed pillow 1 inch wider and longer, and the same depth, 2½ inches

Yarn of your choice

Bind the canvas, work the embroidery, and block. Apply 1 piece of cording as in Figure 5. Allowing about ½ inch seam allowance at the middle of a side, baste the boxing over the cording, wrong side up. Turn over to the wrong side of the canvas, and, starting about 3 inches from the end of the boxing, machine stitch exactly on top of the first line of stitching. Stop about 3 inches from the other end (Fig. 8). Turn back again, and fit the ends of the boxing, and seam them. Baste the last 6 inches in place. Now turn over to the wrong side, and finish sewing the boxing in place

FIG. 8

FIG. 9

(Fig. 9). This is done because it is impossible to measure and seam the boxing exactly for a perfect fit before sewing it to the pillow front. Sew another length of cording to the upper edge of the boxing, overlapping the ends at a different corner (Fig. 10). Baste the backing in place. Machine stitch on 3 sides, including all 4 corners. Stitch on the cording side exactly on top of the stitching of the cording (Fig. 11). Turn right side out, insert the pillow, and hem the opening invisibly (Fig. 12).

FIG. 10

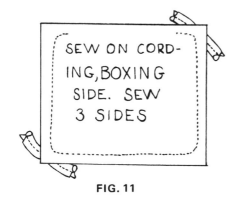

FIG. 11

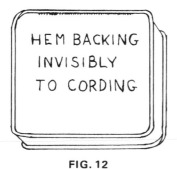

FIG. 12

Style D. Rectangular, Plain, both sides canvas

PLAIN-BOTH SIDES CANVAS

Materials needed

2 pieces of canvas the desired size and proportions, plus 1¼ inch excess canvas all around as in Figure 1
Muslin covered pillow 1 inch larger each way
Yarn of your choice

Bind the canvas, work the embroidery, and block both pieces. Cut off the binding, turn in the excess canvas and hem, mitering the corners (Fig. 13). Place the back and front against the muslin pillow, and hold them together with safety pins. Match the corners carefully (Fig. 14). Sew the

FIG. 13

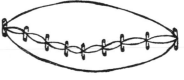

FIG. 14

pieces together with strong thread. Cover the seams with fringe or yarn cording. Tassels can be added. Astrakhan Velvet makes a good fringe. It covers the seams completely (Fig. 15).

END UNFINISHED
CANVAS BOXING EQUAL TO PERIMETER OF PILLOW

FIG. 16

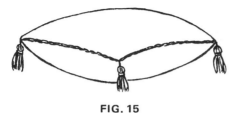

FIG. 15

ADJUST LENGTH OF
BOXING. THEN SEAM

FIG. 17

Style E. Rectangular, both sides and boxing worked in canvas

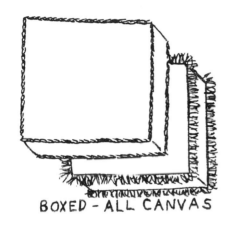

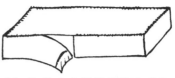

FINISH SEWING
AROUND TOP

FIG. 18

BOXED - ALL CANVAS

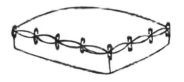

FIG. 19

Materials needed

2 pieces of canvas as in D, plus a strip for the boxing equal to the perimeter of the pillow, plus 3 inches in length, and 1½ inches wider than the desired width
Muslin-covered pillow 1 inch larger and ½ inch deeper
Yarn of your choice

ASTRAKHAN VELVET
FRINGE OVER SEAMS

FIG. 20

Bind the canvas, work the embroidery, and block all 3 pieces. Cut the binding off the front and back, hem and miter (Fig. 13). Cut the binding off the boxing, and hem all but the last 2 inches of the sides. Miter the corners of one end only. Overcast the other end (Fig. 16). Starting with the mitered end, and in the middle of a side, sew the boxing to the pillow front. At the other end you may have to add a few, or rip a few embroidery stitches for a perfect fit. It is impossible to measure the length of the boxing exactly. Adjust the length of the boxing, and hem and

miter the second end (Fig. 17). Seam the boxing and finish, sewing it to the front of the pillow (Fig. 18). Set the pillow down in the casing and "safety pin" the back in place, placing the corners carefully above the corners of the front (Fig. 19). Sew all around with strong thread. Cover the top and bottom seams with fringe or yarn cording (Fig. 20).

Style F. Round, 1 side canvas

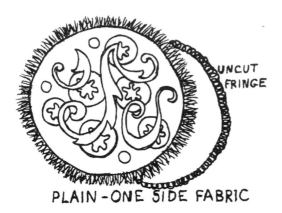

UNCUT FRINGE

PLAIN-ONE SIDE FABRIC

Materials needed

1 square piece of canvas equal to the diameter of the
pillow, plus 1¼ inch excess canvas all around
1 round piece of backing material equal in diameter to the
pillow front, plus ¾ inch seam allowance all around
Muslin-covered pillow 1 inch larger in diameter than the
pillow front
Yarn of your choice

Draw a circle on the canvas, but keep the
piece of canvas square (Fig. 21). Make a paper
pattern like the circle on the canvas. Bind the
canvas, work the embroidery, and block, using the
pattern as a guide.

Put 2 rows of machine stitching, one on top
of the other, about ½ inch out in the excess canvas
all around. Run a gathering thread through the
stitching (Fig. 21). Baste on the backing ¾ of the
way around, right sides together. Machine stitch

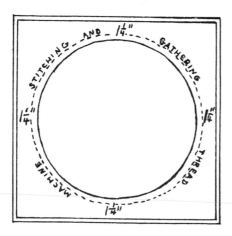

FIG. 21

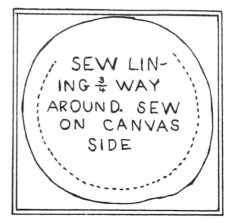

SEW LINING ¾ WAY AROUND. SEW ON CANVAS SIDE

FIG. 22

BACKING

PULL UP GATHERS AND HEM EXCESS CANVAS

FIG. 23

SEW OPENING INVISIBLY COVER SEAM WITH FRINGE OR CORDING

FIG. 24

on the canvas side, sewing as close to the embroidery as possible (Fig. 22). Cut off the binding
and all but 1 inch of the excess canvas. Draw up
the gathering so the excess canvas turns in, and the
edges of the pillow curve up slightly. Hem the
excess canvas in place (Fig. 23). Turn the casing
right side out, insert the muslin pillow, and hem
the opening. Cover the seams with fringe or yarn
cording (Fig. 24).

Style G. Round, 1 side canvas fabric-covered or commercial cording added

PLAIN-FABRIC OR COMMERCIAL CORD ADDED – BUTTON IN CENTER

Materials needed

Same as F, plus fabric covered or commercial cording 3 inches longer than the circumference of the pillow

Bind the canvas, work the embroidery, and block, using the pattern as a guide. See F for machine stitching and gathering thread. Baste the cording to the right side of the canvas, overlapping the ends, and bringing them to the outside. Machine stitch close to the embroidery on the wrong side (Fig. 25). Baste on the backing ¾ of the way around. Stitch on the canvas side on top of the first line of stitching. Cut off the binding and all but 1 inch of the excess canvas. Draw up the

CORDING
BASTE ON
RIGHT SIDE
STITCH ON
WRONG
SIDE

FIG. 25

gathering thread, and hem the excess canvas in place as in Figure 23. Turn right side out, insert the pillow, and invisibly hem the opening. A large fabric button can be set in the middle (Fig. 26).

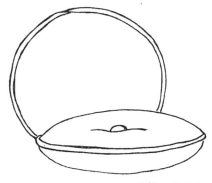

BUTTON IN CENTER

FIG. 26

Style H. Round, both sides canvas

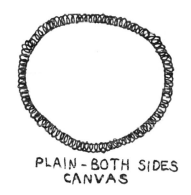

PLAIN-BOTH SIDES CANVAS

Materials needed

2 square pieces of canvas as in F
Muslin-covered pillow as in F
Yarn of your choice

Draw circles on the pieces of canvas, but keep the pieces square. Make a paper pattern (See Fig. 21).

Bind the canvas, work the embroidery, and block, using the pattern as a guide. See F for machine stitching and gathering threads. Cut off the binding and all but 1 inch of the excess canvas.

Draw up the gathering threads, and hem the excess canvas of both pieces (Fig. 27). Place the back and front against the muslin pillow, and hold them together with safety pins (Fig. 28). Sew all around with strong thread. Cover the seam with fringe or yarn cording (Fig. 29).

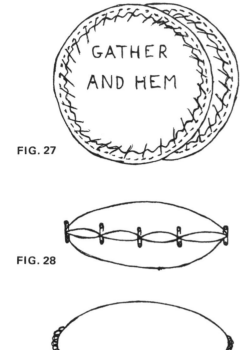

FIG. 27

FIG. 28

FIG. 29

Style I. Round, 1 side canvas, fabric boxing, and fabric covered or commercial cording

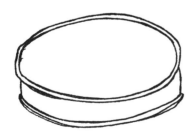

BOXED - FABRIC BACK
AND BOXING - FABRIC OR
COMMERCIAL CORDING

Materials needed

1 piece of canvas as in F
1 piece of fabric backing as in G, plus 2 pieces of cording 3 inches longer than the circumference of the pillow, plus 1 strip for the boxing 1¼ inches wider than the desired width, and 3 inches longer than the circumference of the pillow
Muslin-covered pillow 1 inch larger in diameter than the pillow top, and ½ inch deeper than the finished boxing width
Yarn of your choice

Bind the canvas, work the embroidery, and block. See F for machine stitching and gathering thread. See Figures 25, 8, 9, and 10 for sewing cording, and fitting and sewing the boxing. Trim off the binding, and all but 1 inch of the excess canvas. Draw up the gathering thread, and hem the excess canvas (Fig. 30). Baste the backing to the top of the boxing and cording ¾ of the way around. Stitch on the boxing side exactly on top

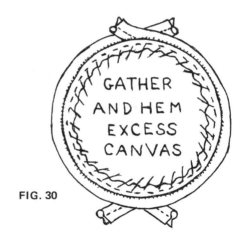

GATHER
AND HEM
EXCESS
CANVAS

FIG. 30

SEW TO
CORDING ON
BOXING SIDE.
SEW ¾ WAY
AROUND
BACKING-
WRONG SIDE

FIG. 31

of the cording stitching (Fig. 31). Turn right side out, insert the muslin pillow, and hem the opening invisibly (Fig. 32).

FIG. 32

Style J. Round, boxed, all canvas

BOXED - ALL CANVAS

Follow the directions for H, but add boxing as in E (Fig. 33).

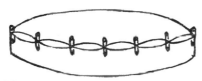

FIG. 33   SEAM ALL AROUND. FINISH WITH YARN CORDING OR FRINGE

Style K. Octagon, boxed, all canvas (Fig. 34)

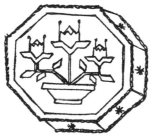

BOXED - OCTAGONAL ALL CANVAS

Simply modify the directions for E. The muslin form is usually stuffed with a firm block of foam rubber about 2 inches deep. If you can't find foam rubber thick enough, tape thinner pieces together. The muslin cover will hold them in place. Other shapes can be made by further modifying some of the above directions.

MODIFY DIRECTIONS FOR PILLOW C-2

FIG. 34

Style L. Rectangular with pleated corners, all canvas, or 1 side fabric

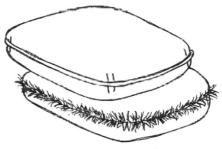

PLEATED CORNERS - ALL CANVAS OR FABRIC BACK

Materials needed

1 or 2 pieces of fine canvas in the desired proportions, plus 1¼ inches excess canvas all around; allow 1 inch extra each way as the sides fold down

Backing if desired, plus fabric or commercial cording equal to the perimeter of the pillow. Yarn cording can be used instead.

Muslin-covered pillow equal to dimensions of the canvas

Yarn of your choice

Note: Fine canvas must be used because of the corner pleats. Coarse canvas would be too bulky.

Bind the canvas. The piece of canvas is rectangular. The worked area has diagonal corners left unworked (Fig. 35). Each diagonal corner edge is 1½ inches long. Work the embroidery, and block.

FIG. 35

To make pleated corners, draw a line along each side into the unworked canvas to complete each corner (A-B and B-C in Fig. 36). Measure diagonally in from the corner 1⅛ inch (B-D). Run a basting thread to this point from the corner. Now, with pins, mark spots ¼ inch each side, like the top of a "T" (E-F). Mark these spots by slipping a straight pin under a stitch. Make short folds roughly perpendicular to the edges. Bring the folds over toward the corners. Line them up from the points marked with pins, and parallel to the basting thread, forming an unsewed dart. They don't need to be too accurate. The sides of the top will curve down, and there will be a continuous

line around the corner. Baste the darts securely in place. Cut off the binding and all but 1 inch of the excess canvas at the corners. Overcast the edges (Fig. 37). Fabric backing can be treated the same way. The corner need not be cut off. Add fabric covered or commercial cording, if desired. Overlap the ends in the middle of a side. Turn under the excess canvas, and hem all around. Join the back and the front over a muslin pillow, pin and sew by hand, adjusting the pleats at the corners, if necessary. A fringe or yarn cording can be added to the pillow (Fig. 38). This produces a softly contoured pillow with no awkward corners.

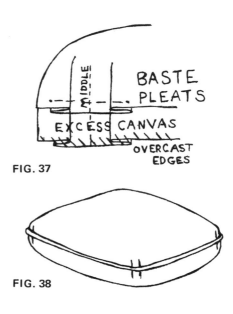

FIG. 37

FIG. 38

Style M. Cylindrical with fabric ends

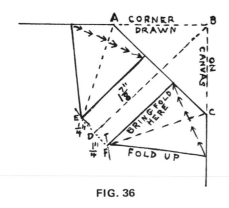

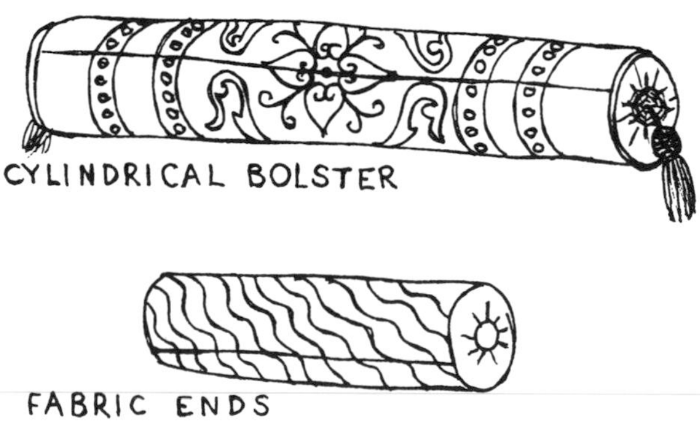

FIG. 36

CYLINDRICAL BOLSTER

FABRIC ENDS

A rectangular piece of canvas equal in length to the length of the cylinder. The width is equal to the circumference of the circular ends. Be careful not to make the circle too small. It is best to try your proportions first with a piece of paper. Add 1¼ inch excess canvas all around (Fig. 39).

2 strips of fabric equal in length to the circumference of the ends, plus 2¼ inches. The extra length is to take care of the slight puckering of the machine stitching. The strips should be 1½ inches wider than the radius of the circle.

Muslin-covered, firmly packed cylindrical pillow, with circular ends. It can be any size but should be quite firm. You can roll a piece of ½ inch foam rubber for a firm straight-sided pillow. Bevel the end of the roll (Fig. 40). When planning the design, make it match across the seam (Fig. 41).

embroidery as possible. Run a gathering thread near the other edge of the fabric. Use large stitches (Fig. 42). Hem the excess canvas along the sides. Seam the sides of the cylinder as invisibly as possible, matching the design across the seam. (See General Directions: "Joining Pieces of Canvas—Seaming.") Seam the fabric ends too. Cut off the binding around the circles, turn under this excess canvas and hem (Fig. 43). No mitering is needed. Draw up one gathering thread very tightly, tucking the seam allowance into the hole. Sew up the hole securely (Fig. 44). Insert the pillow and draw up and sew the other end. Pat the ends flat. The ends can be finished with a large fabric-covered button, or a large Spider Web. A final touch could be a tassel on a "stem" so it will hang down (Fig. 45).

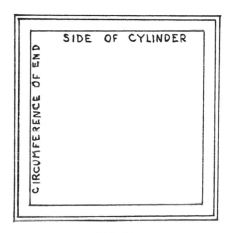

SIDE OF CYLINDER

CIRCUMFERENCE OF END

FIG. 39

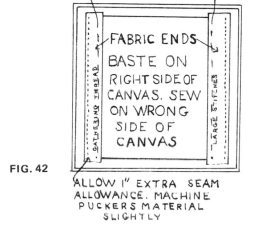

FABRIC ENDS

BASTE ON RIGHT SIDE OF CANVAS. SEW ON WRONG SIDE OF CANVAS

GATHERING THREAD

LARGE STITCHES

FIG. 42

ALLOW 1" EXTRA SEAM ALLOWANCE. MACHINE PUCKERS MATERIAL SLIGHTLY

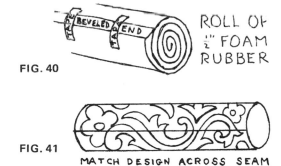

BEVELED END

ROLL OF ½" FOAM RUBBER

FIG. 40

FIG. 41

MATCH DESIGN ACROSS SEAM

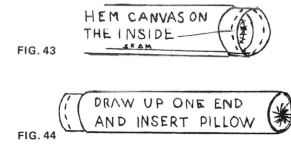

HEM CANVAS ON THE INSIDE

SEAM

FIG. 43

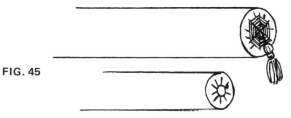

DRAW UP ONE END AND INSERT PILLOW

FIG. 44

FIG. 45

Bind the canvas, work the embroidery, and block. To make fabric ends, baste the strips of fabric along the ends, right sides together. Turn over to the wrong side, and stitch as close to the

Style N. Cylindrical, canvas ends

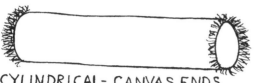

CYLINDRICAL- CANVAS ENDS

Materials needed

Canvas as in M, plus circular pieces to fit in the ends (Fig. 46). Plan the circular ends first. The circumference of the circles must fit the edges of the rectangular piece exactly. (See Figures 39, 40, 41).
Muslin-covered pillow as in M

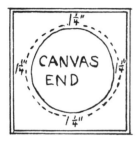 

FIG. 46

Bind the canvas, work the embroidery, and block. Use a paper pattern to make sure the ends are circular. Finish the ends (Fig. 47). (See "Finishing Canvas on a Curve.") Cut the binding off the rectangular piece and hem the sides. Seam the sides on the outside, matching the design across the seam. (See "Joining Pieces of Canvas—Seaming.") It may be necessary to adjust the width of the rectangular piece to fit the circular ends. If so, hem the ends and one side, mitering the 2 corners. Sew on both circular ends. Adjust

PIN ENDS AND SEAM PART WAY

FIG. 47

the fourth side of the rectangular piece to fit perfectly by adding or ripping stitches along the edge. Don't bother to do this unless the fit is really bad. Hem the fourth side mitering the last 2 corners (Fig. 48). Insert the pillow at the side seam, and hem the side seam as invisibly as possible. Finish the circular edges with fringe or yarn cording (Fig. 49).

FIG. 48

FIG. 49

Style O. Other shaped ends

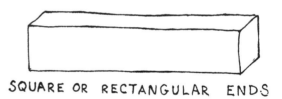

SQUARE OR RECTANGULAR ENDS

A similar cushion to N can be made with square, rectangular, triangular, or elliptical ends. To keep the sides flat, the muslin inner cushion should be stuffed with a firm block of foam rubber. Several pieces can be taped together, if you can't find foam rubber thick enough. The muslin cover will hold them in place (Fig. 50).

SQUARE, RECTANGULAR, TRIANGULAR, OR ELLIPTICAL ENDS CAN BE SUBSTITUTED FOR CIRCULAR ONES

FIG. 50

Swinging Door Plates

Measure the door plates accurately. They vary slightly in size (Fig. 1).

Materials needed

A piece of canvas 1½ inches larger each way than the measurements of the door plate.
Yarn of your choice.

Use fine canvas and flat stitch patterns. The needlework should be as thin through as possible. The worked area must be a tiny bit smaller, about 1-1/16 inches, than the glass plate so as to be sure

it can't extend beyond the glass. Plan your design so as to include, or hide, the screws (Fig. 2).

Bind the canvas, work the embroidery, leaving 4 crossed threads unworked where the screws will go (Fig. 3). Block carefully so as not to stretch the worked area larger than the glass plate measurements.

There are two ways to finish the canvas. (1) You can cut off the binding and hem and miter the excess canvas to the back of the embroidery (Fig. 4). (2) You can work a buttonhole stitch

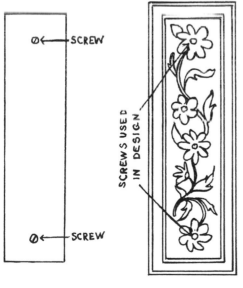

FIG. 1   FIG. 2

FIG. 3

FIG. 4

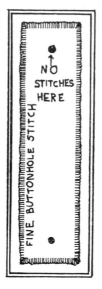

FIG. 5

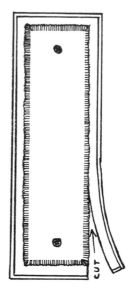

FIG. 6

around the edge, using fine thread in every hole. Make the stitches about ¼ inch wide (Fig. 5). Then trim off all of the excess canvas (Fig. 6). This method will reduce the thickness of the canvas to a minimum. Because the piece will be entirely covered by glass, there won't be any wear, so the usual hemming is unnecessary. The buttonhole stitch will cover the cut edges perfectly.

Enlarge the holes where the screws will go with an awl and insert the screws through the glass and the needlework. Holding the pieces carefully, mount on the door.

Brick Door Stops

Materials needed

Brick—get this first

Canvas to cover 5 sides, plus 1¼ inch excess canvas, see below for 2 positions of brick.

Outing flannel to cover entire brick; see Figs. 5, 6.

Velvet or felt to fit the 6th side, plus 2 inches extra each way

Yarn of your choice

First get your brick. They aren't identical in size or proportions. For example, one brick measures 8¾ inches by 2⅛ inches by 4 inches, and another measures 8⅛ inches by 2¼ inches by 3¾ inches. Next decide whether you want the door stop to lie on its largest side, (Fig. 1) or on its long narrow side (Fig. 2).

Measure the brick carefully, all 3 measurements. Make a paper pattern, allowing ¼ inch extra to make room for the bulk of the canvas and the seams. See the diagrams for patterns for the 2 different positions of the brick (Figs. 3, 4). Place

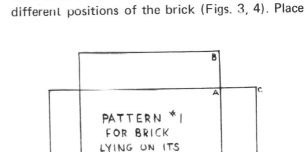

PATTERN *1 FOR BRICK LYING ON ITS LARGEST SIDE

FIG. 3

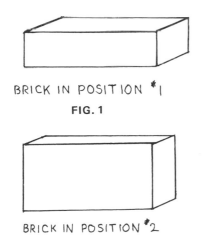

BRICK IN POSITION *1

FIG. 1

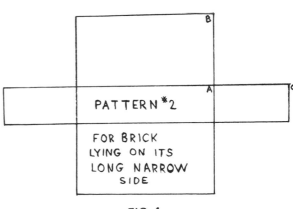

PATTERN *2 FOR BRICK LYING ON ITS LONG NARROW SIDE

FIG. 4

BRICK IN POSITION *2

FIG. 2

the pattern on a piece of white paper and draw a line around the edges. Work out your design on the paper, keeping in mind which parts will be at the bottom when the cover is mounted. If lettering or geometric design is to be used, it is best to plot it out on graph paper.

Trace the outlines of the pattern and the design. Be sure you have the same number of threads between A and B, and A and C in figure 3 or 4 so the seams will be even when the cover is finished.

Bind the canvas, work the embroidery, and block. Cover the brick with the outing flannel. Cover the bottom and 1 inch up the sides with the material you have selected. Seam the 1 inch corners, and sew the top of the piece to the outing

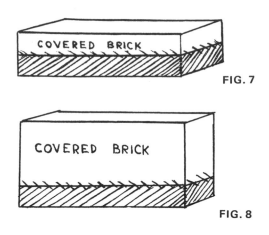

flannel covering (Fig. 7 or 8). Fold the canvas along the lines for the brick edges. This will bring edges AB and AC together. Using heavy thread, and sewing into the unworked canvas only, sew these seams on the right side. Sew ¾ inch into the excess canvas, too (Fig. 9 or 10). You will have double triangles of canvas on the inside (Fig. 11).

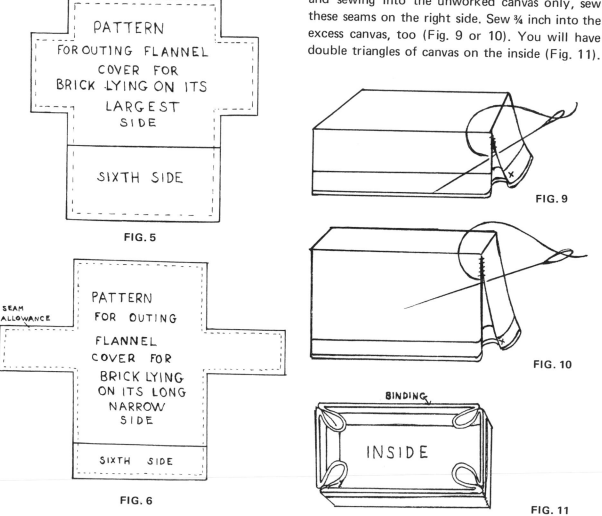

FIG. 5

FIG. 6

Cut away the triangle, leaving about ¾ inch excess canvas. Fold these edges back, and hem them to the back of the needlework (Fig. 12). Don't turn the piece wrong side out, if you can help it. Cut away the binding and all but ¾ inch of canvas around the bottom (Fig. 13). Turn under and hem (Fig. 14). Slip the cover over the brick, and hem the edge (Figs. 15, 16). Go over the side seams with matching yarn, if they show too much.

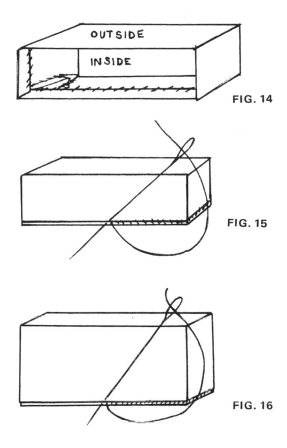

FIG. 14

FIG. 15

FIG. 16

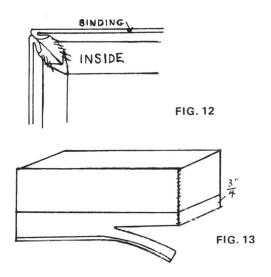

FIG. 12

FIG. 13

House Brick Door Stop

Materials needed

New brick—get this first; bricks vary in size and proportion

2 triangular pieces of wood, ½ inch thick, right (90°) angle at the top, hypotenuse equal to the width of the brick, slanting sides equal in length (Fig. 1) for gables

2 pieces of ⅛ inch plywood for the roof, the length equal to the length of the brick, the width equal to the slope of the gables (Fig. 2)

1 piece of wood 1 inch by ½ inch by thickness of the brick, plus the altitude of the gables, plus 1 inch for the chimney (Fig. 3)

1 piece of felt ¼ inch larger each way than the largest area of the brick (Fig. 4)

1 piece of outing flannel twice the largest area of the brick (Fig. 5)

Glue

12½-inch finishing nails

Masking tape

Canvas for roof—The width equal to the length of the plywood pieces, plus 3 inches. The length equal to twice the width of the plywood pieces, plus 3 inches (Fig. 6); add ¼ inch each way for the thickness of the plywood

Canvas for house sides—1 piece equal to twice the length and width (perimeter) of the brick, add ⅛ inch to each measurement, plus 3 inches; height equal to the thickness of the brick, plus the altitude of the gables, plus 3 inches (Fig. 7); no canvas for the chimney

Yarn of your choice

Bind both pieces of canvas. Plan the design for the sides of the house, doors, windows, shrubbery, flowers, etc. Remember the chimney will be

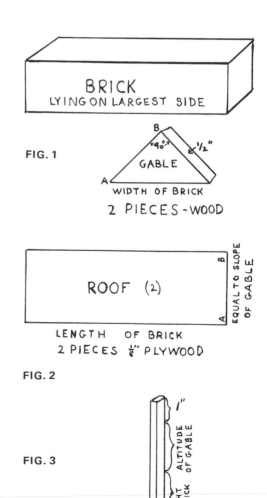

FIG. 1

BRICK
LYING ON LARGEST SIDE

B
90°
½"
GABLE
A
WIDTH OF BRICK
2 PIECES - WOOD

FIG. 2

B
ROOF (2)
A
EQUAL TO SLOPE OF GABLE
LENGTH OF BRICK
2 PIECES ⅛" PLYWOOD

FIG. 3

1"
ALTITUDE OF GABLE
HEIGHT OF BRICK
CHIMNEY

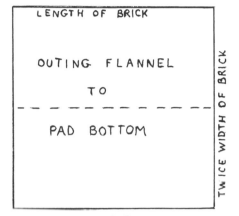

FELT TO PUT
ON BOTTOM

¼" WIDER THAN BRICK

¼" LONGER THAN BRICK

FIG. 4

LENGTH OF BRICK

OUTING FLANNEL
TO
PAD BOTTOM

TWICE WIDTH OF BRICK

FIG. 5

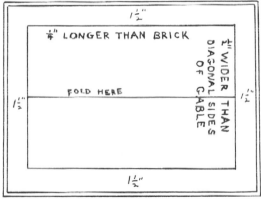

1½"

¾" LONGER THAN BRICK

¼" WIDER THAN DIAGONAL SIDES OF GABLE

FOLD HERE

1½"

1½"

1½"

CANVAS FOR ROOF

FIG. 6

placed against one end of the house. Work in Tent, or stitchery of your choice. Work the stitchery of the roof to simulate shingles. Block the 2 pieces. The overall length of the side piece must be ½ inch longer than the actual perimeter of the brick to allow for the thickness of the embroidery.

Place the wood for the gables on the ends of the brick. Glue and tape them in place (Fig. 8). Cut away the excess canvas from the house sides, leaving 1 inch all around. Wrap the canvas around the house sides, matching the gable points to the tops of the triangles. It may be necessary to glue the canvas to the house sides to make it lie flat. Turn under the excess canvas at a corner, and sew the seam (Fig. 9). Cut away part of the excess

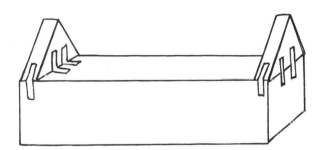

FIG. 8

SLASH

X

Y

SEAM

FIG. 9

BINDING

1½"

1½"

1½"

1½"

¾" LONGER THAN BRICK

¾" WIDER THAN BRICK

1½"

FIG. 7   CANVAS FOR HOUSE SIDES

canvas at the top of the gables so the canvas will lie flat (X in Fig. 9). Glue the excess canvas to the thickness of the gables and to the top of the brick, slashing the canvas ½ inch in from the corners (Y in Fig. 9). Fold the excess canvas on the bottom, and glue to the under side of the brick. Sew mitered corners. Fold the piece of outing flannel in half, and tack it. Glue it to the bottom of the brick. Glue the felt on the bottom. You can sew it to the edges of the canvas, if you wish.

To make the roof, sandpaper or file the top edges of the plywood so the outer edges will meet (Fig. 10). On the right side, hammer in the nails part way, 3 to a side ¼ inch in. Then remove them. Trim off the binding and all but 1 inch of the excess canvas. Lay the plywood pieces on the canvas. Fold the excess canvas over the edges of the plywood. The worked area should cover the thickness of the plywood. Sew mitered corners, and glue or tape down the excess canvas. Leave a little slack where the angle of the roof will come; between the 2 pieces of plywood (Fig. 11).

Place the roof on top of the house sides. Overcast in place with sewing cotton. Work a covering stitch all around the edges of the roof, seaming it to the sides. Using your embroidery needle, poke along the roof edges and find the nail holes. Separate the stitches carefully and hammer in the nails. Use a counter sinker or a metal punch to drive them all the way in so the canvas and the embroidery will cover the heads (Fig. 12).

To make the chimney, put some glue around the top of the piece of wood for the chimney, down about ¾ inch. Place the end of a long piece of yarn against the glue, point down (Fig. 13).

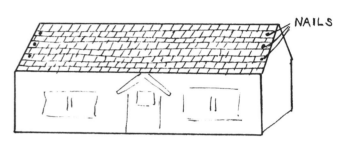

FIG. 12

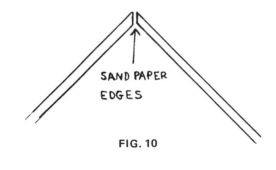

SAND PAPER EDGES

FIG. 10

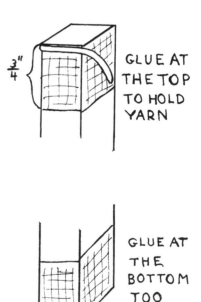

$\frac{3}{4}$"

GLUE AT THE TOP TO HOLD YARN

GLUE AT THE BOTTOM TOO

FIG. 13

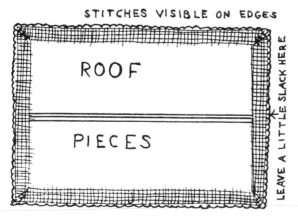

STITCHES VISIBLE ON EDGES

ROOF

PIECES

LEAVE A LITTLE SLACK HERE

FIG. 11

WRAP EVENLY

FIG. 14

BRICK DESIGN

FIG. 15

FIG. 16

Carefully wrap the yarn round and round the piece of wood, gradually covering it (Fig. 14). Put some glue at the bottom end, too. Tuck the end of the yarn in at the bottom with a needle. If you wish to simulate bricks, work white yarn with a needle every third row. Cross over one strand of wrapped yarn on the side that will be next to the house. Work short vertical stitches in and out, joining the horizontal lines in a brick pattern (Fig. 15). This will help keep the wrapped yarn in place. Paint the top of the chimney black. Sew the chimney against the end of the house as invisibly as possible. Climbing vines can be embroidered on the end of the house and part of the chimney, if desired (Fig. 16).

Note: It is not a good idea to make the sides of the house white. They would get dirty very soon.

Rugs

Canvas embroidery or needlepoint rugs are practical as well as beautiful. They wear well if worked in persian rug yarn, and one should not hesitate to walk on them. They can be washed or dry cleaned. They can be made rectangular or round, long and narrow, even octagonal. They can be made into stair carpeting. Diagonal Tent, or a variety of stitch patterns, can be used. Rugs can be conventional in design or as modern as your taste decrees. Large rugs can be made in several pieces, which are then joined together.

To make the following rugs, no special skills or equipment are required.

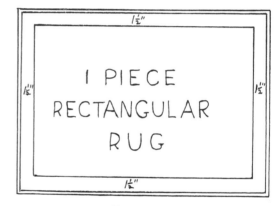

FIG. 1

Style A. 1 Piece, rectangular

Materials needed

1 piece of coarse canvas in the proportion and size desired, plus 1½ inches excess canvas all around (Fig. 1)

2 pieces of padding equal to the rug's measurements

An old woolen blanket is ideal (you can buy summer blankets made of cotton, and if you can find a "second," it would serve perfectly; get something springy, but not too thick)

2-inch-wide rug binding tape for all 4 sides, plus about 10 inches extra. Lining material of some sort. Monk's cloth is good. Don't use burlap; it doesn't wear well

Yarn of your choice

Bind the canvas, work the embroidery, and block. While the binding is still in one piece, wet it thoroughly to shrink it. Press without stretching it. Starting in about ¼ inch from the corner, machine stitch the binding along the edge of the excess canvas, stitching as close to the embroidery as possible. Sew across to the other corner, and then cut the tape ¼ inch short of the other end (Fig. 2). Repeat on the other side (Fig. 3).

For the ends, place the tape so as to have 1 inch excess beyond the corner (Fig. 4). Sew across, and cut the tape, leaving 1 inch excess at the other corner. Repeat on the other end. The tape is sewed before cutting because the sewing machine will pucker the tape slightly, making accurate measuring impossible. Turn the rug over, and fold the excess canvas and the tapes against the back. The tape should lie flat. If you want a plain or machine-stitched edge, one row of stitches should show on the back. If you plan to cover the edges, this is not necessary. Turn the tapes up out of the way, cut off the binding, and hem and miter the excess canvas to the back of the embroidery (Fig. 5).

For the padding, if you have bought a new summer blanket, be sure to shrink it before cutting it. Use hot water. Cut one piece to fit into the space between the excess canvas edges. Hem in place with large stitches (Fig. 6). Tack at intervals. The corners will still be thicker than the rug cen-

ter, so cut another piece of padding to come up to within ½ inch of the edge of the rug. Cut out the corners over the mitering. The rug should be the same thickness throughout. Tack at intervals and hem in place (Fig. 7).

Fold the tapes back in place. Turn under the extra inch and baste the corners, but not to the padding, however. Hem the ends and the bit of the sides where the tapes overlap (Fig. 8). Lay the rug backing in place, tucking the edges under the tapes. Tack at intervals, and hem all around (Fig. 9).

FIG. 2

FIG. 3

FIG. 4

FIG. 5

FIG. 6

FIG. 7

FIG. 8

FIG. 9

Style B. Rectangular, several pieces seamed together

Get several pieces of canvas, identical in size. You will need 1½ inches excess canvas around each piece. Be sure all selvage edges run the same direction. When planning the worked area it is best to make the pieces exactly the same by counting the number of threads each way so the seams will fit together perfectly. If you wish, you can join the pieces by splicing them together as you go along. See "Joining Pieces of Canvas—Splicing," p. 5. You will end your embroidery with the rug in one piece. Then follow the finishing directions for Rug A.

If you wish to seam the pieces together, see "Joining Pieces of Canvas—Seaming." After you have sewn the seams, cut the binding off the seamed edges only, not around the outside edge. Hem and miter these inside edges (Fig. 10). Then follow the directions for Rug A (Figs. 2 through 5).

Cut pieces of preshrunk padding to fit into the spaces between the edges of the turned back canvas. Hem them in place (Fig. 11). The second layer of padding will be in one piece, with square holes cut out over all the corners. Cut it to come up to within ½ inch of the outside edge. Hem and tack it in place (Fig. 12). Now finish the corners of the tapes, and add the backing, following the instructions for rug A (Figures 8 and 9).

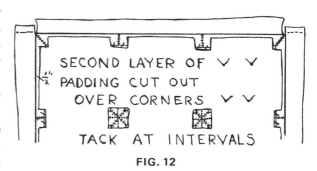

FIG. 12

Style C. Octagonal

A rug made in the shape of an octagon should have 8 equal sides. If the rug is made in 9 pieces, there will be 5 square pieces, and 4 with one diagonal side (Fig. 13). Note that the seams do not coincide with the angles at the edges of the rug. Making some modifications, follow the directions for rug B.

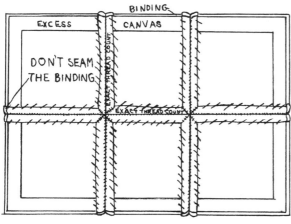

FIG. 10

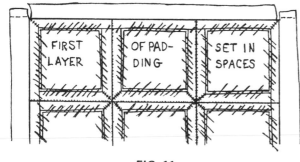

FIG. 11

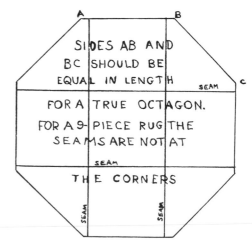

FIG. 13

Style D. Stair carpeting

Stair carpeting is usually made in pieces. Each piece will equal 1 tread and 1 riser, with the tread area at the top of each piece. Place the seams at the backs of the treads, bottoms of the risers. They will be less conspicuous, and will not be where most of the wear comes (Fig. 14).

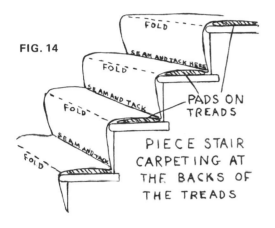

FIG. 14

Style E. Round or elliptical (oval)

Plan and work your rug on a rectangular piece of canvas, with 1½ inches excess canvas at the sides and ends. Before starting to work, make a paper pattern of the area to be covered with stitchery. You will need it when you do the blocking (Fig. 15).

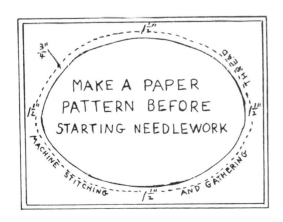

FIG. 15

Bind the canvas, work the embroidery, and block. Next place 2 rows of machine stitching, one on top of the other, ¾ inch out in the excess canvas (Fig. 15). Run a gathering thread through the stitching. (See "Finishing Canvas on a Curve.") Before pulling up the gathering thread, stitch the binding tape around the edges as close to the embroidery as possible. When you have stitched almost all the way around, cut the tape, leaving 1 inch seam allowance (Fig. 16). Then seam the tape and finish the first stitching (Fig. 17). Turn the rug over, cut off the binding, and all but 1¼ inches of the excess canvas. Draw up the gathering thread so the excess canvas turns in and the rug lies flat. Press the resulting pleats, and hem the excess canvas to the back of the stitchery (Fig. 18). You will need 1 or 2 thicknesses of preshrunk padding to match the thickness of the edges. Hem and tack

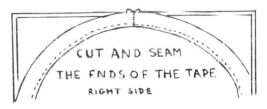

FIG. 16

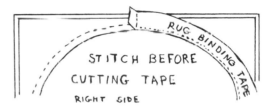

FIG. 17

FIG. 18

them in place (Fig. 19). Run another gathering thread around the edge of the tape. Draw it up so the tape will curve against the back of the rug. Cut the rug backing so the tape will overlap about 1 inch. Hem the tape to the backing (Fig. 20).

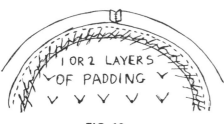

FIG. 19

FIG. 20

Rectangular rug, method 2

The excess canvas of a rectangular rug can be folded under, and the embroidery worked through both layers of canvas around the edges. Baste the canvas in place before beginning the stitchery (Fig. 21). Bring the excess canvas together in a diagonal line at the corners, and sew along the line with carpet thread (Fig. 22). Next cut off the binding.

Slit the top of the excess canvas in the corner, all but a thread or 2. Fold the triangular pieces back and hem them down (Fig. 23). This makes as thin a corner as possible. Apply 1 or 2 layers of pre-shrunk padding to the area between the edges of the turned under canvas (Fig. 23). Cover the whole back of the rug with lining (Fig. 24).

A word of warning: Since this type of rug cannot be blocked, don't use stitch patterns which warp the canvas. If you think it needs it, press the finished rug lightly.

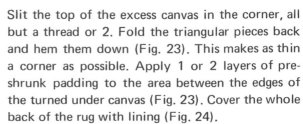

FIG. 22

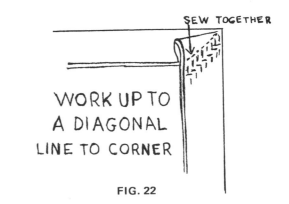

FIG. 23

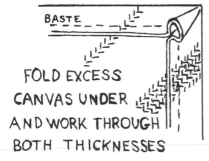

FIG. 21

FIG. 24

Finishing touches

There are several ways to add a finishing touch to your rug. You can work Binding stitch all around (Fig. 25), or only on the long sides, and make fringes at the ends (Fig. 26). You can fringe the rug all the way around, or you can run machine stitching between the last 2 rows of embroidery for a neat sharp edge (Figs. 27, 28).

FRINGE ALL THE WAY AROUND

FIG. 27

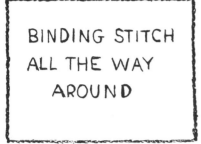

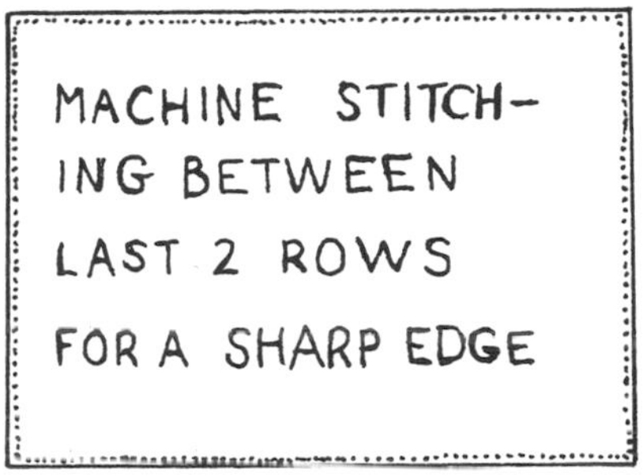

BINDING STITCH ALL THE WAY AROUND

FIG. 25

MACHINE STITCHING BETWEEN LAST 2 ROWS FOR A SHARP EDGE

FIG. 28

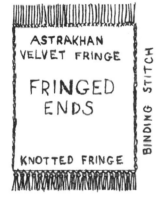

ASTRAKHAN VELVET FRINGE

FRINGED ENDS

BINDING STITCH

KNOTTED FRINGE

FIG. 26

Sizing

It is not necessary to apply glue or any other stiffening material to the back of your needlework before finishing the rug. It might create a problem if the rug is ever washed or dry cleaned. If you wish, a coating of nonskid material can be applied to the backing. This will stiffen the rug slightly.

Luggage Rack Straps

Materials needed

Get the luggage rack first; they vary in size and the length
    of the straps needed

Canvas

Yarn of your choice

Lining material

FIG. 1

If there are old straps on the rack, take them off and measure them carefully. They should be long enough to wrap around the bars at least 1½ times (Fig. 1). If all straps, usually 3, are to be worked on one piece of canvas, be sure to leave 1½ inches of canvas between them so there will be enough to turn under for finishing. Be sure there is about 2½ inches of unworked canvas at each end (Fig. 2).

Bind the canvas, work the embroidery, and block. Cut the straps apart, but don't trim off the excess canvas on the ends, just the binding. Overcast the canvas edges (Fig. 3). Cut the lining to cover the worked area only (Fig. 4).

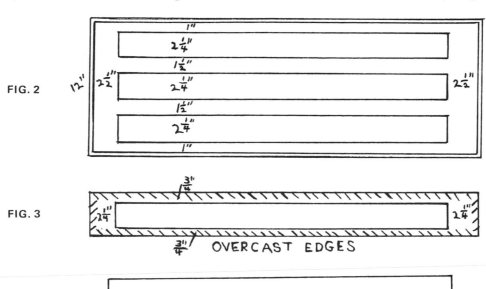

FIG. 2

FIG. 3

OVERCAST EDGES

FIG. 4   LINING

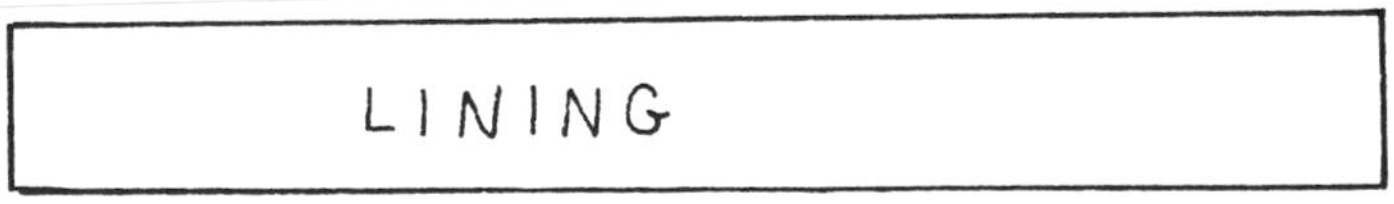

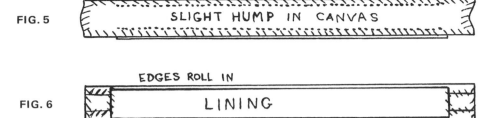

FIG. 5   SLIGHT HUMP IN CANVAS

EDGES ROLL IN

FIG. 6   LINING

If you are careful, you can sew the lining to the straps by machine. Lay the canvas on top of the strip of lining, right sides together. Sew close to the last row of stitching on one side. Before sewing the second side, make a slight hump in the canvas so the lining will be slightly narrower than the canvas (Fig. 5). Carefully turn the strap right side out, and press lightly. The canvas will roll over the edges, and the lining will be completely hidden (Fig. 6). Hem the ends of the canvas and the lining without turning under. Find the place where the old straps were attached to the bars of the luggage rack. It should be on the under side. Nail or tack the end of the excess canvas on one end. Don't use the old nail holes (Fig. 7).

Wrap the strap around the bar 1½ times, and extend it across to the other side. Partially close the rack to allow some slack, and wrap the strap the same number of times at the other end before nailing it to the bar (Fig. 8). The unworked canvas will be completely hidden. It is less bulky than the worked area, improving the appearance of the straps. Be sure all the straps are the same length so as to distribute the weight of luggage evenly (Fig. 9). Work binding stitch along the edges of the straps if you feel it is needed.

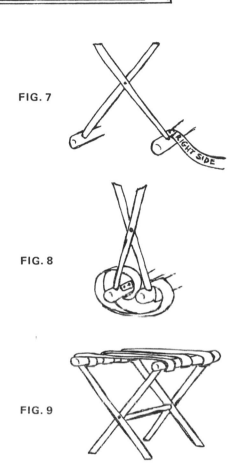

FIG. 7

FIG. 8

FIG. 9

Chair Seats and Backs,
Foot Stools, and Benches

Chair seats

Chair seats vary widely in design and size, so there can be no one pattern for all seats. It is best to make a cloth pattern, not a paper one. Use an old sheet. Lay it on the chair and pin it all around the edges, cutting off the excess (Fig. 1). Cut into the pattern for chair back posts, arms, etc. If the chair is to be reupholstered, the new stuffing will probably be higher than the old, so add an extra inch or two to the worked area of the canvas (Figs. 2,

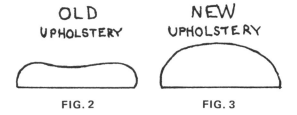

OLD UPHOLSTERY

NEW UPHOLSTERY

FIG. 2   FIG. 3

3). Draw a line on the cloth pattern from back to front, and mark the center. Because the seat of the chair is arched, the far side will be foreshortened when viewed from the front, so center your design ½ inch to 1 inch forward or below the true center of the pattern (Fig. 4). If the upholstered part of the seat extends down the sides, draw a line where the soft fold is between the top and the sides. Limit your design to this area (Fig. 5).

Measure the pattern and buy a piece of canvas at least 3 inches larger each way. Always work with a rectangular piece of canvas. Bind the canvas, and lay the pattern on it, being careful to have the center lined up with a canvas thread from front to back. Allow an extra inch all around for new upholstery. Draw an outline of the pattern. Draw across or around all cutout places for the chair back and arm posts. Work the embroidery across these areas. The upholsterer will cut into the canvas to make way for the posts. Work rounded areas for folded corners. Remember to center your design below the true center of the canvas (Fig. 5).

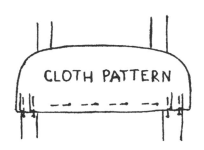

CLOTH PATTERN

CUT INTO PATTERN HERE

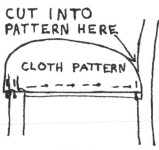

CLOTH PATTERN

FIG. 1

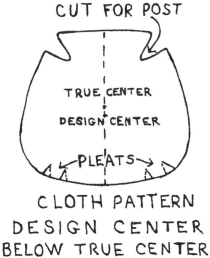

CUT FOR POST

TRUE CENTER

DESIGN CENTER

PLEATS

CLOTH PATTERN
DESIGN CENTER
BELOW TRUE CENTER

FIG. 4

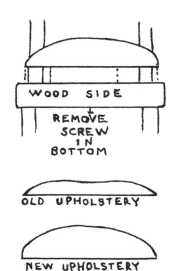

WOOD SIDE

REMOVE SCREW IN BOTTOM

OLD UPHOLSTERY

NEW UPHOLSTERY

FIG. 5

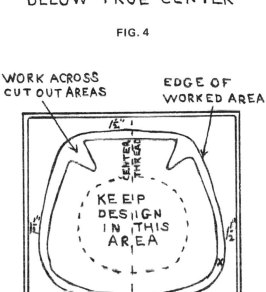

WORK ACROSS CUT OUT AREAS

EDGE OF WORKED AREA

CENTER THREAD

KEEP DESIGN IN THIS AREA

X EXTRA SIZE TO ALLOW
FOR NEW UPHOLSTERY

FIG. 6

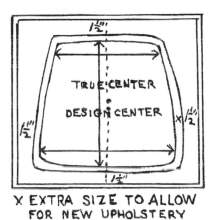

TRUE CENTER

DESIGN CENTER

X EXTRA SIZE TO ALLOW
FOR NEW UPHOLSTERY

FIG. 7

Work the embroidery and block the piece before delivering it to the upholsterer. These people can mount your canvas dry, but if there is much distortion, it would be hard to do. They wouldn't risk washing your piece, as they can't be sure everything is washable, so blocking the piece yourself is best. Use the cloth pattern as a guide.

There is a type of chair with the upholstered seat set in a wooden frame. There is usually a screw in the bottom of the seat. If you remove this screw, the upholstered part lifts out (Fig. 6). A cloth pattern is not necessary for this type, but measure carefully the width at the back and front, and the depth. Allow an extra inch each way for new upholstery, and enough to tuck under the edges (Fig. 7). Remember to center the design about ½ inch forward or below the true center (Fig. 7).

Chair backs

Chair backs shouldn't present much of a problem. If the area is rectangular, and entirely above the chair seat, just allow an extra ½ inch all around for tuck in (Fig. 8). Center the design above the true center of the canvas because of the foreshortening of the bottom of curved area (Fig. 8). Some chair backs have an upholstered area extending down behind the chair seat. A good 2 inches will be hidden, so center your design well above the center of the canvas. Pin the canvas to the chair back to find the best spot for the design center (Fig. 9).

Foot stools and benches

Stools can be treated like chair seats, but, of course there will be no posts to deal with. The design can be placed in the true center. Because stools are usually viewed from all sides, it is best to choose a design with no top or bottom, so any view will be pleasing (Figs. 10, 11).

Some benches have backs and some don't. Use the chair directions for those that have backs, and the stool directions for those that don't.

Stitch pattern choice. Because chairs and foot stools usually get hard wear, it is best to choose stitch patterns with short stitches that cover the canvas well. Some people like to use Florentine (Bargello), or other long stitch patterns, but they run the risk of having a button or buckle snag the threads, spoiling the work. Besides, this type of stitch pattern just doesn't wear as well as a small compact one would.

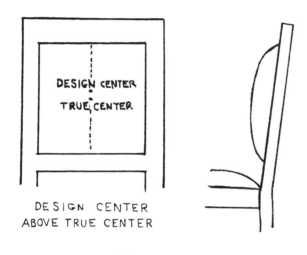

DESIGN CENTER
ABOVE TRUE CENTER

FIG. 8

FIG. 10

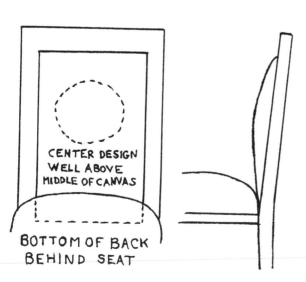

BOTTOM OF BACK
BEHIND SEAT

FIG. 9

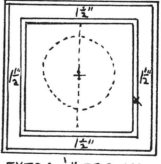

X EXTRA ½" FOR UP-
HOLSTERER'S TUCK-IN

FIG. 11

Director's Chair

Director's chairs are found with the seat attached in 2 different ways (A in Fig. 1). Below the frame that supports the arms are pieces of wood with triangular ends. In the old-style chair, the fabric that forms the seat is brought around these pieces and nailed to the wood. The hinges, which allow the arms to fold down, are fastened through the fabric into the wood (Fig. 2).

In the new-style chairs, the triangular piece has a semicircular groove in it. The cloth seat is hemmed, and a dowel is enclosed in the hem. This dowel and the hemmed seat edge fit into the groove. It is held in place by the bottom of the arm frame (Fig. 3). Because the cloth parts must take the weight of the sitter, they cannot be made of the embroidered canvas only. The heavy material should be retained, and the embroidered canvas sewed onto it. The material makes a good backing. If the cloth on your chair is in bad condition, or is the wrong color, new ones for the new style chair are available for very little cost. An awning company could provide you with the cloth to replace the parts of an old-style chair.

Measure the strip of canvas that forms the chair back. Make your canvas of equal width. Plan to bring your embroidered canvas around the chair back posts to the edges of the hems (A to B in Fig. 4). Add ½ inch for the bulk of the canvas. Don't plan to have the embroidered canvas extend under the arm frames, and around the triangular pieces of wood in the old-style chair, or around the

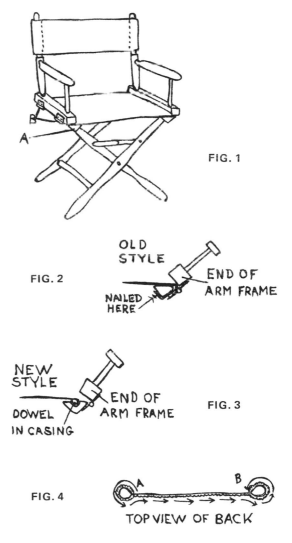

FIG. 1

OLD STYLE

FIG. 2

END OF ARM FRAME

NAILED HERE

NEW STYLE

END OF ARM FRAME

DOWEL IN CASING

FIG. 3

FIG. 4

TOP VIEW OF BACK

dowel hems in the new. Measure the distance across the chair seat between the arm frames. The embroidered canvas is to be hemmed to the cloth seat at these lines (Fig. 5). The 2 pieces of canvas will be equal to these measurements, plus 1¼ inches excess canvas all around (Fig. 6).

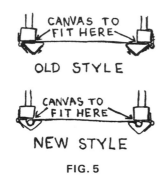

FIG. 5

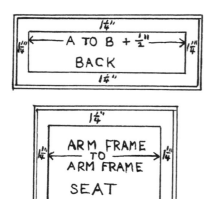

FIG. 6

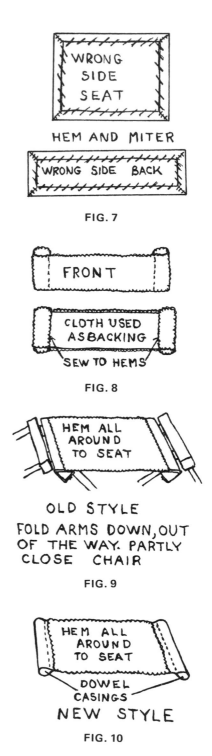

FIG. 7

FIG. 8

FIG. 9

FIG. 10

Bind the canvas, work the embroidery, and block. Trim off the binding, and hem the excess canvas of both pieces, mitering the corners (Fig. 7). Remove the cloth piece from the back of the chair. Using a strong needle and an awl, if necessary, hem the canvas to the chair back piece. It isn't necessary to open the hems in the ends of the cloth. Just hem your canvas to the edges (Fig. 8). In the old-style chair the canvas can be sewed to the piece of cloth right on the seat. Fold the arms down out of the way, and partially close the chair to provide some slack (Fig. 9).

In the new type of chair the seat piece of cloth is easily removed. Take out the dowels, and hem the canvas to the cloth (Fig. 10). Work a decorative stitch pattern along the front and back edges of the seat, and along the top and bottom edges of the back, if you like. Reassemble the chair.

Slip Seat Chair Pads

Slip seat pads are firm cushions, usually boxed, for use on unupholstered chair seats. They are usually filled with block foam rubber, cut to the shape of the seat. The cover can be boxed with canvas, or any appropriate material. Ties are attached above the legs, and tied under the chair seat (Fig. 1). Directions are given for making 4 different styles. In all cases, first make a paper pattern ⅛ inch smaller than the seat on 3 sides, and just meeting the chair back (Fig. 2). Allow 1½ inches excess canvas all around. Keep the piece of canvas rectangular. This makes it a lot easier to block (Fig. 3).

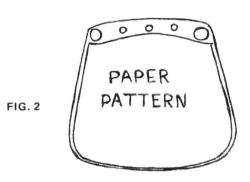

FIG. 2

FIG. 3

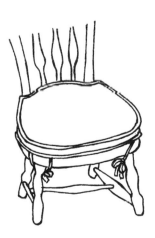

FIG. 1

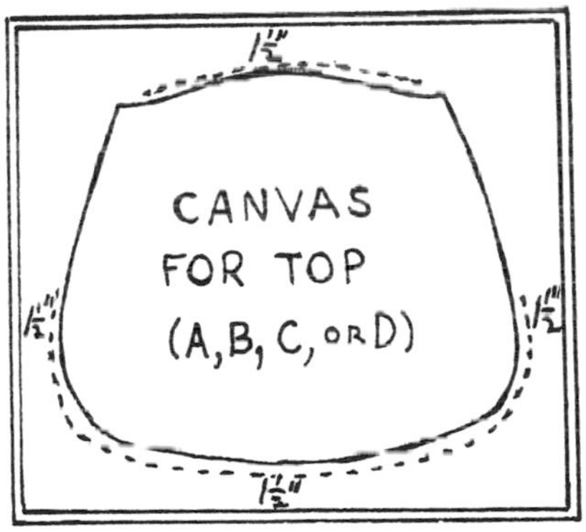

Style A. Canvas boxing

Materials needed

1 piece of canvas to accommodate the pattern of the seat, plus 1½ inches excess canvas all around

A piece 3 inches longer than the perimeter of the pattern, and 3½ inches wide; if you have to piece the boxing, allow 1½ inches extra for each seam (Fig. 4).

CANVAS BOXING – 1½" X PERIMETER OF THE PATTERN (A)

FIG. 4

Have enough muslin for 2 areas the size of the pattern, and 1 piece 5 inches deeper, and also enough for the boxing equal to the canvas boxing; ¾ inch seam allowance for all pieces

2 yd. of tape for the ties; this is approximate; measure to suit your chair

1 piece of 1½ inch foam rubber to fit the seat pattern

Yarn of your choice; if you intend to make yarn cording you will need uncut yarn, as most cords can't be pieced (see "Cords and Braids," p. 213, for lengths).

If you plan to use a geometric design, make sure the center of the pattern from front to back is lined up with the center thread of the canvas, and that the back corners use a common thread. Make the boxing for Style A 1½ inches wide. Make a boxed muslin cover for the foam rubber piece (Fig. 5).

FIG. 5

Bind the canvas, work the embroidery, and block. Use the pattern as a guide. Before cutting off the binding, see "Finishing Canvas on a Curve," and the dotted lines in Figure 3. Prepare the curved edge, and then cut off the binding and all but 1 inch of the excess canvas. Hem and miter the back corners. Small slashes may be needed for the slight concave curves near the back posts (Fig. 6).

FIG. 6

Cut the binding off the sides and off one end of the boxing. Hem the sides, all but the last 3 inches. Miter the corners of the other end (Fig. 7). Sew the boxing to the top, right sides out, starting with the finished end in the middle of the back. You may have to add a few or rip a few stitches at the other end to make the boxing fit perfectly. Adjust the length of the boxing, then finish hemming the excess canvas and miter the 2 corners (Fig. 8). Seam the boxing and finish hemming it to the top (Fig. 9).

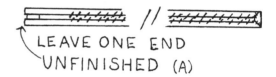

LEAVE ONE END UNFINISHED (A)

FIG. 7

FIT THE END BEFORE SEAMING ENDS OF BOXING (A)

FIG. 8

SEW THE BOXING AND FINISH SEAM (A)

FIG. 9

Style B. Fabric boxing and cording

Materials needed

Enough canvas to accommodate the pattern, plus 1½ inches excess canvas all around (Fig. 3)
Muslin, ties, and foam rubber the same as for Style A
About 1½ yd. of material for the boxing and cord covering 2 yd. cotton cord, and yarn of your choice

Cut a piece of material about 1½ inches longer than the perimeter of the top. You will probably have to piece it. If you do, allow 1½ inches for each seam. Make the strip 2½ inches wide (Fig. 10). Cut bias strips 2 inches wide for the cording. Join the pieces to make 2 long strips equal to the perimeter of the pattern, plus 3 inches. Cover the pieces of cotton cord, using a sewing machine (Fig. 11). Baste 1 piece to the edge of the cushion top with the excess material on the outside. Overlap the ends in the middle of the back, and bring the ends out (Fig. 12). Turn over to the canvas side, and machine stitch carefully around the edge of the worked area, sewing as close to the embroidery as possible. Baste the boxing over the cording, starting in the middle of the back. Don't finish the ends of the boxing yet

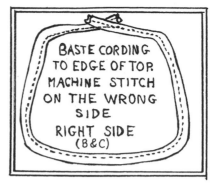

FIG. 12

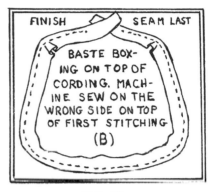

FIG. 13

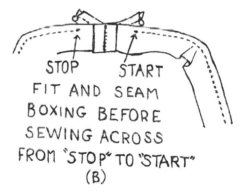

FIG. 14

(Fig. 13). Turn the piece over to the canvas side, and, starting about 3 inches from the end, carefully stitch over your first row of stitching. Stop about 3 inches from the other end (Fig. 14). Turn back to the right side and adjust the 2 ends of the boxing to fit perfectly. Seam them on the machine, and turn back the seam allowance (Fig. 14). Turn to the wrong side and finish sewing the boxing in place. This is done because it is impossible to cut and seam the boxing for a perfect fit beforehand.

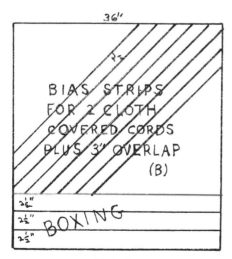

FIG. 10

FIG. 11

Before cutting the binding off the top, see "Finishing Canvas on a Curve," and Figure 3. Follow these directions, and then cut off the binding and some of the excess canvas, leaving about 1 inch. Hem and miter the back corners. Small slashes may be needed for the slight concave curves near the chair back posts (Fig. 15). Stitch the other piece of cording to the bottom of the boxing, overlapping the ends in the middle of the back (Fig. 16).

Fold the paper pattern across the middle (Fig. 18). Cut the piece of muslin that is 5 inches deeper across the middle, having 2½ inches on each part. Pin the folded pattern to the piece for the back half so as to have ¾ inch seam allowance at the back, and the half sides, and the 2½ inches below the fold (Figs. 19, 20). Draw a line around the back part. Sew a 1 inch hem along the straight edge. Do the same with the front half of the muslin (Fig. 21). Overlap and baste the hemmed

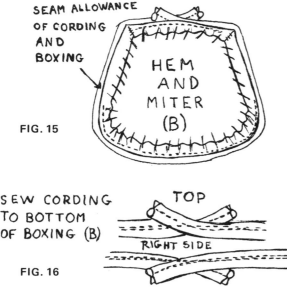

SEAM ALLOWANCE OF CORDING AND BOXING

HEM AND MITER (B)

FIG. 15

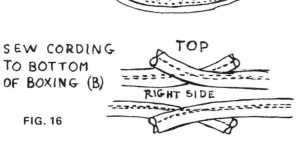

SEW CORDING TO BOTTOM OF BOXING (B)

TOP

RIGHT SIDE

FIG. 16

To finish both styles, cut the tape for the ties into 4 pieces. Fold each piece in half, and attach the fold to the top of the boxing above where the legs of the chair will be. Spread the ends apart about 1½ inches, and sew them to the bottom edge of the boxing (Fig. 17). Sew securely as they will be pulled snug.

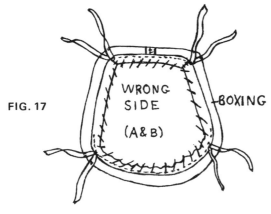

FIG. 17

WRONG SIDE (A&B)

BOXING

FOLD PATTERN IN HALF (A&B)

FIG. 18

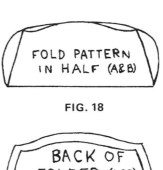

BACK OF FOLDED (A&B) PATTERN

1½

FIG. 19

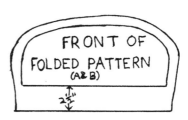

FRONT OF FOLDED PATTERN (A&B)

2½

FIG. 20

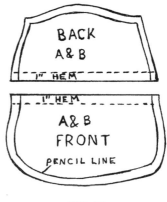

BACK A & B

1" HEM

1" HEM

A&B FRONT

PENCIL LINE

FIG. 21

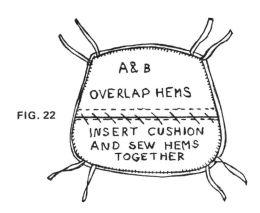

FIG. 22

A& B
OVERLAP HEMS

INSERT CUSHION
AND SEW HEMS
TOGETHER

edges to make the pieces fit the opened out pattern. Sew the backing to the edge of the boxing, using the pencil lines as a guide (Fig. 22).

For the canvas boxing, make 2 round cords and sew them invisibly over the seams. Remove the bastings from the backing. Insert the muslin-covered cushion, and, with large stitches, hem the opening together. This makes the back easy to open in case the cushion ever needs to be removed. The closing is completely concealed, and will not mar the chair (Fig. 23).

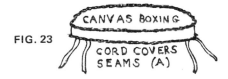

FIG. 23

CANVAS BOXING

CORD COVERS
SEAMS (A)

For false cording, work an extra inch, perhaps in a contrasting color, on either side of the boxing (Fig. 24). Fold this in half and sew the outside edge to the true edge of the boxing before attaching the boxing to the top (Fig. 25). It gives the effect of a cording, although it is really just a fold.

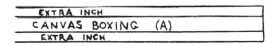

EXTRA INCH
CANVAS BOXING (A)
EXTRA INCH

FALSE CORDING

FIG. 24

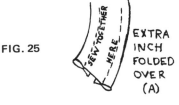

FIG. 25

SEW TOGETHER
HERE

EXTRA
INCH
FOLDED
OVER
(A)

Style C. Fabric covered cording—no boxing

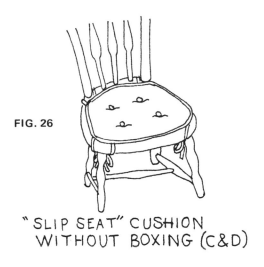

FIG. 26

"SLIP SEAT" CUSHION
WITHOUT BOXING (C&D)

Materials needed

Canvas as in styles A and B
Cording equal to perimeter, plus 3 inches
Muslin-covered pillow
Tapes and backing as in A and B
Buttons (optional)

Make a paper pattern and prepare the canvas as in Figures 2 and 3. This kind of cushion can be finished like a thin pillow. See "Pillows," A, B, or C, p. 19. A thin muslin pillow can be made in the shape of the chair seat, but a little larger. Don't make the pillow too thin. It will flatten with use.

See Figure 12 for attaching the cording. Sew the folded tapes to the cording stitching, with the ends on the inside (Fig. 27). Baste the backing

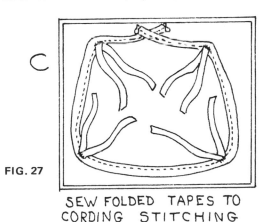

C

FIG. 27

SEW FOLDED TAPES TO
CORDING STITCHING

over the front, right sides together. Turn over and stitch 3 sides on top of the first stitching. Include the back corners. Hem and miter the trimmed canvas. (See "Finishing Canvas on a Curve.") Turn right side out, insert the pillow, and seam the back opening invisibly. Add buttons, if desired (Fig. 28).

FIG. 28

Style D. Yarn cording or fringe edging—no boxing

Materials needed

Same as for C but without the cording
Prepare the canvas as in Figs. 2 and 3

Stitch the folded tapes to the excess canvas next to the embroidery. Baste the backing in place, turn over and stitch 3 sides as close to the embroidery as possible. Include the back corners. Hem and miter the trimmed canvas (Fig. 29). (See "Finishing Canvas on a Curve.") Turn right side

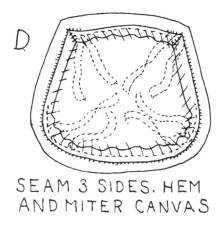

SEAM 3 SIDES. HEM AND MITER CANVAS

FIG. 29

out, insert the pillow, and close the back opening. Make yarn cording, and sew invisibly over the seam, or make a fringe edging. Sew into the canvas only, especially across the back, so that, if necessary the cushion can be opened by removing the slip stitch seam across the back (A in Fig. 30). Add buttons, if desired.

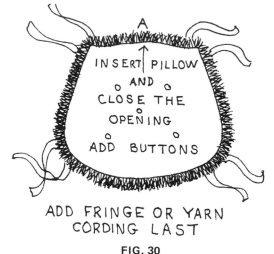

ADD FRINGE OR YARN CORDING LAST

FIG. 30

Note: Yarn cording and canvas boxing makes finishing easier, and will wear longer.

Alternate fastening

Instead of using ties around the chair legs, pieces of tape can be crossed under the chair and snapped in place. Be sure they are good and tight (Fig. 31).

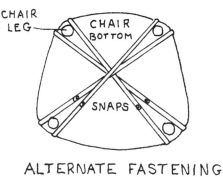

ALTERNATE FASTENING USE INSTEAD OF TIES

FIG. 31

Piano Bench Pad

The following directions and diagrams are for three styles of pads to fit the type of piano bench with a hinged lid over a compartment beneath. For a hard top that doesn't open, see "Slip Seat Chair Pads," p. 53. Adjust these directions to fit your bench. For the upholstered type, see "Chair Seats and Backs, Foot Stools, and Benches," p. 48.

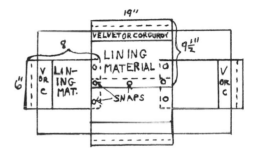

FIG. 3

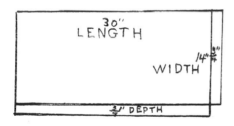

FIG. 1

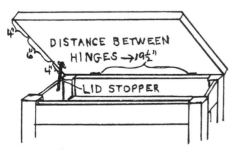

FIG. 2

Measure the top of the bench—length, width, and thickness (Fig.1). Measure the distance between the hinges, and the distance from the corner to the top of the lid support. Measure an equal distance in from the opposite corner (Fig. 2). The following measurements are for a standard modern piano bench:

Width of side straps, 19 inches

Width of end straps, 6 inches

Side straps—add tuck in, ¾ inch, thickness, ¾ inch, ½ the width of the bench, 7 inches, and 1 inch overlap (Fig. 3)

Length of side straps, 9½ inches (Fig. 3)

End straps—Add tuck in, ¾ inch, thickness, ¾ inch, distance from the end to the side strap, 5½ inches, and 1 inch overlap (Fig. 3)

Length of end straps, 8 inches (Fig. 3)

Style A. Canvas top only.
Velvet or corduroy cording, boxing, cushion back, and tops of straps.
Lining material straps.

Materials needed

1 piece of canvas 32½ inches by 16½ inches (Fig. 4)

2 yd. velvet or corduroy. See layout (Figs. 5, 6)

¾ yd. lining material. See layout (Fig. 7)

1 piece firm foam rubber 30 inches by 14 inches, or Dacron padding (get this from an upholsterer; 2 inches will compress to 1 inch)

1 yd. muslin (see pattern in Fig. 8)

5 yd. cotton cord to be covered

9 or 10 gripper snaps

Yarn of your choice

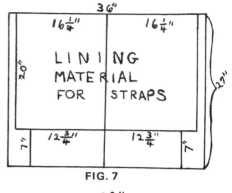

FIG. 7

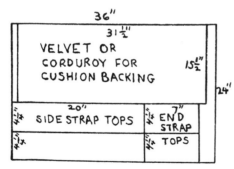

FIG. 4

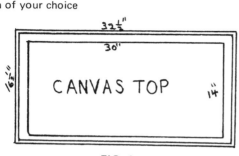

FIG. 5

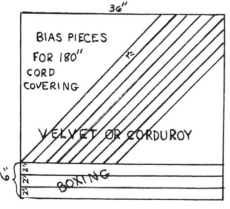

FIG. 6

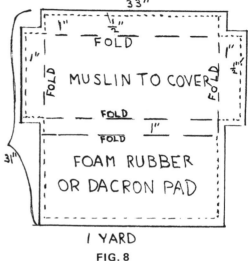

I YARD

FIG. 8

Bind the canvas, work the embroidery, and block. Cut and set aside the velvet or corduroy for the cushion backing. Cut and piece strips for the boxing, piecing at the corners (Fig. 9). Cut and piece bias strips for 180 inches (2 pieces 90 inches each) for velvet or corduroy-covered cording (Fig. 6). Fold and sew over cotton commercial cord (Fig. 10). Baste ½ of cording along the edge of the embroidered top, raw edges out. Bring the ends

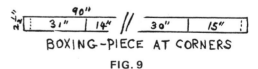

BOXING-PIECE AT CORNERS

FIG. 9

VELVET OR CORDUROY
COVERED CORD 180″(-90″)
BIAS

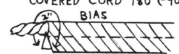

FIG. 10

out at a corner (Fig. 11). Turn over to the canvas side and stitch as close to the embroidery as possible.

Piece the boxing into a long strip so the seams will come at the corners (Fig. 9). Beginning near an end, baste the boxing on top of the cording and canvas, right sides together, leaving seam allowance at the corner. Turn over to the canvas side, and carefully machine stitch on top of your first stitching, stopping about 3 inches from the end (Fig. 12). Turn back again.

Fit the ends of the boxing and seam them. Turn the piece over again and finish stitching the boxing around the corner. This is done so the boxing will be sure to fit perfectly (Fig. 13).

Stitch the other half of the cording to the lower edge of the boxing (Fig. 14). Cut the binding off the canvas, turn back and hem the excess canvas, making modified mitered corners. The corners will be slightly rounded (Fig. 15).

FIG. 14

FIG. 15

Style B. Canvas top and boxing, yarn cording or fringe, velvet or corduroy cushion backing and tops of straps, lining material straps.

Materials needed

Canvas for top and boxing, 1 piece 32½ inches by 16½ inches, 1 strip 3½ inches by 90 inches, or 2 pieces 5 inches by 46 inches for a 2 piece boxing, or 2 pieces 32 inches by 5 inches, and 2 pieces 16 inches by 5 inches for a 4 piece boxing (Figs. 4, 16)

2/3 yd. of 36 inch velvet or corduroy for the cushion backing and the tops of the straps (See layout 5 in Fig. 5)

Lining material, foam rubber, muslin, snaps as in Style A

Yarn of your choice for embroidery, plus enough uncut yarn to make 2 cords 90 inches each. This is for cord edging. Omit if fringe edging is used.

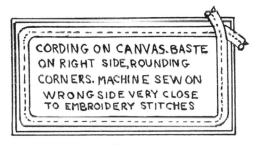

FIG. 11

FIG. 12

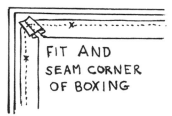

FIG. 13

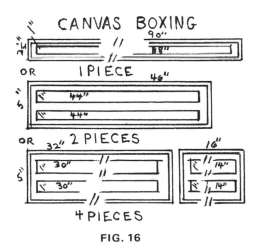

FIG. 16

Bind the canvas, work the embroidery, and block. Cut the binding off the top. Hem and miter the excess canvas to the back of the embroidery (Fig. 17). Cut the binding off the boxing and piece into a long strip. Hem the excess canvas along the sides, and miter the corners of one end only (Fig. 18). Leave the other end unfinished. Beginning at a corner, right sides out, seam the boxing to the top. At the other end it may be necessary to add or rip a few embroidery stitches to ensure a perfect fit. Adjust the boxing to fit, miter the remaining corners, and seam the boxing. Finish sewing the boxing to the top (Fig. 19).

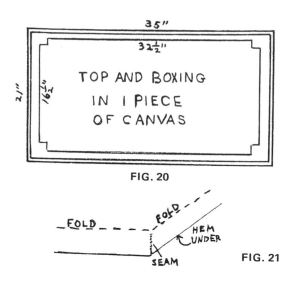

FIG. 20

FIG. 21

Bind the canvas, work the embroidery, and block. Cut off the binding, seam the corners, and hem the excess canvas to the back of the embroidery (Fig. 21).

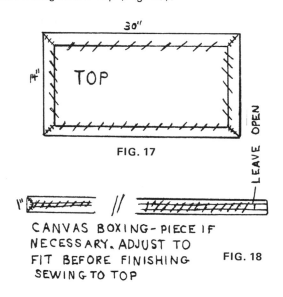

FIG. 17

FIG. 18

CANVAS BOXING- PIECE IF NECESSARY. ADJUST TO FIT BEFORE FINISHING SEWING TO TOP

FIG. 19

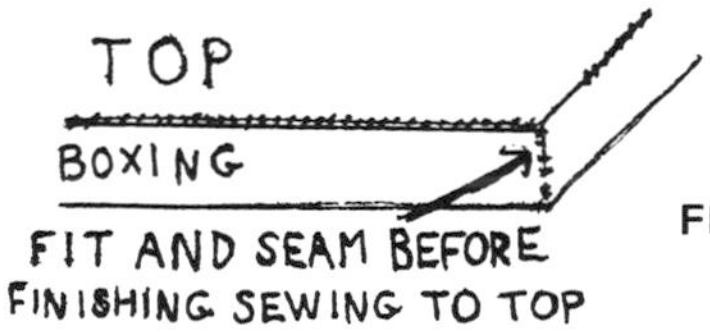

TOP
BOXING
FIT AND SEAM BEFORE FINISHING SEWING TO TOP

Straps

For the side pieces, sew the long edges of the velvet or corduroy to the lining material, right sides together. There is ½ inch seam allowance on each (Fig. 22). Bring the other end of the lining material up in back, right sides together, and seam the sides. There is ½ inch seam allowance on each side (Fig. 23).

Style C. Top and boxing in one piece. No cording or fringe.

Materials needed

1 piece of canvas 35 inches by 21 inches (Fig. 20)
Velvet or corduroy, same as B
Lining material, foam rubber, muslin, and snaps, same as A and B (select the velvet or corduroy and lining material before choosing main color yarn because of limited color choice.

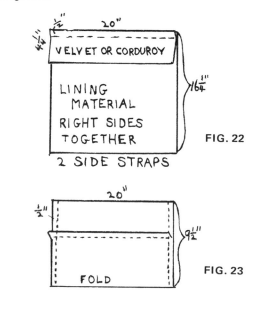

VELVET OR CORDUROY

LINING MATERIAL RIGHT SIDES TOGETHER

2 SIDE STRAPS

FIG. 22

FOLD

FIG. 23

For the end pieces, sew the long edges of the velvet or corduroy to the short edges of the lining material. Bring the end of the lining material up in back, right sides together, and seam the sides. There is ½ inch seam allowance (Figs. 24, 25). Turn all 4 pieces right side out, and press lightly on the wrong side (Fig. 26).

The side pieces will measure 19 inches by 9½ inches. The end pieces will measure 6 inches by 8

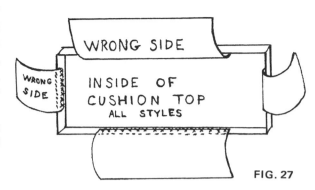

FIG. 27

inches. There is ¾ inch seam allowance for the tuck in. Have the velvet or corduroy side out. Hand sew the ends of the straps securely to the inside of the boxing, centering the pieces on the ends and sides. (Fig. 27).

If yarn cording or fringe is to be added, do so now (Fig. 28). Cover the foam rubber with muslin (Fig. 29). Insert the cushion, cover with the piece

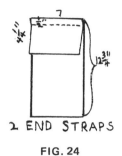

2 END STRAPS

FIG. 24

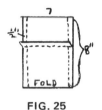

FIG. 25

CORD FINISH

FIG. 28

FRINGE FINISH

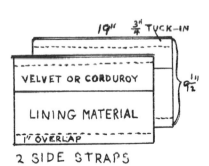

2 SIDE STRAPS

FIG. 26

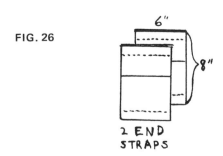

2 END STRAPS

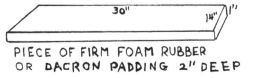

PIECE OF FIRM FOAM RUBBER OR DACRON PADDING 2" DEEP

FIG. 29

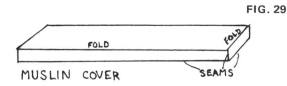

MUSLIN COVER

of velvet or corduroy backing, and hem it to the edges of the boxing and the tops of the straps (Fig. 30). Place the cushion on the bench top, and pull the side straps snug. Insert 3 or 4 gripper snaps in the overlap (Fig. 31). Pull the end straps in, and tuck them under the side straps. Insert 3 gripper snaps in the overlap of the ends, and the sides of the side straps (Fig. 32).

This makes a neat, firm piano bench cushion that will stay in place when the bench top is opened. Finishing with canvas boxing and yarn cording or fringe, Style A, is a lot easier than Style B, and will wear better.

These measurements may have to be adjusted to suit individual piano benches.

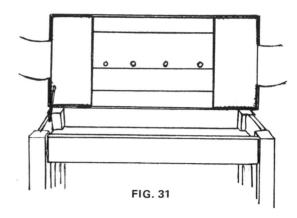

FIG. 31

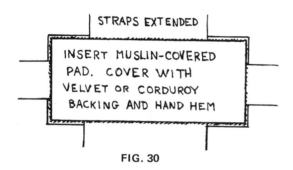

STRAPS EXTENDED

INSERT MUSLIN-COVERED PAD. COVER WITH VELVET OR CORDUROY BACKING AND HAND HEM

FIG. 30

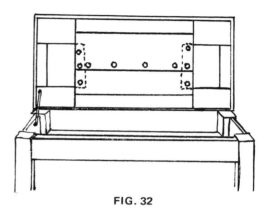

FIG. 32

Bell Pulls and Hangings

Today bell pulls are strictly ornamental. In the days of large houses and many servants, the bell pull, a long narrow panel usually finished, top and bottom, with decorative metal fittings designed for the purpose, hung on a bracket attached to the wall. A cord, fastened to the top and run through the walls, was attached to a bell in the servants' quarters. A yank on the bell pull summoned a servant.

Bell pulls and other hangings are usually lined and fitted to mountings, either hidden or exposed, along the top, and sometimes at the bottom.

Bell Pulls

Materials needed

1 piece of canvas 2 inches wider than the desired width of the worked area, and 3½ inches longer

Lining material equal to the worked area, plus ½ inch on either side, and 2½ inches on the ends

Decorative metal ends, if you plan to use them

Yarn of your choice

Decorative bell pull ends can be purchased at shops specializing in embroidery materials. Plan your bell pull any desired length, usually 50 inches to 60 inches. Measure the width of the metal end to which the embroidery will be attached. Plan the embroidery ¼ inch wider than this measurement (Fig. 1). This is done because, when the piece is blocked, it is best to pull and tack the piece lengthwise only (Fig. 2). This avoids the possibility

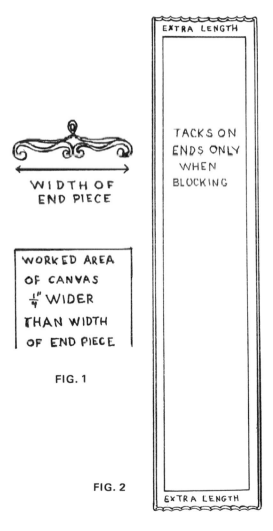

WIDTH OF END PIECE

WORKED AREA OF CANVAS ¼" WIDER THAN WIDTH OF END PIECE

FIG. 1

EXTRA LENGTH

TACKS ON ENDS ONLY WHEN BLOCKING

FIG. 2

EXTRA LENGTH

of crooked sides caused by the pulling of the tacks. Blocking this way will narrow the canvas slightly, making it fit the decorative ends snugly. When hemming and mitering the corners, leave about ¾ inch of plain canvas exposed beyond the worked area at the ends. This reduces the amount of bulk to be drawn through the opening on the back of the metal end (Fig. 3). Bring the lining down to cover the back of the unworked end (Fig. 4). Pull the unworked end through the slot, turn it back against the lined area, and hem it to the lining (Fig. 5).

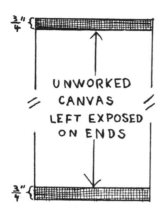

FIG. 3

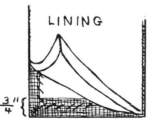

FIG. 4

BRACKET ON BACK OF END PIECE

FIG. 5

Hangings

Materials needed

Plan the shape and size of the hanging, using the various shapes illustrated for suggestions; use a rectangular piece of canvas to accommodate your pattern with 1½ inches all around for excess canvas

Buy the lining material, and necessary hanging bar or bars, weights or whatever before selecting the yarn because of limited color choice and materials

Yarn of your choice

There is an almost unlimited variety in the ways to design and finish hangings. They are almost always straight across the top. Bars to support the top can be metal or wood, decorative or plain, hidden or exposed. Drapery departments will cut bars to any length desired, adding finials for a decorative finish (Fig. 6). The lined hanging can have loops of material or embroidered canvas, added at the top for the bar (Fig. 16). A cord is attached at the ends of the bar for hanging. Cord loops of yarn can be made (Fig. 7). It is necessary to have some small projections near the ends of the bar, over which a small loop of thread can be hooked. A tack or small nail in the wooden bar, or a little screw in the hollow brass bar, will serve (Fig. 8). A solid brass or wrought iron bar is treated differently. Obviously you can't insert a

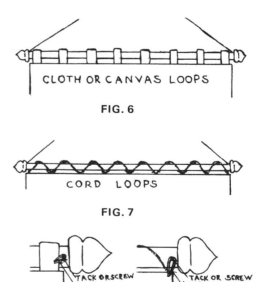

CLOTH OR CANVAS LOOPS

FIG. 6

CORD LOOPS

FIG. 7

TACK OR SCREW LOOP OF THREAD   TACK OR SCREW LOOP OF THREAD

FIG. 8

nail or screw, so instead take a file and make a notch or groove around the bar near the end (Fig. 9). Sew 2 pieces of thread to the corner of the hanging, or to the end loop of material. These should be long enough to wrap around the groove several times and tied in the back (Fig. 10). Don't leave any slack, or the thread won't stay in the groove. These measures are necessary to keep the hanging from sliding together in a bunch at one end of the bar.

Make cloth or canvas loops long enough to accommodate the bar easily, plus an extra inch at each end. Finish the loops with lining material, leaving them open at the ends. Attach them securely to the back of the unlined piece (Fig. 11). Be sure to place a loop near each end so the corners won't sag. Bring the lining up over the ends of the loops, to the top of the hanging, and hem. Sew through the loops to catch the front edge (Fig. 12).

A wooden top can be made at home. Get 2 pieces of wood ¼ inch by 1 inch by ¼ inch longer than the width of the hanging (Fig. 13). Sand and finish one side and all edges of both pieces, rounding the tops of the edges slightly. The pieces can be stained or painted. Lay one piece, unfinished side up, on a table. Lay the top of the hanging, wrong side up, ⅛ inch down from the top edge of the wood, allowing the wood to extend ⅛ inch out at each end (Fig. 14). Tack or glue the wood in place. Attach a hanging cord to the corners of the hanging now. Place the second piece of wood, finished side up over the top of the hanging, and directly over the first piece of wood. Use clamps to hold the pieces of wood together while you insert short screws through the second piece of wood, the top of the hanging and into the first piece of wood. Be careful you don't go all the way through to the front (Fig. 15).

A flat bar of metal or wood can be inserted into a casing made at the top of the lining by simply hand sewing across an inch or so below the top (Fig. 16). This will hold the top of the hanging straight, and won't show. You can add a decora-

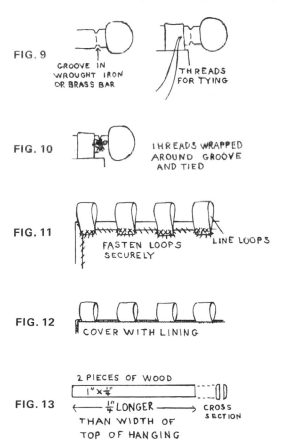

FIG. 9 GROOVE IN WROUGHT IRON OR BRASS BAR THREADS FOR TYING

FIG. 10 THREADS WRAPPED AROUND GROOVE AND TIED

FIG. 11 FASTEN LOOPS SECURELY LINE LOOPS

FIG. 12 COVER WITH LINING

FIG. 13 2 PIECES OF WOOD 1"×¼" ¼" LONGER THAN WIDTH OF TOP OF HANGING CROSS SECTION

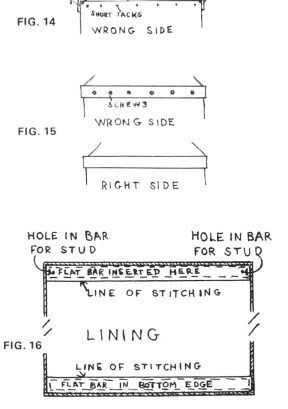

FIG. 14 SHORT TACKS WRONG SIDE

FIG. 15 SCREWS WRONG SIDE RIGHT SIDE

FIG. 16 HOLE IN BAR FOR STUD HOLE IN BAR FOR STUD FLAT BAR INSERTED HERE LINE OF STITCHING LINING LINE OF STITCHING FLAT BAR IN BOTTOM EDGE

tive button or stud at each top corner to support a hanging cord. If studs are used, holes must be bored near the ends of the top bar (Fig. 17). A similar bar can be placed inside the lining at the bottom. You can buy aluminum bars of this type in a hardware store. Your dealer will cut it to any length desired.

If no bar is desired at the bottom, attach lead weights at the corners before lining the piece to keep the corners from curling (Fig. 18). These can be bought in a drapery department or store. Sometimes fringe or tassels are added to the bottom edge. (See "Fringes," p. 220, and "Tassels and Pompons," p. 223.)

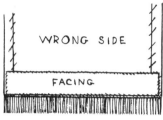

COMMERCIAL FRINGE ADDED BEFORE FACING

FIG. 19

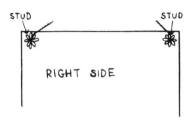

FIG. 17

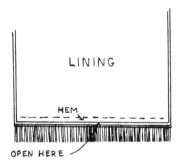

FIG. 20

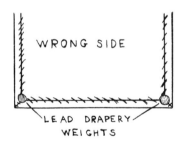

FIG. 18

FIG. 21

To insure a straight hang it is advisable to leave the lining loose at the bottom edge. Cut a piece of lining material 2 inches wide, and face the bottom edge (Fig. 19). Hem the bottom edge of the lining and attach the other 3 sides to the canvas (Fig. 20).

The bottom edge need not be straight. It can be curved or pointed, either a single or several points (Figs. 21, 22, 23). (See "Finishing Canvas on a Curve.") Hem and miter all edges (Figs. 24, 25). A series of oval weights should be placed near the bottom of the curved edge before lining (Fig. 21). Single weights should be placed near the tips

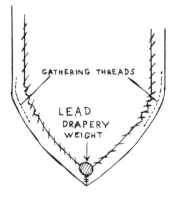

FIG. 22

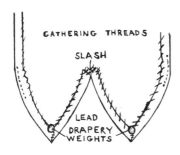

FIG. 23

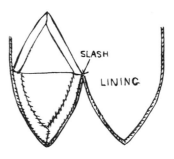

FIG. 27

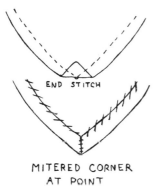

MITERED CORNER
AT POINT

FIG. 24

of the points (Figs. 22, 23). Face the curved edges of a hanging with more than one point, using bias lining material (Fig. 26). Bring the lining down over the facing and hem in place (Fig. 27).

A simple inexpensive top for a bell pull or wider hanging is a hollow brass curtain rod with little balls on the ends. This should be easily available in any drapery department or store. The rod can be cut to any desired length. Or a short flat stick can be inserted in a casing (Fig. 28).

Sometimes unusual materials, such as driftwood, are used to produce special artistic effects.

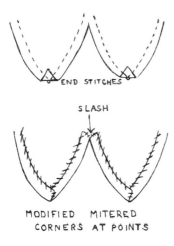

MODIFIED MITERED
CORNERS AT POINTS

FIG. 25

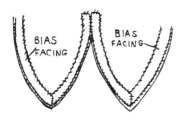

FIG. 26

FIG. 28

Typewriter Cover

This is a cover for a standard typewriter. If you have a cover for one, use it as a pattern. If there is no cover, make a pattern out of paper. One piece serves to cover the back, top, and front. There are 2 pieces to be set in at the sides. Make line A to B equal to line C to D. Most typewriters are narrower in the front than in the top and back, so taper the sides of the main piece so the cover will fit comfortably, but not be too snug at the bottom (Fig. 1).

Materials needed

Canvas to accommodate the 3 pieces, plus 1¼ inches excess canvas around each piece; draw the outlines of the 3 pieces, lining up the straight edges with the canvas threads (Fig. 2)

Interlining and lining for the 3 pieces

Commercial cording with a flange can be set into the seams, or you can work a decorative stitch pattern to cover them (you can make a yarn cording to be sewed on invisibly after you sew the seams; the pieces of cording should be equal in length to the sides of the main part [A to B in Fig. 1]

Yarn of your choice

In planning the design, remember that the back of the main part will have its top and bottom reversed (Fig. 1).

Bind the canvas, work the embroidery, and block. Cut off the binding and all but about 1 inch of the excess canvas. Turn under the canvas, and hem it to the back of the embroidery. Small folds will be needed at the curves. Miter all sharp cor-

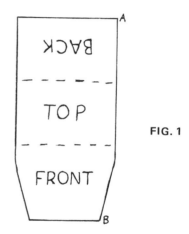

FIG. 1

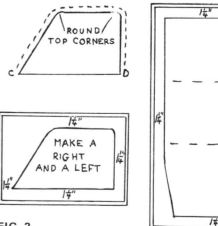

FIG. 2

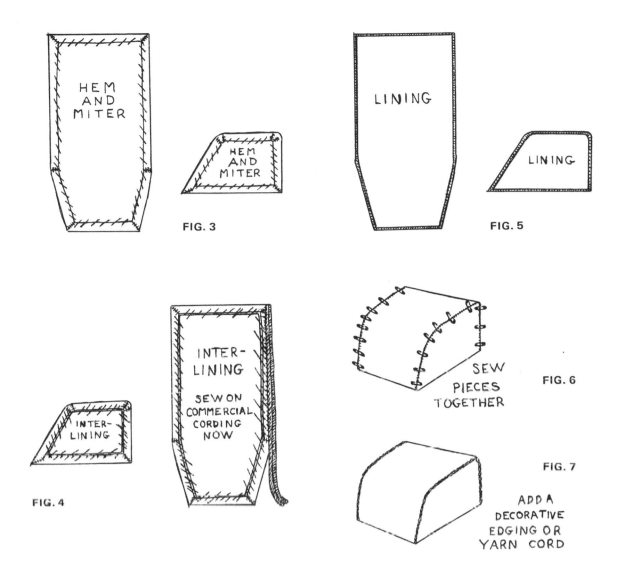

FIG. 3

FIG. 5

FIG. 4

FIG. 6

FIG. 7

ADD A
DECORATIVE
EDGING OR
YARN CORD

ners (Fig. 3). Cut the interlining to fit in the space between the edges of the turned back canvas. Hem it in place (Fig. 4). If you are using commercial cording, sew it to the sides of the main piece now (Fig. 4).

Using your pattern, cut out the lining material, including about ¾ inch seam allowance. Line all 3 pieces (Fig. 5). Using safety pins to help hold the pieces together, seam the 3 pieces together on the right side (Fig. 6). (See "Joining Pieces of Canvas—Seaming.") If you have not used a commercial cording, work a decorative stitch pattern over the seams, or make yarn cording and sew it invisibly over the seams (Fig. 7).

Card Table Covers

Measure the card table; they are not all the same size. Some have square corners, and some have rounded ones (Fig. 1). Measure the depth of the side of the table. This can vary, too (Fig. 2).

The cover should fit snugly, but shouldn't be so tight that there is strain at the corners, so measure carefully. Allow ¼ inch extra each way for the thickness of the canvas, and the bulk at the seams or darted corners, also ¼ inch extra in the depth.

Materials needed

1 piece of canvas the width and the length of the table, plus the depth, plus 1½ inches excess canvas all around
Matching material for the casing 2 inches wide and 3 inches longer than the perimeter of the table. For a square-cornered table, 4 pieces of material 12 inches long by the depth of the top, plus seam allowance, used to face the corners
1 piece of narrow elastic equal to the perimeter of the table
8 pieces of ½ inch tape, and 8 snaps (optional)
4 pieces of ¼ inch elastic equal to the width of the table, minus 16 inches (optional)
Yarn of your choice

Choose stitch patterns that are small and flat, especially in the center. Long stitches are easily caught by fingernails or rings. Stitch patterns around the edges can be more elaborate, but avoid too much "bumpiness." Many people put beverage glasses on the corners. An uneven surface could lead to spills.

SQUARE CORNERED CARD TABLE

ROUND CORNERED CARD TABLE

FIG. 1

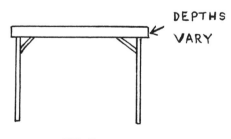

DEPTHS VARY

FIG. 2

Square-cornered table

Plan the worked area with unworked corners the depth of the table, plus ¼ inch. The canvas comes wide enough to make the cover in 1 piece. Add 1½ inches excess canvas all around (Fig. 3).

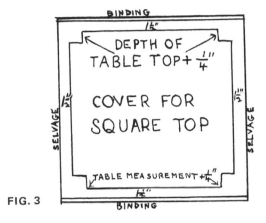

FIG. 3

Bind the canvas, work the embroidery, and block. Pinch the edges of the unworked corners together, and seam on the right side with matching yarn. Continue the seam ¾ inch into the unworked canvas (Fig. 4). On the inside, cut away all but ¾ inch of the triangular piece (Fig. 5). Fold the sides back and hem. There will be a sort of triangular piece at the top (Fig. 6). Cut a long strip of the

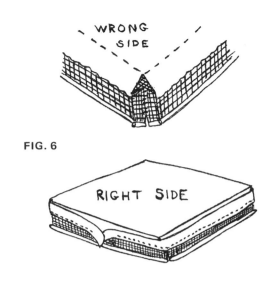

FIG. 6

matching material, piecing it if necessary, 2 inches wide, and 3 inches longer than the perimeter of the table. Starting in the middle of a side, baste the strip, right sides together, to the edge of the worked area. Stop near the other end. Turn to the wrong side, and, starting about 3 inches from the beginning, machine stitch as close to the embroidery as possible, around the corners, and to within 3 inches of the other end (Fig. 7). Turn back to the right side. Fit and seam the ends of the strip. Turn over to the wrong side again, and finish the last 6 inches (Fig. 8). This is done because it is

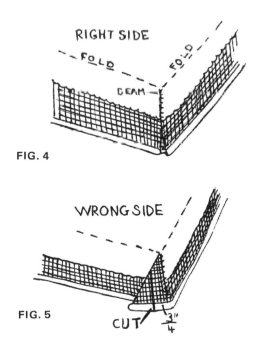

FIG. 4

FIG. 5

CUT ¾

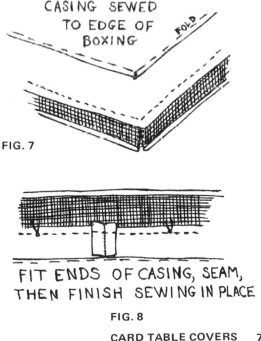

CASING SEWED TO EDGE OF BOXING

FIG. 7

FIT ENDS OF CASING, SEAM, THEN FINISH SEWING IN PLACE

FIG. 8

CARD TABLE COVERS 73

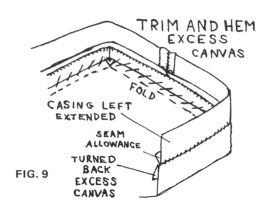

FIG. 9

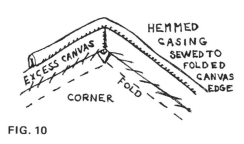

FIG. 10

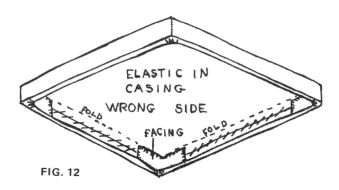

FIG. 12

like a contour sheet. Sew the ends together (Fig. 12). The best way to adjust the tightness of the elastic is to put the cover on the table, and turn it upside down on another table. Then you can get at the casing and the elastic easily. A little of the embroidered boxing should turn in, too.

Round-cornered table

The worked area of the canvas should equal the width by the length of the table, plus the depth, plus ¼ inch each way. Allow 1½ inches excess canvas all around (Fig. 13). Bind the canvas first. Keep it rectangular. Lay the bound canvas on the table, and weight it down so it won't slip. Now pinch 3 darts in each corner, one in the center and one on each side. Try to make them of equal size and 2 inches to 3 inches apart, depending on the sharpness of the curve. Try to make the future sewing lines parallel (Fig. 14). This is as near to achieving a curved fold as you can come. Mark the darts clearly, but don't sew them yet. The embroidery will be omitted in the dart areas.

impossible to figure the exact length of the strip for a perfect fit. Now cut the binding off the canvas, turn it up, and hem, leaving the strip of material extended (Fig. 9). Turn under ½ inch seam allowance of the strip, and securely hand hem it to the folded edge of the canvas (Fig. 10). Use fairly strong thread. There will be strain on these stitches.

It is not necessary to line the whole cover, but a facing at each corner will protect the seam area from the corners of the table. Turn in the seam allowance of the facings and sew them into the corners, 6 inches on each side (Fig. 11). Put a small safety pin in one end of the piece of elastic, and, slipping in between your hand-sewn stitches, thread the elastic through the casing all the way around. Pull the elastic up just enough to turn the corners under, and make the cover snug, somewhat

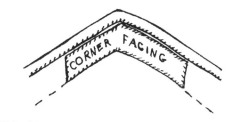

FIG. 11

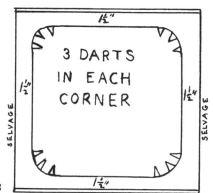

FIG. 13

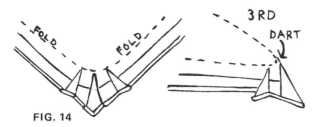

FIG. 14

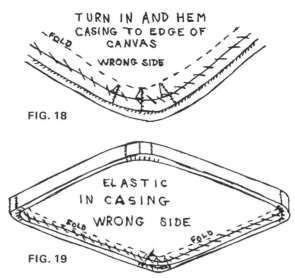

TURN IN AND HEM CASING TO EDGE OF CANVAS

FOLD WRONG SIDE

FIG. 18

ELASTIC IN CASING WRONG SIDE

FOLD   FOLD

FIG. 19

Work the embroidery, and block. Sew up the darts on the right side, using matching yarn. Sew about ¾ inch into the unworked canvas (Fig. 15). Cut a long strip of the matching material, piecing it, if necessary, 2 inches wide, and 3 inches longer than the perimeter of the table. Sew it to the edge of the embroidery (Fig. 16). (See "Square-Cornered Table" directions.)

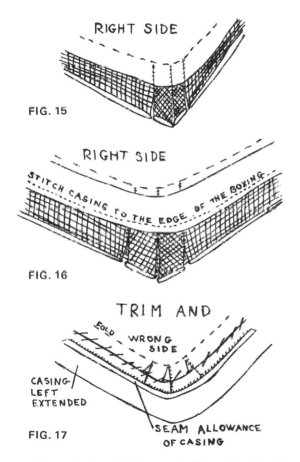

RIGHT SIDE

FIG. 15

RIGHT SIDE

STITCH CASING TO THE EDGE OF THE BOXING

FIG. 16

TRIM AND

FOLD   WRONG SIDE

CASING LEFT EXTENDED

SEAM ALLOWANCE OF CASING

FIG. 17

Trim off the binding and all but 1 inch of the excess canvas. Turn under the excess canvas and hem, leaving the casing extended (Fig. 17). Turn under the seam allowance of the casing, and hem it to the edge of the folded edge of the canvas. Use strong thread and sew securely. There will be strain on these stitches (Figs. 18, 19). (See "Square-Cornered Table" for inserting the elastic.)

If you feel the sides are a little loose, you can make straps to snap to the casing across from one side to the other under the table. Put 8 inch pieces of tape on the ends of the ¼ inch elastic, with half a snap at each end, and the other half snap on the under side of the casing. Stretch the elastic just enough to provide a little tension, but not enough to pull the edges of the cover out of a straight line (Fig. 20).

Note: If your card table cover becomes soiled, take it off and wash it as you would any fine woolen product. Cover the table with a single piece of plastic, and put the cover back on after you have squeezed out as much water as possible with towels. It will dry in perfect shape.

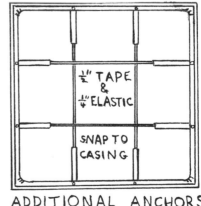

½" TAPE & ¼" ELASTIC

SNAP TO CASING

FIG. 20

ADDITIONAL ANCHORS USE IF NECESSARY. COVER SHOULD BE TIGHT.

Trays

Make an attractive tray out of a wood picture frame, old or new. If you use an old one be sure the corners are firm. Not all wood frames will do. The outside edge must be wide and thick enough to support a pair of handles (Fig. 1). If the frame is unfinished, you can finish it with stain, paint, varnish, wax, or any way you wish.

Materials needed

A suitable frame with glass

A piece of canvas equal in measurements to the glass, plus 1½ inches excess canvas all around (Fig. 3)

A piece of heavy stiff cardboard ⅛ inch smaller each way than the measurements of the glass (there is a flange against which the glass rests; this makes the glass larger than the frame opening [Fig. 4])

A piece of thin composition board, or a piece of ⅛ inch plywood equal to the outside measurements of the back of the frame (Fig. 5)

10 to 20 small flat head screws, depending on the size of the frame

A piece of felt to cover the plywood or board

A pair of decorative metal handles, with suitable small screws (Fig. 2)

Rubber cement, glue, heavy thread or string, and a small drill

Yarn of your choice

A word about borders. An attractive border adds much to the appearance of many designs. Just don't put one too close to the edge. Any slight deviation from an exact straight line would show if the border is close to the edge of the frame. If you want to use one, choose a border

FIG. 1

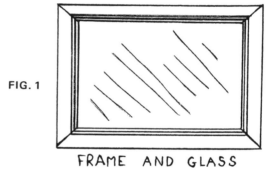

FRAME AND GLASS

FIG. 2

WORKED AREA EQUAL TO MEASUREMENTS OF GLASS

FIG. 3

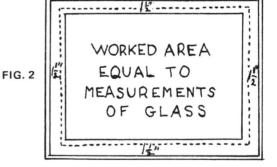

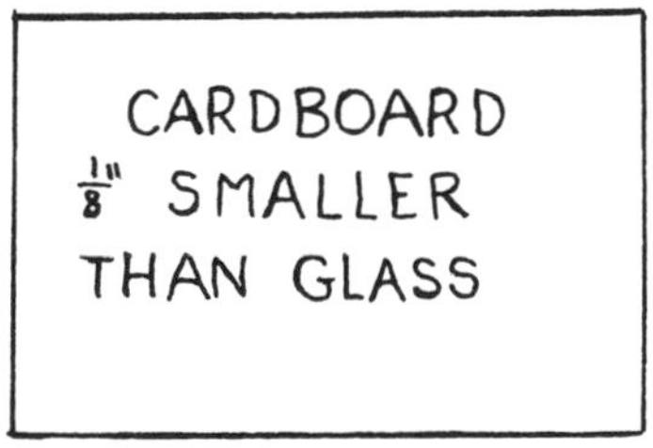

CARDBOARD ⅛" SMALLER THAN GLASS

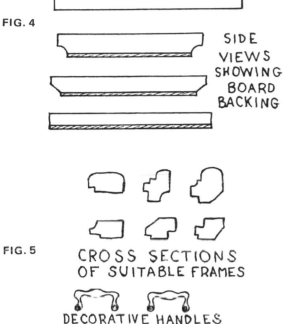

FIG. 4

STIFF COMPOSITION BOARD OR ⅛" PLYWOOD EQUAL TO MEASUREMENTS OF OUTSIDE OF BACK OF FRAME

FELT THE SAME SIZE

SIDE VIEWS SHOWING BOARD BACKING

FIG. 5

CROSS SECTIONS OF SUITABLE FRAMES

DECORATIVE HANDLES

that has many open spaces, or irregular edges, such as a floral one. This will make blocking much easier.

Place the composition board or plywood on the back of the frame. Tape it to hold it in place. Mark spots, evenly spaced, about 3 inches apart around the edges of the board. With a very small drill, make holes through the board, into the back of the frame. Set this aside until later (Fig. 6).

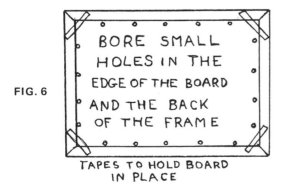

FIG. 6

BORE SMALL HOLES IN THE EDGE OF THE BOARD AND THE BACK OF THE FRAME

TAPES TO HOLD BOARD IN PLACE

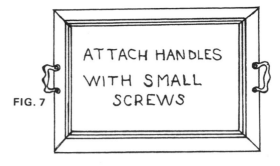

FIG. 7

ATTACH HANDLES WITH SMALL SCREWS

Attach the handles in the middle of the short sides, using small screws. These will probably come with the handles (Fig. 7).

Bind the canvas. Mark off an area equal to the measurements of the glass. Be sure you draw your line along the canvas threads. Run 2 rows of machine stitching, one on top of the other, around this area, about ½ inch out in the excess canvas. Work the embroidery, and block, using the glass as a guide. Be sure the corners are square (Fig. 8). Cut off the binding, and with heavy thread or string, stretch the canvas over the heavy cardboard. Sew into the line of machine stitching. Pull tight enough to make the top side even and smooth, but not tight enough to make peaks along the folded edge. Make modified mitered corners (Fig. 9). (See "Mounting Canvas for Framing," p. 11.)

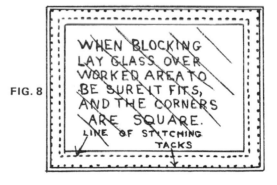

FIG. 8

WHEN BLOCKING LAY GLASS OVER WORKED AREA TO BE SURE IT FITS, AND THE CORNERS ARE SQUARE.

LINE OF STITCHING

TACKS

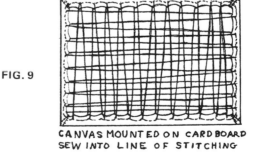

FIG. 9

CANVAS MOUNTED ON CARDBOARD SEW INTO LINE OF STITCHING

If your embroidery has depth and you don't want it squashed flat against the glass, glue or sew narrow strips of felt along the edges. Be sure it is narrow enough so it won't show. Use a color to match the background color of the embroidery (Fig. 10). You will want to seal the space between the edges of the glass and the frame so an accidental spill won't run under the glass and ruin the embroidery. This can be done with a generous strip of rubber cement. Be sure all edges and corners are covered. The rubber cement is waterproof. It can't dry out and let go because of the pressure of the glass against it, yet the glass can be easily removed later, if necessary. Put the rubber cement along the flange on the back of the frame, and press the glass firmly against it. If any cement oozes out onto the front of the glass, it can easily be removed with a razor blade or sharp knife (Fig.11).

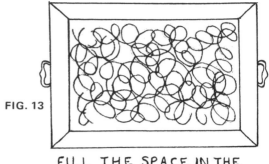

FIG. 13

FILL THE SPACE IN THE BACK, IF NECESSARY

will want to fill the space firmly so the cardboard and canvas can't slip down (Fig. 13).

Now set the composition board or plywood in place, and put the screws in the holes you made earlier. Be sure they are screwed down even with the surface of the board so the back will be smooth (Fig. 14). Don't try to use nails; you'll break the glass. Last, glue the piece of felt on the back so there will be no danger of scratching anything you might lay the tray on (Fig. 15).

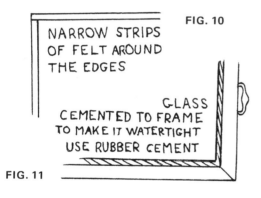

FIG. 10

NARROW STRIPS OF FELT AROUND THE EDGES

GLASS CEMENTED TO FRAME TO MAKE IT WATERTIGHT USE RUBBER CEMENT

FIG. 11

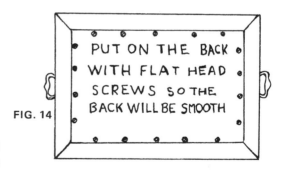

PUT ON THE BACK WITH FLAT HEAD SCREWS SO THE BACK WILL BE SMOOTH

FIG. 14

Set the canvas-covered board in place. It should fit snugly (Fig. 12). If there is a small space between the back of the cardboard and the back edge of the frame, fit in layers of newspaper. If the space is quite large, you can fill it with tightly crumpled newspaper, excelsior, or nylon net. You

GLUE FELT ON THE BACK

FIG. 15

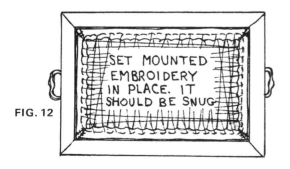

FIG. 12

SET MOUNTED EMBROIDERY IN PLACE. IT SHOULD BE SNUG

The same procedure can be followed for an oval (elliptical), or round tray. You will need smaller handles to fit the curved sides. See "Mounting Canvas for Framing—Oval," p. 12.

Picture or Mirror Frame

Measure the picture or mirror to be framed. Decide how wide you want the frame to be. Allow 1¼ inches all around for excess canvas (Fig. 1). The measurements in Figure 1 are for standard photograph sizes. Adjust them to suit your individual needs.

Materials needed

1 piece of fairly fine canvas as above
2 pieces of thin but stiff cardboard equal to the outside measurements of the frame, and a piece for an easel
Lining material for the frame, plus seam allowance, and a piece 1¼ inches larger all around than the picture opening
Heavy thread or string
Yarn of your choice

Bind the canvas. Draw a line for the outside edges. Draw a rectangle for the opening ¼ inch (⅛ inch on each side) smaller than the measurements of the picture. Be sure you have at least 1¼ inches excess canvas around the edges (Fig. 1 and 2). Work the embroidery and block.

Run 2 rows of machine stitching, one on top of the other, ¼ inch out from the outer edge of the frame. On the right side, lay the small piece of lining material over the opening, allowing the 1 inch extra to extend over the frame. Baste it in place. Turn to the wrong side, and machine stitch along the edge of the opening as close to the embroidery as possible. Sew with very small stitches around the corners. Reverse your machine,

FIG. 1

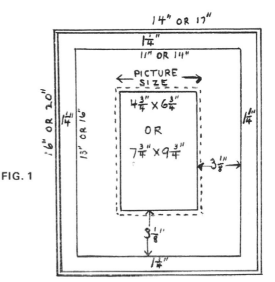

FIG. 2

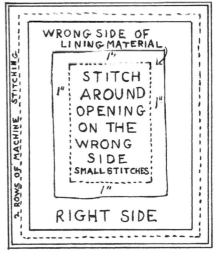

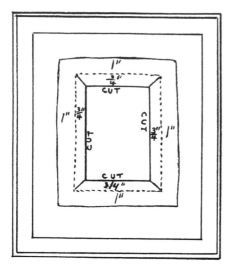

FIG. 3

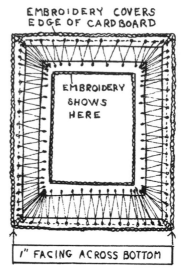

EMBROIDERY COVERS EDGE OF CARDBOARD

EMBROIDERY SHOWS HERE

1" FACING ACROSS BOTTOM

FIG. 5

if you can. This stitching has to hold the short canvas threads where the slash comes (Fig. 3). Cut away part of the canvas and the lining in the opening, leaving about ¾ inch excess around the edges. Slit to the corners, being careful not to cut the machine stitching. Cut off the binding (Fig. 3).

Cut one piece of cardboard ½ inch (¼ inch each way) smaller than the outside of the frame. Cut a hole in the center the exact size of the picture. Round the outside corners slightly (Fig. 4). Lay this on the back of your embroidery. Pull the facing through the hole over the cardboard, pressing it back with your fingers so the facing lies

flat. The embroidery should cover the thickness of the cardboard. Using the heavy thread and a sharp needle, lace back and forth between the excess canvas on the outer edge, and the facing around the opening. Sew into the line of stitching you made around the outer edge. Pull fairly tight. The embroidery around the outer edge should cover the thickness of the cardboard, too, and be visible on the back. Make modified mitered corners. Cut and sew on a facing across the bottom. It should be about 1 inch wide, finished (Fig. 5).

Cut the second piece of cardboard the same size as the first, but with no hole in the middle

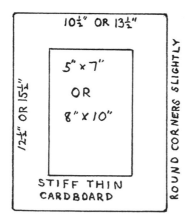

10½" OR 13½"

5" x 7" OR 8" x 10"

STIFF THIN CARDBOARD

ROUND CORNERS SLIGHTLY

12½" OR 15½"

FIG. 4

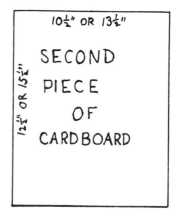

10½" OR 13½"

SECOND PIECE OF CARDBOARD

12½" OR 15½"

FIG. 6

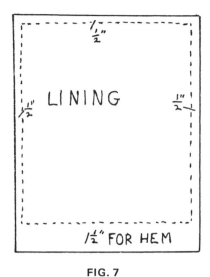

FIG. 7

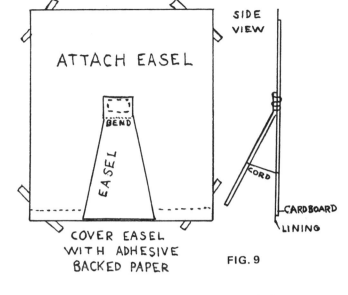

FIG. 9

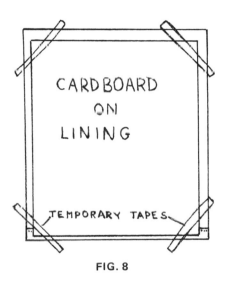

FIG. 8

bottom edge even with the bottom of the cardboard, and with a strong needle and thread, sew the top of the easel through the lining material to the cardboard. Bend the easel to the desired distance and attach a cord made with sewing thread across to keep the easel from bending too far (Fig. 9).

Remove the tapes and hem the lining around the outer edges of the frame, with the opening at the bottom (Fig. 10). The picture should slip up into place. If the corners catch on the string lacing, slide a ruler up between the picture and the frame to free them.

(Fig. 6). Cut a piece of lining material with seam allowance at the top and sides, and about 1½ inches at the bottom for a hem. Hem the bottom (Fig. 7). Using cellophane tape, fasten the second piece of cardboard temporarily to the wrong side of the lining. Have the bottom edge about ¼ inch up from the hemmed edge (Fig. 8). Cut a piece of cardboard for the easel rest. Cover it with adhesive-backed paper, if you like. Bend it about 1 inch down from the top. Turn the lining and cardboard over to the lining side. Place the easel with its

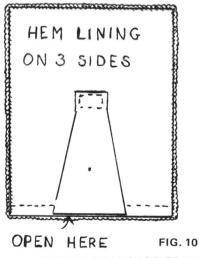

FIG. 10

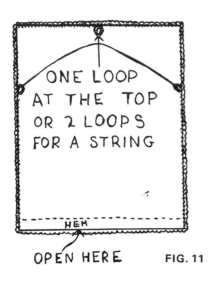

ONE LOOP AT THE TOP OR 2 LOOPS FOR A STRING

HEM

OPEN HERE

FIG. 11

If you wish to hang the picture or mirror, eliminate the easel, and work small buttonhole loops on the lining, either one at the top, or one on each side, part way down, for a string (Fig. 11).

The same procedure can be followed for a round or elliptical frame. You will need to follow the directions for "Finishing Canvas on a Curve," both "Convex" and "Concave."

Church Kneeling Cushions

Kneeling cushions are made in two main styles. Style A is one piece with cutout corners, which are seamed. Style B has a separate top and boxing, with a cording usually added in the seam.

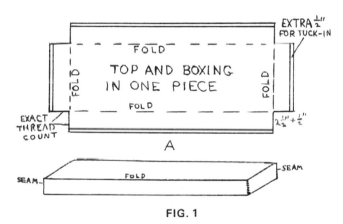

FIG. 1

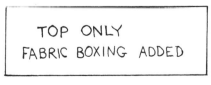

FIG. 2

Style A

Materials needed

Canvas to accommodate the length, width, and boxing, plus 1¼ inches excess canvas all around (Fig. 1)

Firm foam rubber block the length and width of the cushion

3 inch deep muslin to cover the rubber, if desired

A piece of thin plywood the length and width of the cushion, if desired

Backing

Yarn of your choice

For a long altar rail kneeler that is to be pieced, see measuring suggestions below. The block of foam rubber and the plywood should fit the measurements of the assembled cushion. The backing should be in one piece, too.

This type of cushion is preferred. It is simple to make, as it is in one piece. There is no seam where most of the wear comes, along the front edge. The seams at the corners are short and inconspicuous. Make the cushion 2½ inches deep, no more. Deeper cushions will cause people to teeter, and perhaps lose their balance. Firm block foam rubber is used for padding. A 3-inch-deep block can be compressed to 2½ inches.

Style B

Materials needed

Canvas to accommodate the top of the cushion, plus 1¼ inches excess canvas all around (Fig. 2)

Appropriate matching commercial cording, or cotton
    cording to be covered with material to match the
    fabric boxing
Appropriate matching material for the boxing
Backing
Firm foam rubber block the length and width of the
    cushion
Muslin to cover the rubber, if desired
A piece of thin plywood, the length and width of the
    cushion, if desired
Yarn of your choice

For a long cushion that is to be pieced, the separate sections should be seamed before the cording and boxing are added. The foam rubber, plywood, and backing should equal the measurements of the assembled cushion. The cording and boxing should be pieced as infrequently and as inconspicuously as possible.

In this style only the top is usually worked in canvas embroidery. A fabric-covered or commercial cording is placed between the canvas top and the fabric boxing, which is usually made of velvet. Make these up like Style C, "Pillows," p. 19, but stuff with block foam rubber 3 inches deep, compressed to 2½ inches.

Church altar rail kneeling areas vary widely in design and measurements. It is best to do the measuring for kneeling cushions yourself. Use a metal ruler, not a cloth tape, the latter are notoriously inaccurate (Fig. 3). If it is impossible for you to do your own measuring, have someone in the church get a roll of shelf paper. Unroll it on the step on which the kneeling cushions will rest, marking the exact width of the step, the positions of the railing posts, the exact width and position of the gate, etc. (Fig. 4). The cushions can be made to fit accurately by using this pattern.

The cushions are usually made in 3 sections, one long cushion on either side, and a separate one for the gate, so it can be removed when necessary. The long cushions are usually made in several pieces, seamed together at regular intervals (Fig. 5). This makes it possible for many church members to share in the needlework. When planning the pieces for a long cushion, make the total length a couple of inches short. This will allow for the slight bulge in the boxing, and the thickness of the canvas work. We call this "Breathing Room" (Fig. 6).

The type of design used will be subject to the style of the church, the taste of the people who will approve the designs, and the skill of the needleworkers. There is a wealth of design in the

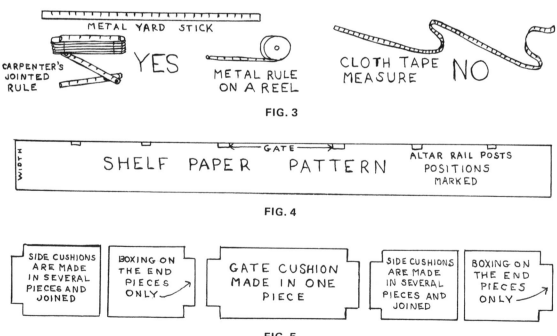

METAL YARD STICK

CARPENTER'S JOINTED RULE

YES

METAL RULE ON A REEL

CLOTH TAPE MEASURE

NO

FIG. 3

WIDTH

GATE

SHELF PAPER PATTERN

ALTAR RAIL POSTS POSITIONS MARKED

FIG. 4

SIDE CUSHIONS ARE MADE IN SEVERAL PIECES AND JOINED

BOXING ON THE END PIECES ONLY

GATE CUSHION MADE IN ONE PIECE

SIDE CUSHIONS ARE MADE IN SEVERAL PIECES AND JOINED

BOXING ON THE END PIECES ONLY

FIG. 5

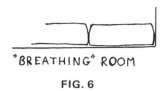

"BREATHING" ROOM

FIG. 6

symbolism of both churches and synagogues. Your church or public library may be able to help you select appropriate ones. Designs can be copied from the church windows or carvings. Geometric forms should be worked out on graph paper, and transferred clearly to the canvas. Paint the design with oil or acrylic paints, applied sparingly. If possible, plan the design so it will hide the seams (Fig. 7). In selecting a stitch pattern, the ever popular Diagonal Tent is used widely, but there are many others that will work just as well, and give more richness and variety to the work. Choose patterns with small units and fairly short stitches so they will wear well. There is a large variety in the encyclopedia. If borders are desired around the edges, set them in about an inch from the fold between the top and the sides. They look better if they are placed this way. Try to plan the border so there is no break in the repeat at the seams. This may require a lot of thread counting, but perfection is worth it (Fig. 8).

After the needleworkers have done their part, the pieces should be blocked, seamed, and the corners of the boxing joined. Check with your measurements or the paper pattern for size accuracy. (See "Joining Pieces of Canvas—Seaming,") Use 3 inch foam rubber made for the purpose. Muslin covering is not absolutely necessary, but it will make mounting the backing easier, as the compression of the extra ½ inch of the foam rubber can be done with the muslin. Besides it will help keep any soil from penetrating to the foam rubber.

Fold under the extra ½ inch of worked canvas, and back the cushions with matching velvet (Fig. 9). If the step on which the cushions will lie is smooth, it may be necessary to attach inconspicuous tapes to be tied or snapped to the altar rail posts to keep the cushions in place. Sometimes the padding is laid on thin plywood boards, and the whole covered with the canvas and backing. This gives the cushions a solid base, which makes them stay in place very well (Fig. 10).

There are other church furnishings frequently made in canvas embroidery, such as altar frontals, pulpit falls, and Bible markers. The finishing of these can vary widely, and are best put in the hands of an expert. Of course, chairs and benches can be treated like those for lay purposes.

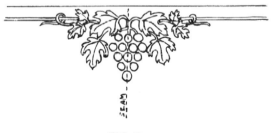

FIG. 7

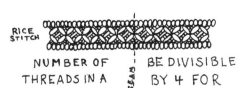

RICE STITCH

NUMBER OF THREADS IN A SECTION MUST | BE DIVISIBLE BY 4 FOR RICE STITCH

FIG. 8

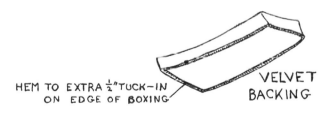

HEM TO EXTRA ¼" TUCK-IN ON EDGE OF BOXING

VELVET BACKING

FIG. 9

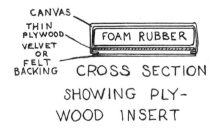

CANVAS
THIN PLYWOOD
VELVET OR FELT BACKING

FOAM RUBBER

CROSS SECTION SHOWING PLYWOOD INSERT

FIG. 10

Book Cover

Materials needed

1 piece of fairly fine canvas as wide as the front, back, and spine, A to B, plus ½ inch by the depth of the book, C to D, plus ¼ inch, plus 1 inch excess canvas all around

Lining material for the above, plus seam allowance, and 2 pieces the depth of the lining material by the width of the book cover (Fig. 4, 5)

2 pieces of thin elastic the depth of the book

1 piece of ribbon 2 inches longer than the depth of the book

Yarn of your choice

Book covers, obviously, can't be made to fit all books, so it is best to choose one of some permanence, such as a Bible, address book, diary, etc. Measure the distance from a top corner, around the spine, to the other top corner with the book closed. Allow ½ inch extra for the thickness of the embroidery, and the book covers. Add ¼ inch to the depth for the thickness of the book covers (Fig. 1). In planning the design, remember the front will be on the right (Fig. 2).

Bind the canvas, work the embroidery, and block. Cut off the binding, hem and miter the corners. Fold the excess canvas in so the first row of the stitchery will show from the back (Fig. 3). Attach the pieces of elastic about ½ inch out from the spine area. Stretch them a little. Attach one end of the ribbon to the top of the spine area (Fig. 6). Hem the lining to the canvas, passing it under

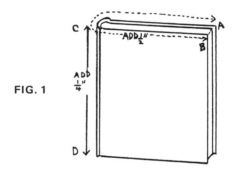

FIG. 1

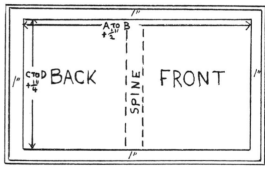

FIG. 2

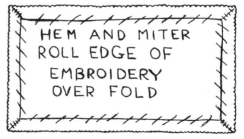

FIG. 3

FIG. 4

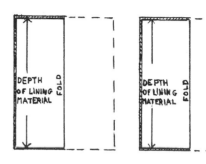

FIG. 7

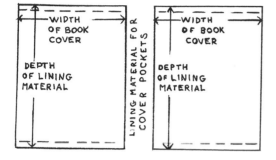

FIG. 5

FIG. 8

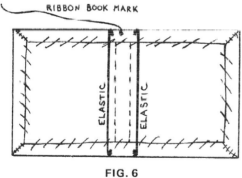

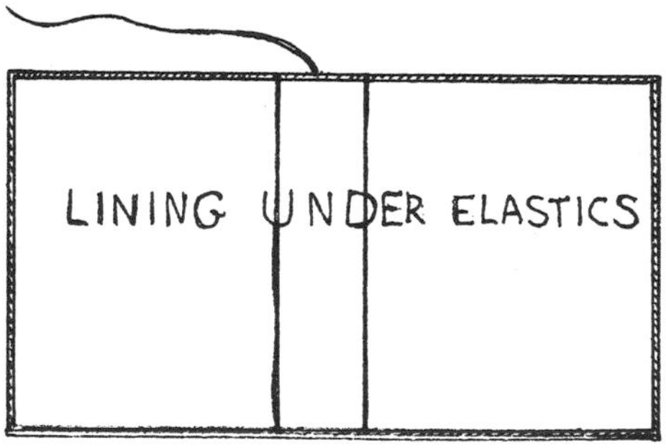

FIG. 6

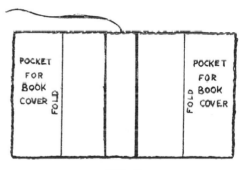

FIG. 9

the elastics (Fig. 7). Fold the extra pieces of lining material lengthwise, and hem them on the other 3 sides (Fig. 8).

With the folded edge toward the spine, hem them to the ends of the book cover. If the canvas shows along the edges, or if you want to cover the seams, work a fine Binding stitch all around (Fig. 9).

Open the book covers, folding them gently all the way back. Pass them under the elastics and into the pockets at the ends. They should be fairly snug (Fig. 10).

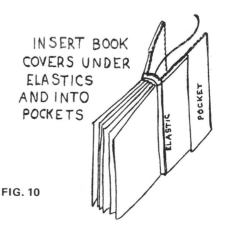

INSERT BOOK COVERS UNDER ELASTICS AND INTO POCKETS

FIG. 10

Telephone Book Cover

Materials needed

1 piece of canvas as wide as the front, spine, and back, A to B, plus ½ inch by the depth of the book, C to D, plus ¼ inch, plus excess canvas of 1¼ inches all around

Lining material for the above (Fig. 5), plus seam allowance, and 2 pieces the depth of the lining material, and twice the width of the book cover (Fig. 6)

2 or 3 pieces of thin elastic the depth of the book

2 pieces of heavy stiff cardboard ¼ inch smaller each way than the front or back

Heavy thread or string

Yarn of your choice

Measure the distance from one top corner, around the spine, to the other top corner. Add ½ inch for the thickness of the embroidery and the cardboard (A to B in Fig. 1). Measure the depth and add ¼ inch. Then add 2½ inches each way, that's 1¼ inches on each side. This is the size of the piece of canvas needed (Fig. 2). When designing the cover, remember the front is on the right side (Fig. 2).

Bind, work the embroidery, and block. Before cutting the binding off, make 2 rows of machine stitching, one on top of the other, about ½ inch out from the embroidered area (Fig. 2). Cut 2 pieces of cardboard ¼ inch smaller each way than the front or back areas of the embroidery (Fig. 3). Lay the pieces of cardboard on the wrong side of the canvas and, cutting off the binding a little at a time as needed, lace back and forth across the

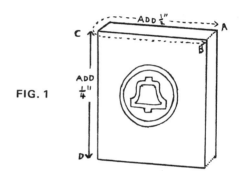

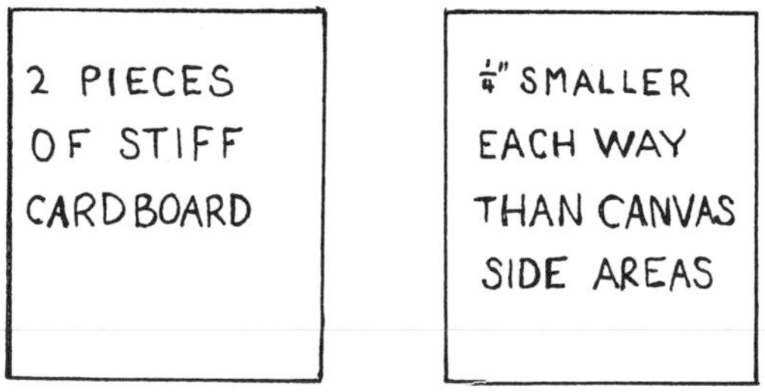

FIG. 1

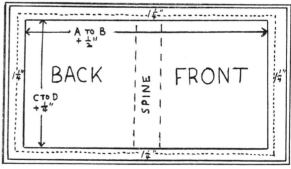

FIG. 2

FIG. 3

2 PIECES OF STIFF CARDBOARD

¼" SMALLER EACH WAY THAN CANVAS SIDE AREAS

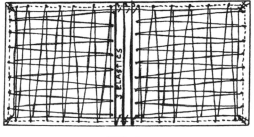

FIG. 4

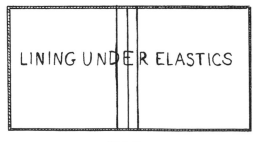

LINING UNDER ELASTICS

FIG. 7

LINING

FIG. 5

2 PIECES FOLDED IN HALF. SEAM THE OTHER 3 SIDES

FOLD

FIG. 8

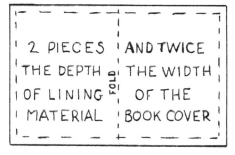

2 PIECES THE DEPTH OF LINING MATERIAL

FOLD

AND TWICE THE WIDTH OF THE BOOK COVER

FIG. 6

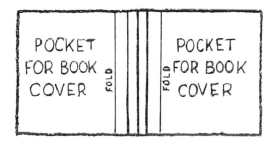

POCKET FOR BOOK COVER

FOLD

FOLD

POCKET FOR BOOK COVER

FIG. 9

cardboard from top to bottom, and from the side to the edge of the spine area. Use heavy thread or string, sewing into the line of machine stitching. Pull your lacing fairly snug. Hem the excess canvas at the top and bottom of the spine area (Fig. 4). Make modified mitered corners.

Sew 2 or 3 pieces of elastic, depending on the thickness of your telephone book, across the spine. Stretch them a little (Fig. 4). Passing the lining material under the elastics, hem it all the way around (Fig. 7).

Fold the 2 extra pieces of lining material in half, and hem the other 3 sides (Fig. 8). With the folded edges toward the spine, hem them to the ends of the cover. Work Binding stitch all around the edges to hide the seams (Fig. 9).

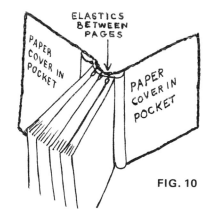

ELASTICS BETWEEN PAGES

PAPER COVER IN POCKET

PAPER COVER IN POCKET

FIG. 10

Open the book at regular intervals for the elastics, and press them in close to the binding. Slip the paper covers of the book into the pockets at the ends (Fig. 10).

Desk Blotting Pad Ends

Materials needed

1 piece of heavy stiff cardboard; you can use an old pad if the cardboard is in good condition

Adhesive backed paper 2 inches wider and 2 inches shorter than the board

2 pieces of fairly fine canvas. Make the worked area ¼ inch longer than the width of the board, and about 2½ inches wide

2 pieces of lining material the same size as worked area of canvas, plus seam allowance

2 pieces of lining material the same length as the width of the board by 5 inches, plus seam allowance

3 pieces of 1 inch elastic the length of the board, minus about 7 inches (get a dark color, it won't show dirt so soon)

1 piece of blotting paper

Yarn of your choice

If you use an old blotting pad, cut off the triangular corners (Fig. 1). You can start from scratch with a piece of ⅛ inch thick stiff card-board. Cover the back, and 1 inch of the front, top and bottom, with adhesive-backed paper. Leave 1 inch at each end uncovered (Fig. 2). Measure the ends, and add ¼ inch to the length of the worked area of the canvas. A good width for a medium-sized pad is 2½ inches. You can make the pieces wider or narrower to suit the pad ends you're making. Both ends can be worked on one piece of canvas. Be sure to have about 1¼ inches excess canvas around the outside, and at least 2 inches between the pieces (Fig. 3). The reason the worked area is ¼ inch longer than the board is to allow for the thickness of the board and the blotting paper. You will want the canvas to curve over the edges of the cardboard.

Bind the canvas, work the embroidery, and block. Cut off the binding, and cut the pieces apart through the middle of the 2 inch excess canvas. Turn under the excess canvas, hem, and

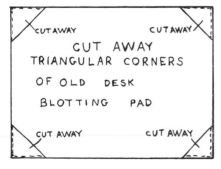

FIG. 1

FIG. 2

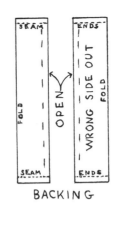

FIG. 3

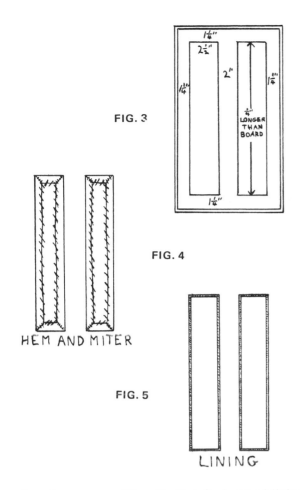

FIG. 4

HEM AND MITER

FIG. 5

LINING

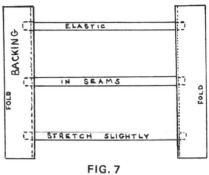

FIG. 6

BACKING

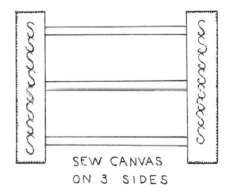

FIG. 7

SEW CANVAS ON 3 SIDES

FIG. 8

SLIP ENDS OVER ENDS OF CARDBOARD. INSERT BLOTTER

FIG. 9

miter the corners (Fig. 4). Cut 2 pieces of lining material and line the pieces (Fig. 5). Cut 2 pieces of lining material the actual width of the board by twice the width of the canvas pieces, plus seam allowance. For 2¼ inch wide canvas that would be about 6¼ inches. Fold the piece in half lengthwise, wrong side out, and seam the short ends (Fig. 6). Turn the pieces right side out. Baste the elastic in the long openings about 2 inches in from the ends, and one in the middle. Adjust their length so they will stretch slightly when they are in place. Turn under the seam allowance of the long openings, and seam the edges, sewing across the pieces of elastic (Fig. 7). Hem the other 3 sides to the edges of the lined canvas (Fig. 8). Binding stitch might be needed to cover the seams. By stretching the elastic, slip the canvas ends over the board. The elastic should stretch just enough to hold the ends snug, but not buckle the board. Cut the blotting paper to fit, and slip it under the canvas ends (Fig. 9).

Book Ends and Paper Weight

It is possible to buy at very little cost the simple black metal book ends often seen in libraries. Or a piece of metal about 4½ inches by 10 inches can be bent across the middle. A sort of slipcover can be made to cover the vertical part (Fig. 1). Make a pair, one for each end of a row of books.

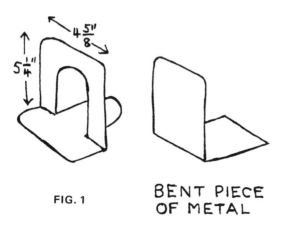

FIG. 1

BENT PIECE OF METAL

Materials needed

2 pieces of fairly fine canvas, 1 inch larger all around than the dimensions of the upright parts

Lining material for the above, plus seam allowance on 3 sides, and 1 inch at the bottom for a hem; also 2 pieces to make 1 inch facings at the bottoms of the canvas pieces

2 pieces of felt to glue on the bottoms of the horizontal parts

Yarn of your choice

Draw a pattern by tracing the outline of the vertical part on a piece of paper. Allow ⅛ inch extra each way. Draw this pattern on a piece of canvas, lining up the straight bottom with the canvas threads (Fig. 2). Plan a design to suit this shape.

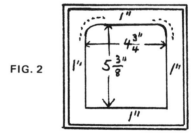

FIG. 2

Bind the canvas, work the embroidery, and block, using the paper pattern as a guide. Put 2 rows of stitching, one on top of the other, ⅜ inch out around the curved corners. Cut off the binding, and a little of the excess canvas at the top corners. Turn in and hem, mitering the bottom corners (Fig. 3). (See "Finishing Canvas on a Curve" for the top corners.)

FIG. 3

HEM AND MITER

FIG. 4

FIG. 5

FIG. 6

FIG. 7

Half a brick book ends

Have a new brick sawed in half to use as a pair of book ends. Or break it with a hammer and cold chisel or a smart rap with the edge of a mason's trowel. You can use the directions for a brick door stop, standing on its narrow side, or you can cover all six sides with embroidery (Fig. 10).

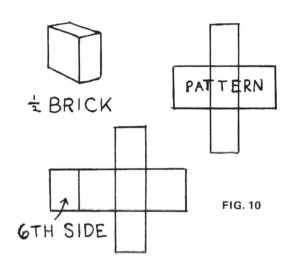

½ BRICK

PATTERN

6TH SIDE

FIG. 10

Hem a 1 inch facing along the bottom edge. A piece of 1 inch wide tape can be used instead (Fig. 4). Cut a piece of lining material with ½ inch seam allowance at the top and sides, and 1 inch extra at the bottom for a hem (Fig. 5). Turn up the hem, making the lining ⅛ inch shorter than the canvas part (Fig. 6). Right sides out, sew the other 3 sides to the canvas, leaving an opening at the bottom (Fig. 7).

Work Binding stitch, or sew a fine cord over the seams on all 4 sides (Fig. 8). Glue pieces of felt on the bottoms of the horizontal parts. Slip the covers over the upright parts. They should be fairly snug (Fig. 9).

Half a brick paper weight

You can use the directions for a brick door stop, lying on its largest side, or you can cover all 6 sides with embroidery (Fig. 11).

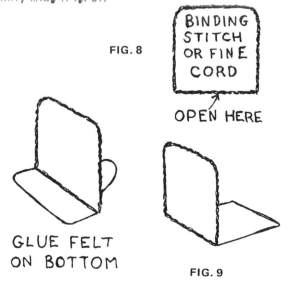

FIG. 8

BINDING STITCH OR FINE CORD

OPEN HERE

GLUE FELT ON BOTTOM

FIG. 9

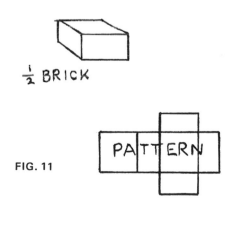

½ BRICK

PATTERN

FIG. 11

Wastebasket Cover

It is possible to cover the sides of a wastebasket with canvas embroidery. This works best if the sides are straight. The bottom can be round, elliptical, rectangular, etc. Most modern baskets are made of metal or cardboard. Baskets with tapered sides can be covered but care should be taken to make an exact pattern. The canvas will have to be glued or sewed to the sides.

Metal—elliptical base

Metal baskets usually have a rolled or bead edge at the top. Measure your canvas to come up to this edge, but not overlap it. You can paint the edge if you like (Fig. 1).

Materials needed

Canvas, the width equal to the depth of the basket up to the bead edge, the length equal to the circumference of the basket, plus ¼ inch to allow for the thickness of the canvas. Include 1¼ inches excess canvas all around (Fig. 2)

Adhesive-backed paper to line the basket—not really paper, but very thin plastic; it comes stuck to heavy paper, and is peeled off when you apply it. You could use any sturdy waterproof material that can be glued on, such as coated wall covering fabrics. It should be waterproof so that it can be wiped with a damp cloth if it should get soiled. The adhesive-backed self-sticking plastic "paper" would be the easiest to handle, however. Buy this first because of the limited choice in colors
A piece of cardboard equal to the size of the bottom on the inside
A piece of felt to glue on the bottom
Yarn of your choice

Remember the 2 ends of the canvas will be brought together and seamed, so plan your design to match across the seam (Fig. 3).

Bind the canvas, work the embroidery, and block. Cut off the binding, and hem back the excess canvas on the ends. Then seam them on the right side (Fig. 4). (See "Joining Pieces of Canvas—Seaming.") Turn in the excess canvas at the top and bottom, and hem (Fig. 5). Cover the top edge with Binding stitch if the canvas shows (Fig. 6).

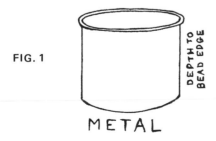

FIG. 1

METAL

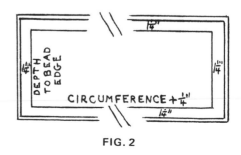

FIG. 2

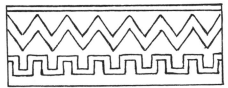

MATCH DESIGN ACROSS SEAM

LINE THE INSIDE SIDES WITH
ADHESIVE BACKED "PAPER"
OR OTHER MATERIAL

FIG. 3

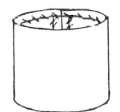

HEM, THEN SEAM
SIDES TOGETHER
RIGHT SIDE OUT

FIG. 4

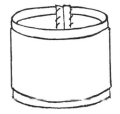

HEM TOP AND
BOTTOM EDGES
NO MITERING

FIG. 6

COVER TOP EDGE
WITH BINDING STITCH

FIG. 6

Line the inside sides of the basket with the adhesive-backed "paper" or other material. Cut a piece of cardboard to just fit in the bottom. Cover this with the paper, too (Fig. 11). Set it in the bottom.

Slide the canvas cover over the outside, and glue a piece of felt on the bottom. If the canvas is a little loose, you will have to glue it in place. Apply a coating of glue about 2 inches wide at the top and bottom of the sides. Wrap the basket tightly with broad pieces of nylon net and allow to dry. Use the net because air can get through.

Cardboard—elliptical base

The canvas is made the true depth of the basket, flush with the top and bottom (Figs. 7, 8).

You can cover the top edge with adhesive-backed paper or other material. Cut a long strip 2½ inches wide and about 1 inch longer than the circumference of the top. Draw a line 1 inch down from the top of the basket as a guide. Carefully

DEPTH TO TOP

CARDBOARD

FIG. 7

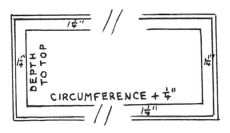

DEPTH TO TOP

CIRCUMFERENCE + ¼"

FIG. 8

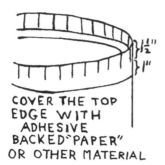

COVER THE TOP
EDGE WITH
ADHESIVE
BACKED "PAPER"
OR OTHER MATERIAL

FIG. 9

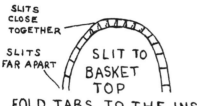

SLITS
CLOSE
TOGETHER

SLITS
FAR APART

SLIT TO
BASKET
TOP

FOLD TABS TO THE INSIDE,
OVERLAPPING THE EDGES.
LINE THE INSIDE SIDES.

FIG. 10

COVER A PIECE OF
CARDBOARD TO SET
IN THE BOTTOM

FIG. 11

Cardboard—rectangular base

You can start from scratch with this style. Just get a small sturdy carton. Cut the top off cleanly to the desired height (Fig. 12). You will need an extra piece of cardboard to set in the bottom.

Plan separate pieces of canvas for each side (Fig. 13). If 2 pieces are to be put on one piece of canvas, remember to allow at least 2 inches excess canvas between them.

Bind the canvas, work the embroidery, and block. Hem back the canvas for the side seams, then sew the seams on the right side (Fig. 14). (See

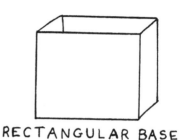

RECTANGULAR BASE

FIG. 12

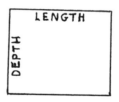

LENGTH   WIDTH

DEPTH   DEPTH

MAKE 4 PANELS
2 OF EACH SIZE
DECORATE INDIVIDUALLY

FIG. 13

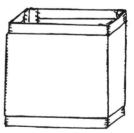

HEM, THEN SEAM SIDES
TOGETHER — NO MITERING
HEM TOP AND BOTTOM

FIG. 14

apply the paper along this line, leaving 1½ inches extended above the top. Cut this part in slits about 1 inch apart on the flatter sides, and ½ inch apart at the ends (Fig. 9). Fold these tabs down over the top of the basket one at a time. The edges of the tabs will overlap (Fig. 10). Line the inside and cover an elliptical piece of cardboard to fit into the bottom (Fig. 11).

See Figures 3, 4, 5, and 6 for working the embroidery, and finishing.

"Joining Pieces of Canvas—Seaming.") Turn under and hem the canvas at the top and bottom. Cut the adhesive paper 1¼ inches deeper, and ½ inch wider than the inside measurements, so when you fold the paper over the top, and down the outside, the corners will be covered (Fig. 15). A little careful snipping will do this neatly (Fig. 16). Cover the extra piece of cardboard, and set it in the bottom (Fig. 17). Go over the edges and seams of the canvas with a decorative stitch pattern (Fig. 18).

It may be necessary to glue the canvas to make it stay against the flat sides. Wrap with the net, and stuff the basket tightly so the sides stay straight. If you like, you could work a stitch pattern around the top through the cardboard and all. This would hold the canvas in place, and it wouldn't be necessary to cover the top edge with the adhesive paper.

Glue a piece of felt on the bottom.

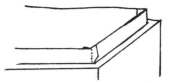

LINE WITH ADHESIVE BACKED "PAPER", FOLDED OVER THE TOP. CUT THE PIECES ½" TOO WIDE SO THE CORNERS ARE COVERED OVERLAP ON THE INSIDE.

FIG. 16

COVER A PIECE OF CARD-BOARD TO, SET IN BOTTOM

FIG. 17

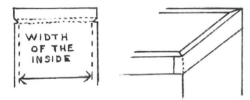

WIDTH OF THE INSIDE

MAKE DIAGONAL CUTS EQUAL TO THE THICKNESS OF THE EDGE

FIG. 15

WORK A DECORATIVE STITCH OVER ALL EDGES

FELT CAN BE GLUED TO THE BOTTOM

FIG. 18

PERSONAL ACCESSORIES

Eyeglass Cases

Included here are four styles of cases. For ordinary size glasses, a square 6½ inches is large enough (Fig. 1). For smaller or larger glasses, lay the glasses on a piece of paper and draw a rectangular pattern on which they will fit comfortably. The measurements for the canvas will be double the short end of the rectangle (Fig. 2). Allow an inch of excess canvas all around.

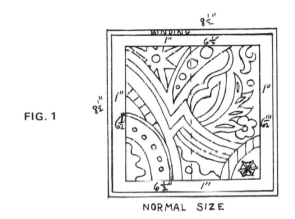

FIG. 1

NORMAL SIZE

Style A

Materials needed

1 piece of canvas 2 inches larger than a rectangle that is the length of the glasses and twice the width

1 piece of lining material the same size as the canvas (choose a closely woven sturdy material, cotton broadcloth, rep, faile, a piece of moiré ribbon, etc.; don't use satin—it's too slippery—or velvet or felt as they're too bulky and aren't washable)

1 piece of interlining material that is somewhat smaller than the above measurements

Yarn of your choice

Bind the canvas and put on the design. When planning your design, keep in mind that only one side will be seen at a time. Work the embroidery and block. Trim off the binding and hem the excess canvas to the back of your stitchery, mitering the corners (Fig. 3). Cut a piece of interlining to fit up to but not overlap the turned back excess canvas. Hem in place (Fig. 4). Hem the lining over the interlining up to the outside edges. Leave 1 canvas thread exposed (Fig. 5).

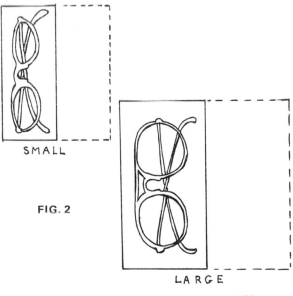

SMALL

FIG. 2

LARGE

If you would like a slight opening at the top of the seam, start the Binding stitch edging about 1 inch down on the side. Work across the top and down the same distance on the other side. Use the canvas thread you left exposed (Fig. 6).

Fold the case together and continue the Binding stitch down the side, joining the 2 sides. Be careful to watch that the 2 corners will match. Continue across the bottom, and the eyeglass case is done (Fig. 7).

Figure 8 shows a handy way to keep your sunglasses in your car.

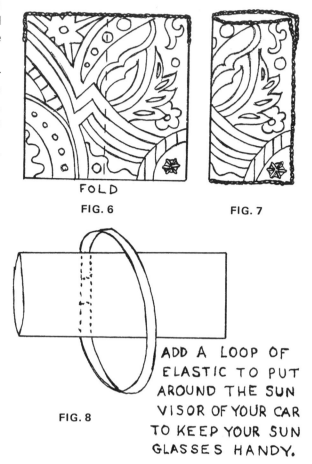

BINDING STITCH ON THE EDGES

FOLD

FIG. 6   FIG. 7

FIG. 8

ADD A LOOP OF ELASTIC TO PUT AROUND THE SUN VISOR OF YOUR CAR TO KEEP YOUR SUN GLASSES HANDY.

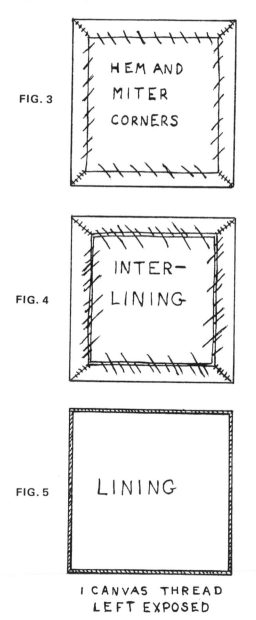

FIG. 3   HEM AND MITER CORNERS

FIG. 4   INTER-LINING

FIG. 5   LINING

I CANVAS THREAD LEFT EXPOSED

Styles B, C, and D

Except for the shape of the tops and bottoms, eyeglass cases B, C, and D are made the same way. Be sure to measure the canvas large enough to allow an inch all around, and 1½ inches between the pieces. When they are cut apart that will allow ¾ inch for each one (Fig. 9).

Before cutting away the canvas for No. D, run machine stitching and gathering threads around the curves. (See General Directions: "Finishing Canvas on a Curve.")

Finish each piece separately, mitering or folding the corners where needed (Fig. 10). Apply the interlining and the lining as illustrated (Figs. 11, 12). Work Binding stitch across the tops of both pieces (Fig. 13). Join the pieces on the other 3 sides with Binding stitch (Fig. 14).

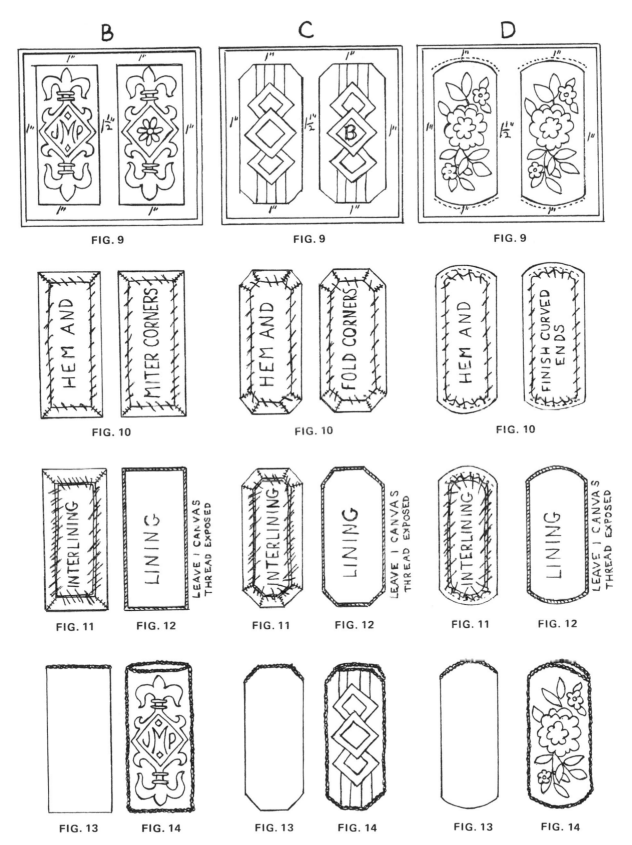

B

FIG. 9

FIG. 10
HEM AND — MITER CORNERS

FIG. 11 INTERLINING
FIG. 12 LINING
LEAVE 1 CANVAS THREAD EXPOSED

FIG. 13
FIG. 14

C

FIG. 9

FIG. 10
HEM AND — FOLD CORNERS

FIG. 11 INTERLINING
FIG. 12 LINING
LEAVE 1 CANVAS THREAD EXPOSED

FIG. 13
FIG. 14

D

FIG. 9

FIG. 10
HEM AND — FINISH CURVED ENDS

FIG. 11 INTERLINING
FIG. 12 LINING
LEAVE 1 CANVAS THREAD EXPOSED

FIG. 13
FIG. 14

Pin Cushion

Pin cushions can be rectangular, circular, or elliptical. You may work both sides, or only one, and finish with a cloth backing.

Materials needed

One or two pieces of canvas 2 inches larger each way than the desired measurements

Yarn of your choice

Muslin for inside cushion

Filling: sand, sawdust, or rice (if sand is used, the cushion will be washable; be sure it is clean)

Bind the canvas, work one or both sides, and block (Fig. 1). Make a muslin cushion the same size as the canvas measurements. Fill with one of the above materials. Pack it in very full so the cushion is hard. Close the opening with heavy thread and fine stitches to prevent the filling from leaking out (Figs. 2, 3).

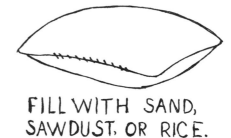

FILL WITH SAND, SAWDUST, OR RICE. PACK TIGHT

FIG. 2

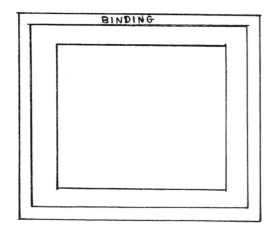

FIG. 1

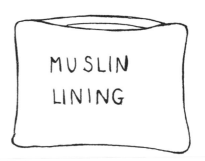

MUSLIN LINING

FIG. 3

Cut the binding off the piece or pieces, and hem back excess canvas, mitering corners, or turning under curved edges (Fig. 4). (See "Finishing Canvas on a Curve.") If both sides have been worked in canvas, place the two sides against the muslin cushion, matching the corners carefully. Pin in place, and sew securely around all four sides. You will have to use strong thread, and pull it tight to make the cushion cover very snug (Fig. 5).

If cloth backing is used, hand sew the edges to the canvas on three sides (Fig. 6). Turn right side out, and insert the muslin cushion. It should be a snug fit. Pulling hard, close the fourth side with strong thread (Fig. 7). Cover the seam with binding stitch or a fine cord (Fig. 8).

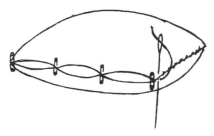

FIG. 5

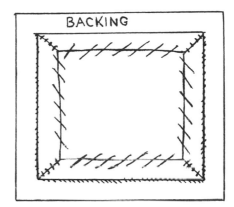

BACKING

FIG. 6

HEM
AND
MITER

RIGHT SIDE

FIG. 7

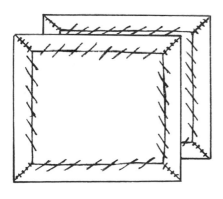

FIG. 4

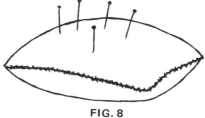

FIG. 8

Needle Book

Materials needed

One piece of fine canvas large enough for both front and
back, plus ½ inch for hinge (fine canvas is best; it
makes the book less bulky)

Two pieces of stiff cardboard equal in measurement to
front or back

Heavy thread or string

Lining material, plus small piece for pocket

Outing flannel for interlining

Flannel or felt for 2 or 3 pages

Tiny button

Bind the canvas. Work the embroidery for the
front, back, and hinge. Remember to put the design for the front on the right side (Fig. 1). Block.
On a sewing machine, sew 2 rows around all 4
sides, one row on top of the other, about ⅜ inch
out from worked area (Fig. 1).

Lay the pieces of cardboard in place on the
wrong side. Cutting off the binding a little at a
time to prevent fraying, fold the excess canvas
over the cardboard, lacing the heavy thread or
string back and forth, top to bottom, and from
one side to the hinge. Sew into the machine stitching, and the back of the stitchery on the hinge.
Pull snug. Make modified mitered corners (Fig. 2).
Place a layer of outing flannel over the string
lacings, hemming it to the edges of the turned-
back canvas (Fig. 3).

Make a pocket large enough to hold several
folders of needles, and sew to the right side of the

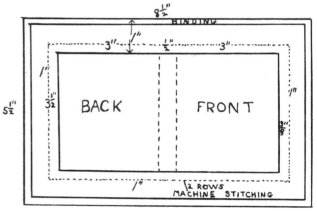

FIG. 1

FIG. 2

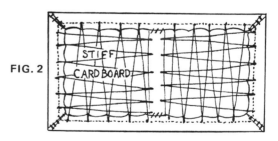

FIG. 3

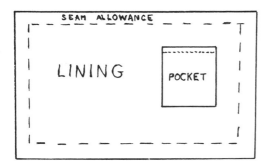

FIG. 4

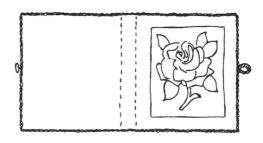

FIG. 6

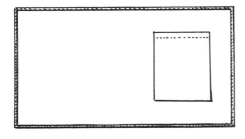

FIG. 5

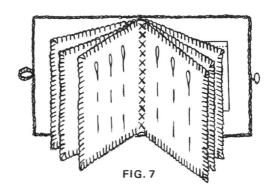

FIG. 7

FIG. 8

lining (Fig. 4). Place the lining over the interlining, and hem all 4 sides, leaving 1 thread of canvas exposed. The pocket will be against the back (Fig. 5).

Work a fine Binding stitch around all 4 sides, making a loop buttonhole on the edge of the front, and attaching a tiny button on the edge of the back. The button and loop can be omitted, if desired (Fig. 6).

If the pages are made of felt you may cut the edges with pinking shears. If they are to be made of a material that would fray, such as outing flannel, work a fine buttonhole stitch along the edges (Fig. 7). Baste the pages in place, and turn over so the outside of the book is up. Using the plucking method, work a decorative stitch pattern along the hinge through all thicknesses (Fig. 7). Close the book and button the button in its loop. This will keep the book closed when it is in your work bag (Fig. 8).

Travel Sewing Kit

Materials needed

Small pair of scissors
Thimble
A few needles and some thread
A few pins, safety and straight
A small piece of flannel, 1 inch by 2 inches
A small button
Fine canvas
Interlining and lining materials
Yarn of your choice

Lay the scissors on a piece of paper and slip the thimble over the points. Draw a pattern to extend out ½ inch and up to make a flap about 2/3 the depth of the scissors. Draw another pattern to match the bottom of the back-flap and extending up to within ¼ inch of the tops of the handles of the scissors (Fig. 1). Lay these patterns on a piece of canvas large enough to allow 1 inch all around, and 1½ inches between the pieces (Fig. 2). Fold the pattern pieces down the middle to line them up with the canvas threads. Draw pencil or ball-point lines around the edges of the pattern pieces (Fig. 2). Bind the canvas, work the embroidery, and block. Cut away the binding and some of the excess canvas, leaving about ¾ inch of canvas around each piece. Turn the excess canvas under and hem to the back of the embroidery. Fold the canvas carefully on the curved ends, following the edge of the worked area. Sew the folds securely (Fig. 3). Sew the button on. Attach the interlining to the front. Attach the interlining

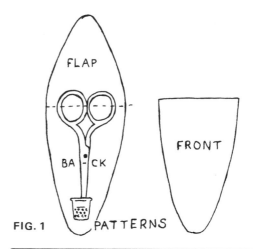

FIG. 1   PATTERNS

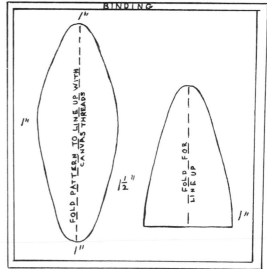

FIG. 2

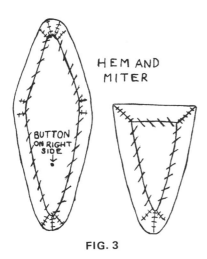

HEM AND MITER

BUTTON
ON RIGHT
SIDE
↓

FIG. 3

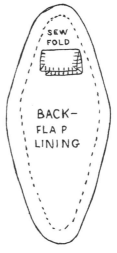

SEW
FOLD

BACK-
FLAP
LINING

FIG. 5

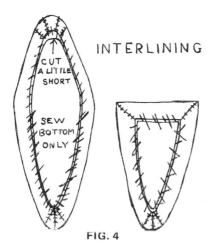

INTERLINING

CUT
A LITTLE
SHORT

SEW
BOTTOM
ONLY

FIG. 4

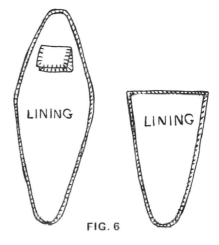

LINING

LINING

FIG. 6

to the back flap at the bottom only, not in the flap. Trim away a little of the interlining at the top. When the flap is folded over, the interlining will slide a little so this part must be left loose (Fig. 4).

Attach the small piece of flannel to the lining of the flap. You can work a small Buttonhole stitch around the edges, if you wish. Sew it across the middle to make 2 "pages" (Fig. 5). Line both pieces of canvas (Fig. 6).

Overcast the 2 pieces together. Work Binding stitch across the top of the front and then up around the flap. Make a loop buttonhole at the top of the flap. Continue on around the edges, joining the front to the back. Make a few extra stitches at the point of strain where the front and back meet (Xs in Fig. 7).

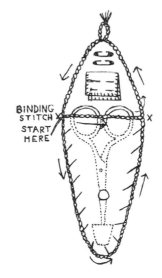

BINDING
STITCH
START
HERE

FIG. 7

TRAVEL SEWING KIT   109

FIG. 8

Tuck the thimble in the bottom and put the points of the scissors into it. Put the needles and a few pins in the "pages" on the flap. You can wrap a few lengths of thread around a card and tuck it in with the scissors (Fig. 8).

This makes an attractive, neat, compact sewing kit, completely equipped. The thimble serves a double purpose. It protects the points of the scissors, so they can't damage the case or stick your fingers.

Clothes Hanger Covers

There are many ways to make decorative padded clothes hangers, and one of them is with canvas embroidery. Use a standard plastic or wood, or a common wire hanger (Fig. 1). Draw a paper pattern, allowing about an inch around the edges but narrowing to ¼ inch on the ends so as not to make the shoulders too wide. Draw half of the pattern, fold the paper in half, and cut both sides at once to be sure the sides match (Fig. 2).

Materials needed

A hanger
2 pieces of canvas to accommodate the pattern, plus 1½ inches excess canvas all around
Yarn of your choice

Design the canvas any way you wish. Bind the canvas, work the embroidery, and block. Sew the machine stitching and put in the gathers. (See "Finishing Canvas on a Curve.") Work with a rec-

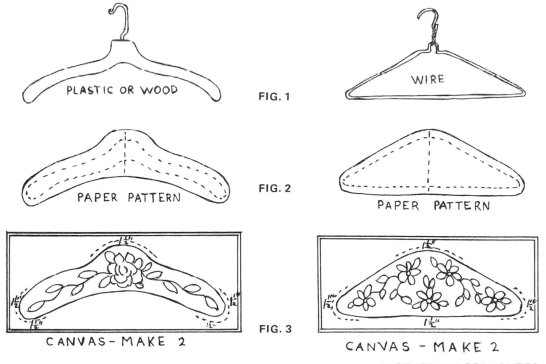

PLASTIC OR WOOD   FIG. 1   WIRE

PAPER PATTERN   FIG. 2   PAPER PATTERN

CANVAS—MAKE 2   FIG. 3   CANVAS — MAKE 2

tangular piece of canvas (Fig. 3). Trim off the binding and all but 1 inch of the excess canvas. Draw up the gathers, and slash the canvas along the curves of the plastic or wood. It is not necessary to face the concave curves of the plastic or wood cover. Slash the excess canvas just enough so the seams don't pucker. Hem the excess canvas of both pieces (Fig. 4).

On the outside, seam the ends and the slopes up to the hook. Leave a small space at the top for the hook to go through. Safety pins are a help in holding the pieces together while you sew. Leave the bottom open (Fig. 5). Use polyester fiber or kapok for stuffing. Wrap some of the fibers around the sloping parts of the hanger, especially if you are using a wire hanger. Tie it on with thread. Then pass the hook through its opening. Don't pull the hook all the way out as far as it will go. Stuff the rest of the casing moderately full, and seam the bottom (Fig. 6).

Cover the seams with a decorative stitch pattern, using a sharp needle. Van Dyke, or Feather, stitch would be appropriate. Put a final touch of decoration around the hook. Ribbon bows or pompons would look nice (Fig. 7).

Don't cover the hook. Any cover would soon get dirty and worn from contact with the hanger bar.

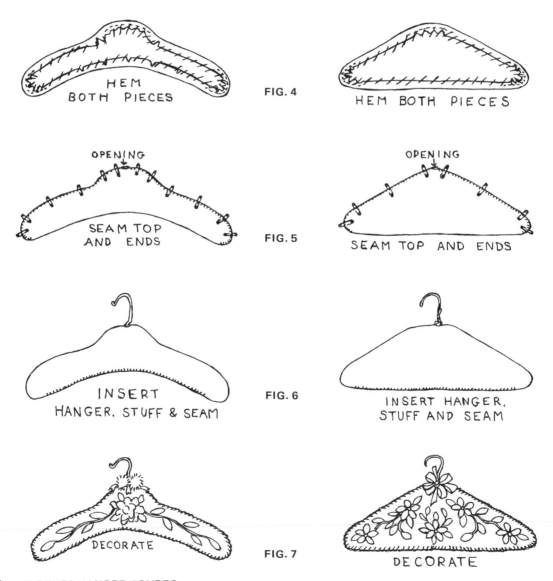

HEM BOTH PIECES   FIG. 4

HEM BOTH PIECES

OPENING

SEAM TOP AND ENDS   FIG. 5

OPENING

SEAM TOP AND ENDS

INSERT HANGER, STUFF & SEAM   FIG. 6

INSERT HANGER, STUFF AND SEAM

DECORATE   FIG. 7

DECORATE

Clutch Bags

Style A

The simplest form of clutch bag, Style A, is a folded rectangular piece (Fig. 1).

Materials needed

3 or 4 corset stays, ½ inch shorter than the width of the bag (obviously, you may have difficulty finding these; if so use straight strips cut from the side of a plastic bleach or milk bottle [7½ inches])

1 piece of canvas 2 inches longer than the combined length of the front, back, and flap (6 plus 6, plus 5 equals 17), plus 2 inches for excess canvas; the width will be 8 inches plus 2 inches; the piece will measure 19 inches by 10 inches (Fig. 2)

2 pieces of canvas 5½ inches by 8 inches, plus 2 inches each way for ends, if you plan to use them (Fig. 3)

¼ yd. stiff waterproof interlining at least 26 inches long, for 2 pieces; one piece ½ inch shorter and ½ inch narrower than the bag measurements (6½ inches by 15½ inches); the second piece is for the zipper pocket (7¼ inches by 10 inches) (Figs. 9, 13)

½ yd. of lining material, something fairly firm and closely woven, coat lining material is good (it is a good idea to choose your lining material before selecting the yarn because of the limited color choice; get matching sewing thread)

7 inch zipper

An attractive button (don't use a snap, the hand-sewn ones look amateurish, and the gripper type can pull out—you can omit the button, if you wish)

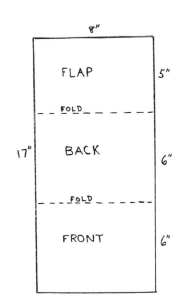

FIG. 1

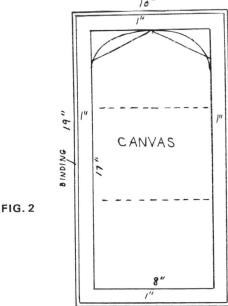

FIG. 2

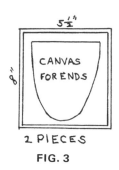

5 ½"

8"

CANVAS
FOR ENDS

2 PIECES

FIG. 3

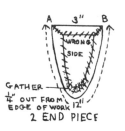

A   3"   B

WRONG
SIDE

GATHER
¼" OUT FROM
EDGE OF WORK   12"

2 END PIECE

FIG. 6

In planning the design, you can use an allover (diaper) pattern of combined stitch patterns, or an arrangement of stripes, or one of the more decorative stitch patterns by itself. If you are planning a design, especially if it is realistic, remember the piece will be folded so that only about 1/3 will be visible at a time. The rectangular shape can be treated as a whole, but the design must have 3 parts that are pleasing separately. Also be sure the middle part won't suffer by being upside down (Figs. 4, 5). The edges of the flap can be rounded or pointed, if desired (Fig. 2). The extra pieces to give the bag depth are set in the sides (Fig. 3). Make the top of each piece 3 inches wide or less. The curve from A to B must equal the length of the front, plus the back of the bag (12 inches— Fig. 6).

Bind the canvas, work the embroidery, and block. Sew 2 pieces of tape across where the folds will come. Insert the stays or plastic strips, and sew the ends of the tape securely. Cut off the binding and all but ¾ inch of the excess canvas. Turn back and hem the excess canvas, mitering the corners. Enclose the other 2 stays or strips in the hems at the ends, omitting the bottom stay for a flat bag, or the top stay for a pointed or rounded flap (Fig. 7). For a rounded flap, see "Finishing Canvas on a Curve" (Fig. 8). For a pointed flap, make a modified mitered corner. Sew the button on the right side 5 inches up from the bottom of the piece (Fig. 7).

To make the ends, cut off the binding and all but ¾ inch of the excess canvas. (See "Finishing Canvas on a Curve" for the bottoms of the pieces.)

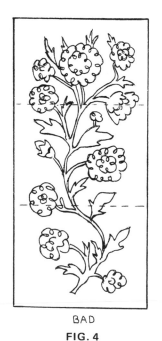

BAD

FIG. 4

GOOD

FIG. 5

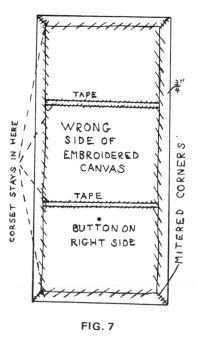

TAPE

WRONG
SIDE OF
EMBROIDERED
CANVAS

TAPE

BUTTON ON
RIGHT SIDE

CORSET STAYS IN HERE

MITERED CORNERS

¾"

FIG. 7

FIG. 8

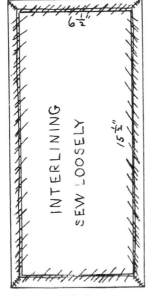

FIG. 9

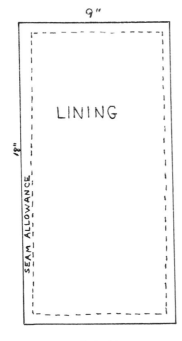

FIG. 10

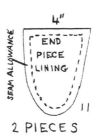

2 PIECES

FIG. 11

Hem all around, mitering the top corners (Fig. 6). Cut the piece of interlining to fit between the edges of the turned back canvas. Sew it loosely to the excess canvas. It must be able to move slightly when the bag is folded (Fig. 9). Cut a piece of lining material 1 inch larger than the bag, allowing ½ inch all around for the seams (9 inches by 18 inches—Fig. 10). Line the end pieces (Fig. 11).

To make a zipper pocket, cut 2 pieces of lining material 8½ inches by 12 inches. Right sides together, sew along the sides only. Seam allowance ½ inch (Fig. 12). Turn right side out. Cut a piece of interlining 1¼ inches by 10 inches (Fig. 13). Insert it between the pieces of lining material, centering it so 1 inch of lining is at each end. Fold it across the middle, open ends up, and sew the sides together (Fig. 14). Turn under the 4 edges of

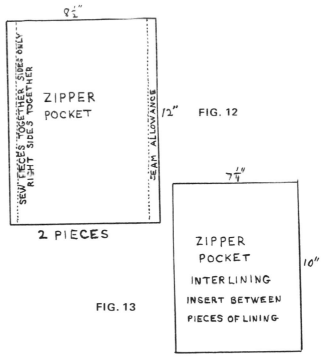

FIG. 12

2 PIECES

FIG. 13

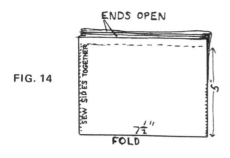

FIG. 14

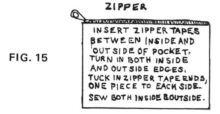

FIG. 15

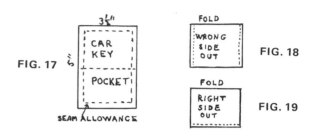

FIG. 17   FIG. 18

FIG. 19

the top opening, and baste, but not together. The pocket should be 5 inches deep. Insert the tapes of the zipper into the 2 openings. Tuck the excess tape at the ends into the openings too. Hand sew the edges of the pocket to the zipper tapes, inside and out, so no raw edges will be exposed (Fig. 15).

Place the pocket against the lining so the bottom fold will be just about where the fold in the lining between the front and the back will come. Sew the pocket securely to the lining along the sides (Fig. 16).

To make a small (car key) pocket, cut a piece of lining material 3½ inches by 5 inches (Fig. 17). Fold it in half, wrong side out, and seam the 2½ inch sides (Fig. 18). Turn right side out, and seam the third side (Fig. 19). Place it on the lining, open end down, 2½ inches from the bottom of the lining material (Fig. 16). Sew it in place. The pocket is upside down now because the front of the bag will be turned up.

Place the lining on the bag and hem all around. Pull the lining a little tight lengthwise so it won't buckle when the bag is folded (Fig. 20). Set the end pieces in place, matching the tops with the edge of the front. Overcast the ends in place. Safety pins will help to hold them while you do the overcasting (Fig. 21). Sew the end pieces in place on the right side. Work Binding stitch along the top of one end piece, across the front of the

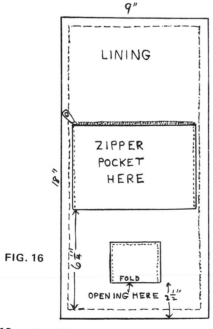

FIG. 16

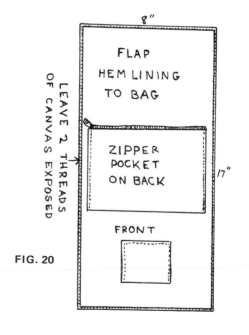

FIG. 20

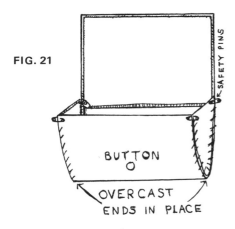

FIG. 21

BUTTON
○

OVERCAST
ENDS IN PLACE

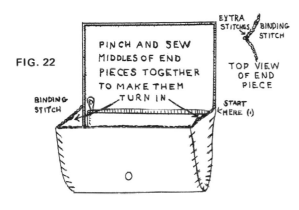

FIG. 22

PINCH AND SEW
MIDDLES OF END
PIECES TOGETHER
TO MAKE THEM
TURN IN

BINDING
STITCH

EXTRA
STITCHES BINDING
STITCH

TOP VIEW
OF END
PIECE

START
HERE (1)

○

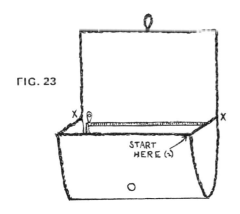

FIG. 23

X   X

START
HERE (2)

○

bag, and along the top of the other end piece (Fig. 22). Starting at the front corner, work Binding stitch over the seam, down around the curve, and up the other side. At the top of the end piece make a few extra stitches. This is where strain will come (X in Fig. 23). Continue along the flap to the center of the top, and work a buttonhole to fit the button. (See "Loop Buttonholes," p. 228).

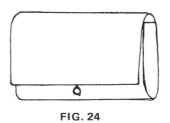

FIG. 24

Continue on across the top and down the other side, adding strengthening stitches at X. Work the Binding stitch over the second seam, finishing at the front corner. Push the end pieces toward the center, and fold the flap down (Fig. 24).

Flat style

If the bag has no end pieces, seam the front to the back after the bag is lined. Work Binding stitch across the front. Starting at a lower corner, work Binding stitch up the side, over the seam. Put in a few strengthening stitches at X, and continue on up to the middle of the top. Work a loop button-hole, and then continue on around and down to the other corner, adding a few strengthening stitches at X (Fig. 25).

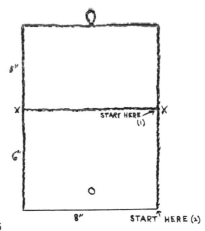

5"

X   X

START HERE
(1)

6"

○

8"   START HERE (2)

FIG. 25

○

Small bags of the flat type can be made for cards, cosmetics, change, etc. Just reduce all measurements to the desired size, and omit the stays. Because everything used is waterproof, the bag can be washed carefully.

Style B

Style B is a second type of clutch bag with curved edges. The proportions diagramed are for a small dressy bag (6½ inches by 5 inches). Enlarge everything proportionally for a larger bag. Because of the curved edges, it is best to use fine canvas, 14 threads to the inch, or finer.

Materials needed

2 corset stays, or 2 strips cut from a plastic bleach or milk bottle (6 inches)

½ yd. canvas

½ yd. tape

A piece of stiff waterproof interlining, 19 inches by 11 inches

½ yd. lining material; choose something fairly firm and closely woven, but thin. Coat lining material is good (it is a good idea to choose the lining material before selecting the yarn to work the embroidery because of the limited color choice)

Sewing thread to match

Decorative button (optional); don't use a snap; hand-sewn snaps look amateurish, and the gripper type can pull out

5½ inch zipper

Yarn of your choice; for a dressy bag, consider yarn other than wool—silk, mercerized cotton, beads, sequins, or combinations

The bag is made in 3 pieces, front, back and flap, and boxing or gusset (Fig. 26). Cut rectangular pieces of canvas, 13 inches by 9 inches, 8 inches by 9 inches, 18 inches by 2½ inches (Fig. 27). Make paper patterns of the 3 pieces, center, and draw their outlines on the canvas, making the straight lines follow the canvas threads.

You can use an allover (diaper) pattern, an arrangement of stripes, or one of the more decorative stitch patterns by itself. If you are planning a design, remember the back and flap will be viewed separately, and, viewed flat, the flap design will be upside down (Fig. 28). Bind the canvas, work the embroidery, and block, using the patterns as a

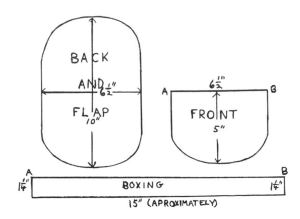

FIG. 26

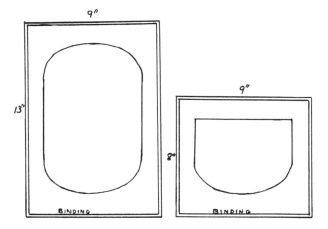

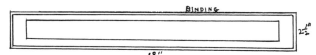

FIG. 27

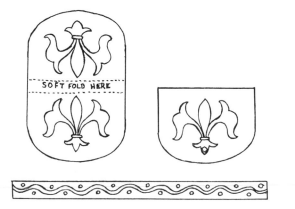

FIG. 28

guide. Sew the piece of tape across where the fold will come between the back and the flap. Sew into the back of the embroidery stitches. Insert the stay, fastening the ends of the tape securely (Fig. 29). See "Finishing Canvas on a Curve" for directions for turning in and hemming the curved edges. Cut off the binding, and all but ¾ inch of the excess canvas, and hem the excess canvas, mitering the upper corners of the front. Enclose the second stay in the top hem of the front.

Sew the button to the front 1 inch up from the bottom (Figs. 30, 31).

Cut 2 pieces of interlining for the front and the back-flap to fit in between the edges of the turned back canvas. Hem the pieces in place, sewing the piece for the back-flap loosely. It will have to move slightly when the bag is folded (Fig. 32). Cut a piece of interlining 1 inch wide, and 4 inches shorter than the length of the gusset. Hem this to the edges of the embroidery in the middle, leaving 2 inches at each end without interlining (Fig. 33). Trim off the binding, hem, and miter the ends, making sure the boxing is exactly the same length as the curved line of the front. Sew across the interlining in the middle (Fig. 34).

Cut 3 pieces of lining allowing ½ inch all around for the seams (Fig. 35). Sew the lining to the front and the boxing (Fig. 36).

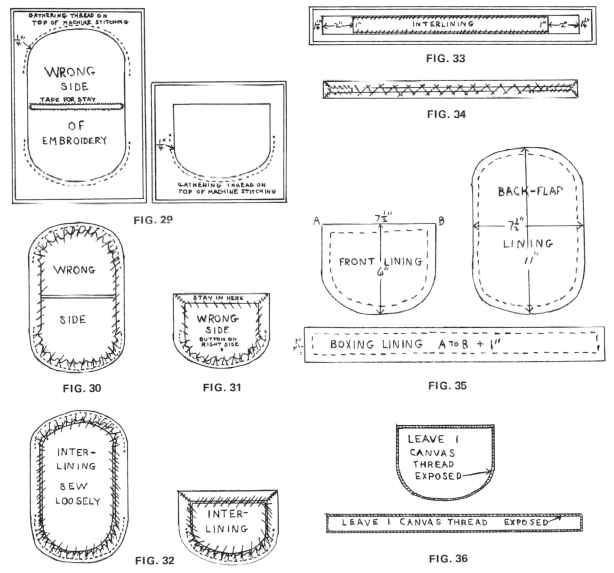

FIG. 29

FIG. 33

FIG. 34

FIG. 30

FIG. 31

FIG. 35

FIG. 32

FIG. 36

To make a zipper pocket, cut 4 pieces of lining material, using the bag front pattern. For a larger bag cut 2 pieces of interlining ½ inch smaller all around. Right sides together, sew the pieces together in pairs, around the curves, leaving the tops open. Turn them right side out (Fig. 37). For the larger bag, insert the pieces of interlining between the layers, and baste in place, leaving 1 inch of lining at the top (Fig. 38). Turn under about ¾ inch of lining material around the 2 openings. Don't sew them shut (Fig. 39). Lay the pieces so the openings are toward each other, and insert the tapes of the zipper into the openings. Tuck the tape ends into the openings, too (C and D in Fig. 40). Sew by hand or machine, both sides of both pieces, so no raw edges are exposed (Figs. 40, 41). Remove the basting threads. Fold the 2 sides of the pocket together, and sew around the curved bottom of the pocket (Fig. 42). Place the pocket against the back of the lining, centering it, and leaving ¾ inch at the bottom. Hem securely to the back of the lining around the curve (Fig. 43).

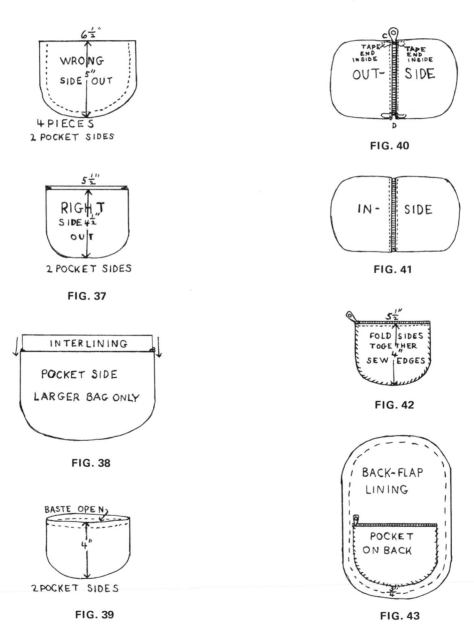

FIG. 37

FIG. 38

FIG. 39

FIG. 40

FIG. 41

FIG. 42

FIG. 43

Place the lining on the back-flap, turn under the seam allowance, and hem all around. Pull the lining fairly tight lengthwise so it won't buckle when the bag is folded (Fig. 44). Join the boxing to the front, using safety pins to hold it in place (Fig. 45). Work Binding stitch along front and top edges (Fig. 46). Pin and seam the boxing to the bag back (Fig. 47). Work Binding stitch over all seams and edges, making a loop buttonhole at the top of the flap. Add a few strengthening stitches where the boxing joins the back. This is where strain will come (X's in Fig. 48). Fold the flap down, pushing ends of the boxing in (Fig. 49).

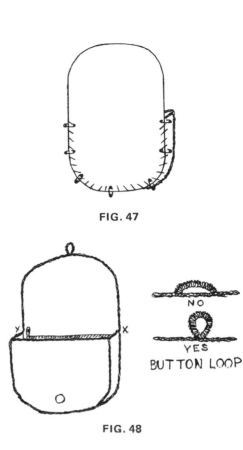

FIG. 47

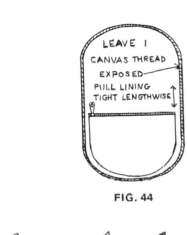

FIG. 44

FIG. 48

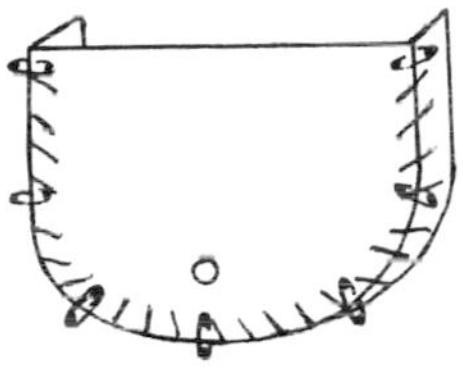

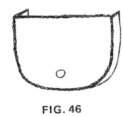

FIG. 45   FIG. 46

FIG. 49

Handbags

The following directions for four styles of handbags are diagrammed for canvas embroidery. With slight modifications, they can be used for surface stitchery, as well.

The conventional needlepoint bag has to be professionally mounted and lined after you have worked the embroidery for the 2 sides and the gusset. This is very expensive. There is an alternative if you can find a top, either with or without a handle, that allows you to finish the bag yourself. It is a good idea to buy your lining material, and any other parts which must match, before selecting the yarn because of the limited choice of color and appropriate material. There are several varieties of bag tops. Some have tiny eyeletlike holes along the edges to which the canvas or cloth parts are sewn (Styles A and B, Fig. 1). There are some with bars to be run through casings and secured with a nut at each end (Style C, Fig. 2). Both of these come in metal and plastic, and sometimes in wood. There is a third kind consisting of 2 pieces of spring steel, hinged at each end. The material is folded over the steel pieces, covering them completely. The bag is opened by pulling the centers of the steel pieces apart (Style D, Fig. 3). Bag tops are not available everywhere, but can be sometimes ordered from mail order houses. Some embroidery shops carry them. It is best to buy the top first, so the bag can be made to fit. Some people have antique bag tops, often in sterling silver (Fig. 4).

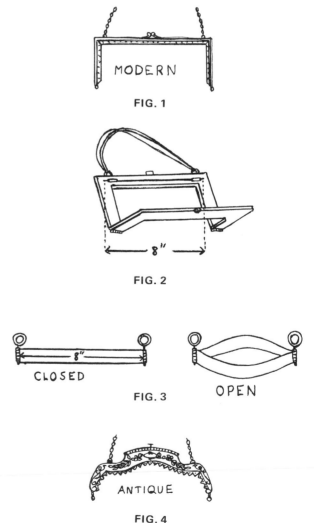

MODERN

FIG. 1

FIG. 2

CLOSED

FIG. 3

OPEN

ANTIQUE

FIG. 4

Style A

Materials needed

Bag top, either old or new

3 pieces of canvas, 2 for the sides, and a long narrow piece for the boxing or gusset

Interlining for the above, plus a piece 4 inches by 5 inches for a pocket

Lining material for the 3 pieces, plus ¼ yd. for the pockets

6 inch zipper, closed at both ends

Yarn of your choice, and matching no. 8 pearl cotton, if you can find it.

Make a paper pattern to fit the size and shape of the bag top (Fig. 5). If the bag top is 8 inches wide, inside measurement, a depth of 8 inches is in good proportion. Curve the sides out to a measurement of about 10 inches (Fig. 6). It is easier to get both curves alike if you fold the pattern in half and cut them at the same time. Measure 2 pieces of canvas to accommodate the pattern, with at least 1 inch all around for excess canvas (Fig. 7).

Measure the distance from one top corner of the pattern, around the bottom, and up the other side to the other top corner (A to B in Fig. 8). This is the length of the boxing. Cut a piece of canvas to accommodate this length, by about 2¼ inches in width, plus an extra inch all around (Fig. 9). Both pieces for the sides can be worked on 1 piece of canvas, but they are easier to handle if they are separate. If both sides are to be worked on 1 piece of canvas, be sure to allow at least 1½ inches excess canvas between them.

Measure the length of the sides of the top (A to C, or B to D in Fig. 5) from the corner down to the hinge. Draw a "V" from the corners of the boxing ends so it will be ¼ inch shorter than this measurement (Fig. 9). The distance from the point of one V, across the boxing, to the point of the other, should be ½ inch longer than a similar distance on the pattern. Leave the area inside the Vs unworked.

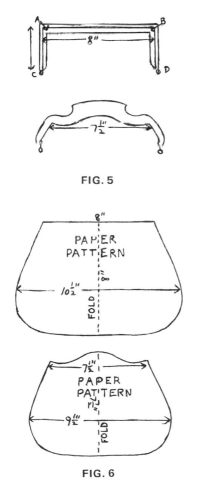

FIG. 5

FIG. 6

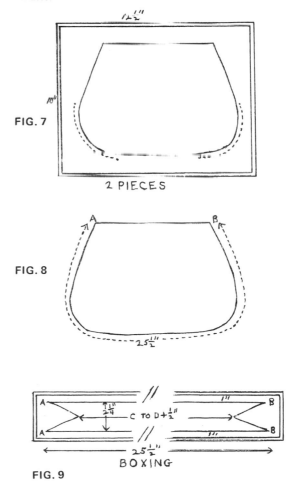

FIG. 7

2 PIECES

FIG. 8

FIG. 9

Bind the canvas, work the embroidery, and block. Before cutting the binding and part of the excess canvas off the side pieces, see "Finishing Canvas on a Curve." See dotted lines in Figure 7. Hem back the excess canvas, mitering the top corners (Fig. 10). Attach the interlining to the side pieces, sewing it only half way up the sides (Fig. 11).

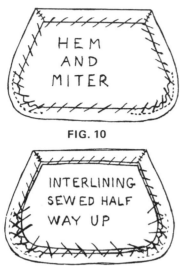

FIG. 10

FIG. 11

For the boxing, on the wrong side, attach a piece of interlining to the area between the Vs (Fig. 12). Right sides together, baste the lining to the canvas. Turn over to the canvas side, and machine stitch along the sides of the Vs, sewing as close to the embroidery as possible. Round the tip of the V slightly (Fig. 13). Continue the stitching into the unworked canvas, out to the binding. Cut the binding off, and turn back the excess canvas along the sides, making zigzag stitches across the interlining (Fig. 14). Cut out some of the excess canvas in the Vs, and lining material, leaving about ¾ inch of canvas. Slash to the bottom of the

Vs (Fig. 14). Turn right side out. Turn the excess canvas near the points to the outside (Fig. 15). Hem the lining to the boxing along the sides, leaving the excess canvas extended near the points (Fig. 16). This is done because canvas is much too bulky to bring to a point without excessive lumpiness. Cut out the pieces of lining material for the sides, allowing about ⅝ inch for seams.

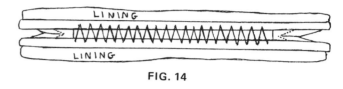

FIG. 14

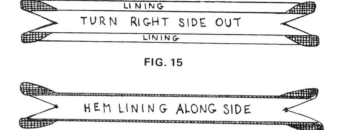

FIG. 15

FIG. 16

Zipper pocket

For a zipper pocket, cut a piece of lining material 2 inches wider than the length of the zipper, and about 10 inches deep. About 2 inches down from the top edge, run a basting thread on one side of the lining material the length of the zipper (Fig. 17). Right sides together, baste the piece for the pocket over the basting thread. Place the narrow end ¼ inch down from the top. Baste a rectangle about 7 inches by 2½ inches (Fig. 18). Turn to the wrong side, and carefully stitch a long

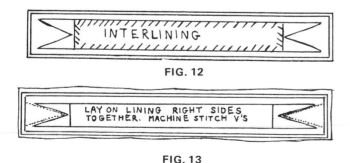

FIG. 12

FIG. 13

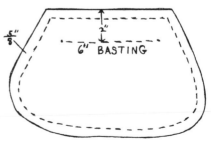

FIG. 17

rectangle around the first basting line about ⅜ inch wide. Start and end your stitching on the side (Fig. 19). Remove the basting threads. Carefully cut a slit through the middle of the long rectangle to within ¼ inch of each end, then diagonally to the corners. Be careful you don't cut the stitching threads (Fig. 20). Pull the pocket material through the slit, pressing back the sides and the triangular end pieces. This will make a long rectangular hole (Fig. 21). The pocket material will be on the wrong side. Set the zipper in this hole, baste and carefully stitch along the sides and across the ends

of the opening (Fig. 22). Fold the pocket material up behind the zipper, matching the edges. Stitch up one side, across above the zipper, and down the other side (Fig. 23). This makes a set in zipper pocket.

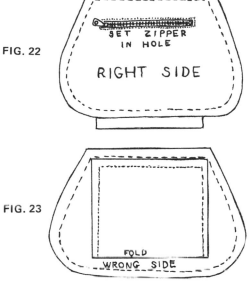

FIG. 22

FIG. 23

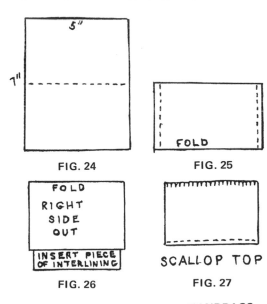

For a patch pocket, prepare a piece of lining material twice the size desired (Fig. 24). Fold it in half and seam the sides (Fig. 25). Turn it right side out, and insert a piece of interlining material slightly smaller than the pocket (Fig. 26). Turn in the open end and seam. For an added touch, work an embroidery stitch pattern, such as Buttonhole along the top folded edge (Fig. 27).

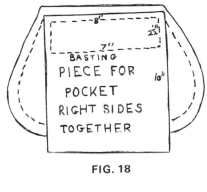

FIG. 18

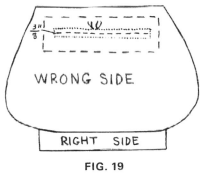

FIG. 19

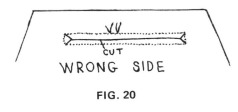

FIG. 20

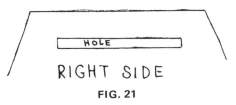

FIG. 21

FIG. 24

FIG. 25

FIG. 26

SCALLOP TOP

FIG. 27

For a scalloped edge patch pocket, you will need 2 pieces of lining material the desired size, plus ½ inch seam allowance all around (Fig. 28). Draw a pattern with a scalloped edge, no seam allowance (Fig. 29). Cut a piece of interlining material ⅛ inch smaller than the pattern (Fig. 30). Lay the pattern on the wrong side of one of the lining pieces and draw a pencil line around the edges. Pin the 2 pocket pieces, right sides together, and stitch along the sides and scalloped edge (Fig. 31). Trim off some of the excess material, and slash to the points of the scallops. Turn the pocket right side out, and carefully pull up the material to the stitching of the scallops. Insert the piece of interlining, fitting it into the scalloped edge. Turn in the bottoms of both sides, and seam the bottom edge. Work Buttonhole stitch along the scalloped edge with pearl cotton or embroidery floss (Fig. 32). Set the patch pocket against the other side of the lining about 3 inches down from the top (Fig. 33).

Place the pieces of lining against the bag sides, and hem across the bottom and halfway up the sides (Fig. 34). Right sides out, and using safety

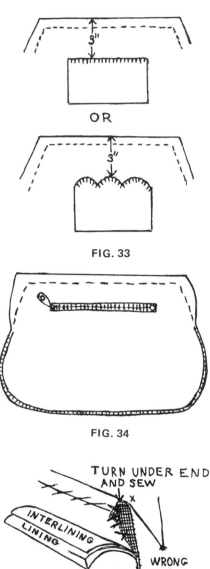

FIG. 33

FIG. 34

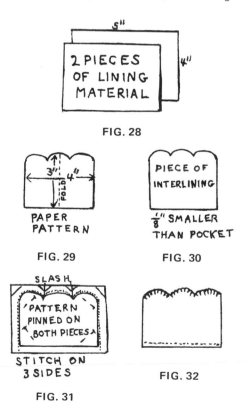

FIG. 28

FIG. 29   FIG. 30

FIG. 31   FIG. 32

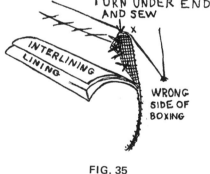

TURN UNDER END AND SEW

INTERLINING

LINING

WRONG SIDE OF BOXING

FIG. 35

pins to help hold things together, overcast the bottom of the boxing to the bag sides. Overcast up the sides to the extended excess canvas. Bring the extended excess canvas over against the back of the embroidery of the sides, folding the tips down, if necessary. Line up the points of the boxing with the corners of the sides (X in Fig. 35), and sew the extended canvas in place. Sew the boxing in place on the right side.

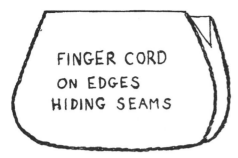

FIG. 36

FINGER CORD ON EDGES HIDING SEAMS

OVERCAST BASTING TO HOLD BAG TOP IN PLACE

BOTTOM OF BOXING "V" BEHIND HINGE

FIG. 37

PERMANENT STITCHING

FIG. 38

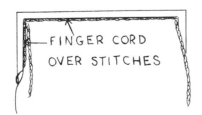

FINGER CORD OVER STITCHES

FIG. 39

Turn the interlining back up and finish sewing it in place. Bring the lining back up, and finish hemming it, sewing into the seam at the top of the boxing. Using the pearl cotton or 1 or 2 plies of yarn, make enough finger cord to sew around over the seams to cover them (Fig. 36). Don't put any in the boxing Vs. Fit the bag top to the sides of the bag, and the Vs of the boxing. Bring the hinges to the outside. Don't put any stitches in this area. With basting thread, overcast the bag top to the frame by bringing the basting thread over the top of the frame at intervals to hold the needlework in place while you are making the permanent stitches (Fig. 37). Using strong but fairly fine matching thread, pass the needle through the bag top and a hole in the frame beneath. Then back again through the next hole to the outside. Work from one end of the frame, across the top, and down the other side. Then reverse direction, going through the bag top and the holes in the frame a second time. This will make a continuous row of neat stitches both inside and out (Fig. 38). If you think it needs it, put a fine finger cord along the edges of the top to hide the stitches (Fig. 39).

Style B

Materials needed

Bag top, either old or new (Fig. 40)

2 or 3 pieces of canvas, 1 for the main part, and either 1 or 2 for the set in end pieces (Fig. 41)

Interlining for the above, plus a piece 4 inches by 5 inches for a pocket

Lining material for the 3 pieces, plus ¼ yd. for the pockets

6 inch zipper, closed at both ends

Yarn of your choice, and no. 8 pearl cotton, if you can find it

A piece of thin stiff material, such as heavy cardboard for the bottom (Fig. 42).

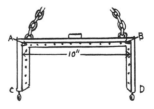

FIG. 40

This type of bag uses the same kind of top as Style A, but the pattern of the bag is different. The 2 sides and the bottom are made in 1 piece, with inset pieces on the ends. The result is a bag that is flat on the bottom (Fig. 43). This pattern is usually used for a fairly large bag.

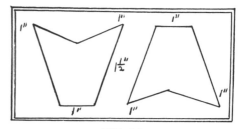

FIG. 44

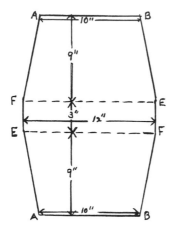

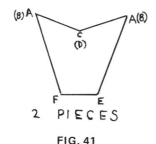

2 PIECES

FIG. 41

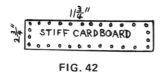

FIG. 42

FIG. 43

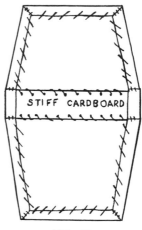

FIG. 45

Bind the canvas. Make paper patterns in good proportion for the size of the top (Fig. 41). The end pieces can be worked on one piece of canvas (Fig. 44). If you work them on 1 piece, be sure to leave at least 1½ inches excess canvas between them. The top and bottom of the main part must fit the measurements of the bag top. The V-shaped parts on the end pieces must be ¼ inch shorter than the distance from A to C, or B to D (Fig. 41). Be sure to lay out the patterns on the canvas so all horizontal lines are lined up with the canvas threads, and that you have at least 1 inch excess canvas all around. Draw the outlines of the 3 pieces.

Work the embroidery and block. Cut away the binding and some of the excess canvas of the main part, leaving about ¾ inch. Cut the cardboard about ¼ inch smaller than the bottom of the bag, and make perforations 1 inch apart, and about ¼ inch in from the edges (Fig. 42). Sew this to the back of the embroidery stitches on the bottom. Fold the excess canvas in and hem, mitering the 4 corners, and making little folds at the corners of the bottom (Fig. 45). Cut a piece of interlining to

FIG. 46

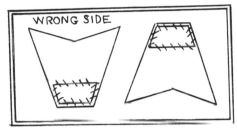

FIG. 47

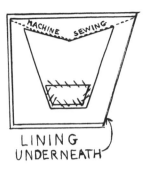

FIG. 48

FIG. 49

FIG. 50

fit between the edges of the turned back canvas, and hem along the middle of the sides only (Fig. 46).

For the end pieces, cut 2 pieces of interlining about 2 inches wide, and about ¼ inch smaller than the width of the end pieces at the bottom. Hem in place (Fig. 47). Cut 2 pieces of lining material to fit the end pieces, allowing ⅝ inch for seams. Baste to the end pieces, right sides together. On the canvas side, machine stitch along the sides of the Vs, sewing as close to the embroidery as possible. Round the bottom points slightly (Fig. 48). Stitch on up into the excess canvas to the binding. Cut off the binding and hem and miter the excess canvas. Hem as far up as you can go without overlapping the V. Cut away all but ¾ inch excess canvas in the Vs. Cut a slash through the canvas and the lining to the point of the V (Fig. 49). Bring the lining over onto the wrong side, press the V with your fingers, and pin. Put a few reinforcing yarn stitches at the point of the V. Turn the seam allowance of the lining in and hem, leaving the excess canvas at the points extended (Fig. 50).

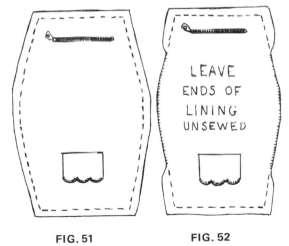

FIG. 51   FIG. 52

Prepare and make 2 pockets on the sides of the main part lining. (See pockets under directions for Style A bag.) Be sure to reverse the bottom one (Fig. 51). Place the lining against the main part, and hem along the middle of the sides only (Fig. 52). Place the end pieces against the middles of the sides of the main part, matching the Es and

Fs. Using safety pins to hold the pieces together, overcast the ends in place, up to the pieces of canvas you left extended (Fig. 53). Fold the tops of the lining and interlining down out of the way. Bring the extended pieces of canvas of the end pieces over against the back of the main part, fold under at the top and sew in place, making the pieces as flat as possible (Fig. 54). Bring the interlining up, and finish sewing it in place. Bring the lining up and sew it in place, sewing into the seams at the tops of the end pieces (Fig. 55). Sew the end pieces to the main part on the right side (Fig. 56). Make 2 pieces of finger cord of pearl cotton, or 1 or 2 plies of yarn, and sew invisibly over the seams to cover them (Fig. 57).

Fit the bag top to the ends of the main part, and the Vs of the ends. Put the hinges on the outside. Sew all around into the holes in the bag top. (See Figs. 37, 38). Leave a small space unsewed by the hinges (Fig. 58). If you feel it is necessary, make 2 more pieces of finger cord to put over the top edges to hide the stitches (Fig. 59).

The bottoms of the end pieces can be rounded (Fig. 60). This produces a softer bag. No stiffening piece is needed in the bottom.

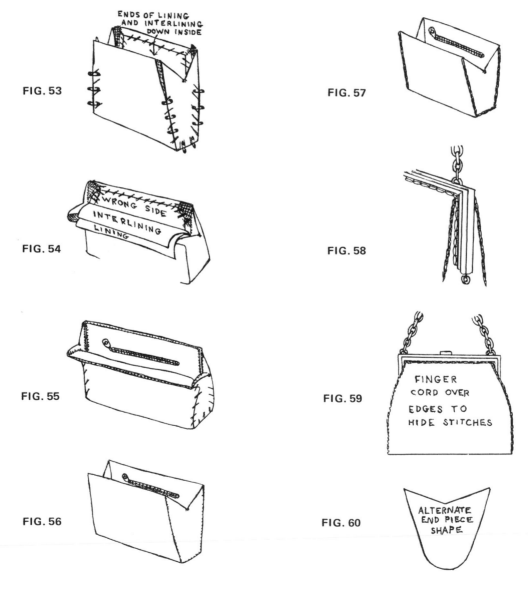

FIG. 53

ENDS OF LINING AND INTERLINING DOWN INSIDE

FIG. 54

WRONG SIDE
INTERLINING
LINING

FIG. 55

FIG. 56

FIG. 57

FIG. 58

FIG. 59

FINGER CORD OVER EDGES TO HIDE STITCHES

FIG. 60

ALTERNATE END PIECE SHAPE

Style C

Materials needed

Bag top

Canvas: 2 pieces 1 inch larger all around than the measurements of the side pieces; 1 piece 1 inch larger all around than the measurements of the boxing

Interlining for the above, plus 1 piece 4 inches by 5 inches for a pocket

Lining for the 3 pieces, plus ¼ yd. for pockets

6 inch zipper, closed at both ends

Yarn of your choice, and no. 8 pearl cotton, if you can find it

The top used for this type of bag is usually made of plastic (Fig. 2). The pattern and proportions for the sides can be similar to Style A (Fig. 6). Make the top of the sides ¼ inch longer than the length of the bar for a snug fit (Fig. 61). The boxing will be different, since it will not be fastened to the sides of the bag top (Fig. 62). Make the boxing as long as the line around the curve of the sides (A to B in Fig. 63). Leave an unworked space 4 threads wide, and ¼ inch shorter than the distance from the bar to the hinge on the side of the frame (Fig. 64).

Bind the canvas, work the embroidery, and block. Before cutting off the binding and the excess canvas off the sides, see the dotted line in Figure 61 and "Finishing Canvas on a Curve." Then cut off the binding and all but ¾ inch of the excess canvas, and hem and miter it to the back of the embroidery (Fig. 65). Hem pieces of interlining to the backs of the sides (Fig. 66). Make pockets in the pieces of lining for the sides (see

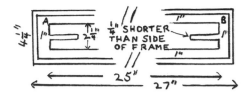

FIG. 62

FIG. 63

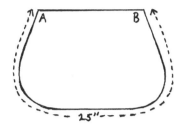

FIG. 64

FIG. 65

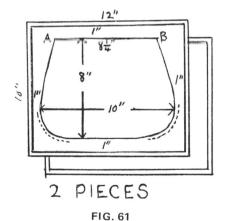

FIG. 61

FIG. 66

pockets instructions for Style A bag). Hem the lining to the sides, leaving about ¼ inch unsewed at the tops of the sides. Place a line of hand sewing into the back of the embroidery ½ inch or ¾ inch down from the top edges (Fig. 67).

Attach a piece of interlining to the wrong side of the boxing between the 2 unworked areas at the ends (Fig. 68). Pin or baste the lining to the boxing, right sides together, and, on the canvas side, machine stitch down the side of the unworked area, across the bottom, and up the other side (Fig. 69). Do not sew into the excess canvas on the ends. Stitch as close to the embroidery as possible. Trim off the binding, turn back the excess canvas, and hem, mitering the corners. Sew

across the interlining (Fig. 70). Don't carry the thread across the unworked area on the ends, as it will be cut. Overcast the 4-thread area to the edge of the embroidery, 2 threads to each side. This will widen the space between the 2 center threads (Fig. 71). Cut through the lining and the space between the 2 center threads (Fig. 72). Turn the boxing right side out, and press lightly on the lining side. Hem the lining all around. Add a few reinforcing stitches of yarn at the bottom of the slot. It will be slightly rounded (Fig. 73).

With the help of safety pins, overcast and hem the boxing to the 2 sides, right side out. Leave an opening at the top corners for the bars (Xs in Fig. 74). Make 2 finger cords, or use Binding stitch to

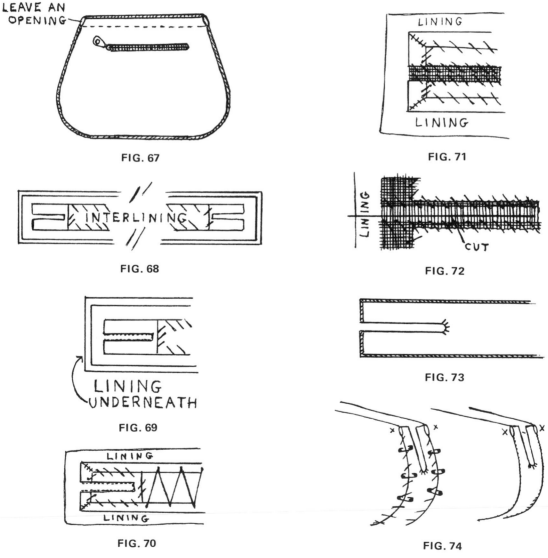

FIG. 67

FIG. 68

FIG. 69

FIG. 70

FIG. 71

FIG. 72

FIG. 73

FIG. 74

cover the seams (Fig. 75). Be careful not to close the openings at the top for the bars. Turn the square ends of the boxing in against the top corners of the sides, and sew securely in place. This will make the top of the boxing turn in (Fig. 76).

Slip the bars through the casings and tighten the nuts (Fig. 77). The sides of the frame and the hinges will be on the outside (Fig. 78).

FIG. 75

FIG. 76

BAR IN CASING

FIG. 77

FIG. 78

Style D

Materials needed

Bag top

Canvas: 2 pieces 1 inch larger all around than the measurements of the side pieces; 1 piece 1 inch larger all around than the measurements of the boxing

Interlining for the above, plus a piece 4 inches by 5 inches for a pocket

Lining for the 3 pieces, plus ¼ yd. for pockets

6 inch zipper, closed at both ends

Yarn of your choice, and no. 8 pearl cotton, if you can find it

½ yd. of grosgrain ribbon, more for a large bag (if possible get a dark color, as the top of the bag will be handled every time the bag is opened)

This type of bag has 2 flat spring steel pieces that are entirely covered with material. Only the hinged ends are left exposed. They come in several sizes, 7½ inches, 8 inches, 10 inches, and 12 inches. The 8 inch size is used for the average size bag (Fig. 3). Make the bag about 1 inch deeper than the other types (9 inches deep for the 8 inch top), and about ¼ inch longer at the top than the length of the steel pieces for a snug fit (Fig. 79). The tops of the sides should be straight for 1½ inches. Make the boxing wider in the middle and tapered to 1 inch at each end (Fig. 80). It should

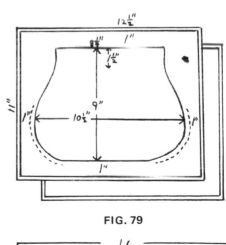

FIG. 79

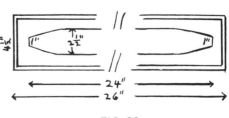

FIG. 80

be as long as the curve around the sides from A to B in Figure 81. Make paper patterns.

Bind the canvas, work the embroidery, and block. Before cutting the binding and excess canvas off the sides, see Figure 79 and "Finishing Canvas on a Curve." Then cut off the binding and all but ¾ inch of the excess canvas. Hem and miter the excess canvas to the back of the embroidery (Fig. 82). Cut and sew in pieces of interlining for the sides to come up to 1½ inches from the top (Fig. 83).

Sew a piece of interlining to the wrong side of the boxing up to 3 inches from each end (Fig. 84). Cut the binding off, and a little excess canvas at the ends so as to leave ¾ inch all around. Turn back the excess canvas and hem at the ends. Sew across the interlining in the middle (Fig. 85). Then line it completely (Fig. 86).

Using the pattern for the sides, measure the depth for the lining to come up to 1½ inches from the top. Add seam allowance, and cut 2 pieces of lining material for the sides. (See pockets directions for Style A.) Sew the lining pieces to the bag sides, leaving 1½ inches at the top uncovered (Fig. 87).

Hem the 2 ends of 2 pieces of grosgrain ribbon 1½ inches wide, so it will be the same length as the top of the sides when it is finished (Fig. 88). Sew the bottom edge to the top of the lining, leaving the top and the ends open (Fig. 89).

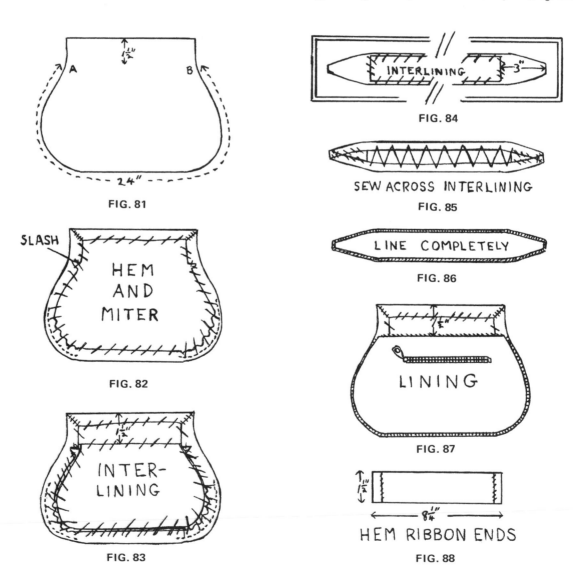

FIG. 81

SLASH

HEM AND MITER

FIG. 82

INTER-LINING

FIG. 83

INTERLINING   3"

FIG. 84

SEW ACROSS INTERLINING

FIG. 85

LINE COMPLETELY

FIG. 86

LINING

FIG. 87

HEM RIBBON ENDS

FIG. 88

With the help of safety pins, overcast the boxing to the bag sides (Fig. 90). Seam the pieces together on the right side (Fig. 91). Cover the seams with Binding stitch or Finger Cord. Use pearl cotton, if you have any (Fig. 92). Pinch in the ends of the boxing, and tack firmly (Fig. 93).

Insert the 2 steel pieces of the bag top into the space between the canvas and the grosgrain ribbon. You will have to open the top to do this (Fig. 94). Sew the canvas and the ribbon together over the bars (Fig. 95). Work Binding stitch over the seams (Fig. 96).

For a soft bag, omit the interlining.

If there are rings at the ends of the top, a handle can be added. Figure 97 shows an alternate pattern, somewhat similar to style B.

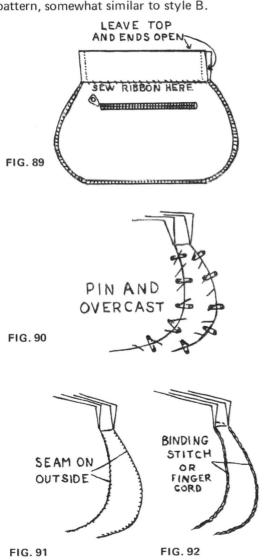

FIG. 89

PIN AND OVERCAST

FIG. 90

SEAM ON OUTSIDE

FIG. 91

BINDING STITCH OR FINGER CORD

FIG. 92

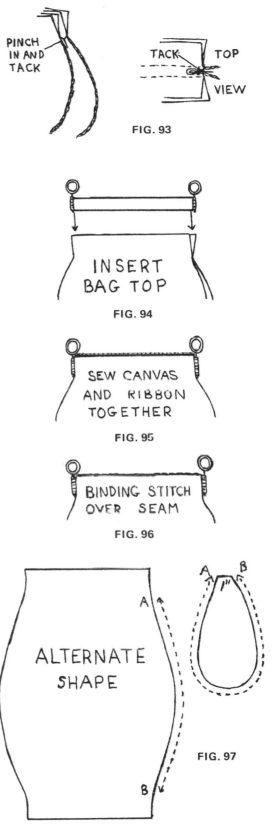

PINCH IN AND TACK

TACK TOP VIEW

FIG. 93

INSERT BAG TOP

FIG. 94

SEW CANVAS AND RIBBON TOGETHER

FIG. 95

BINDING STITCH OVER SEAM

FIG. 96

ALTERNATE SHAPE

FIG. 97

Tote Bags

There are several ways to make the ever-useful tote bag, and directions are given here for twelve of them. Some are soft; made entirely of canvas. Some are stiffened to stand erect. Some are made with readily available supplies, and some require materials that may be a little hard to find.

The ideal aids to making a bag stand erect are corset stays. They are made of springy steel, finished on the ends, and are completely washable. If you can't find any, a passable substitute is strips of stiff plastic cut from the sides of bleach or milk bottles. Some specialty shops may carry the plastic ring handles. They are readily available from New York wholesale houses. If there is enough demand, more shops and art needlework departments may carry them. Be sure to buy your lining, ribbon, and buttons before selecting the yarn, because of the limited choice of materials and colors.

Style A. Soft, all canvas, 1 piece, flat

Materials needed

1 piece of canvas twice the length of the bag and handle, by the width, plus 1½ inches excess canvas all around (Fig. 1)
1 piece of lining material for the above, plus 2 pieces for facings for the concave curves, plus material for pockets, if desired (see Style A, "Handbags," p. 122), plus seam allowance
5 inch zipper, closed at both ends, if you want a zipper pocket
Interlining if desired
Yarn of your choice

When designing the needlework, keep in mind that the upper part must have the design upside down (Fig. 1). Work with a rectangular piece of canvas. Make a paper pattern, folding the handle part over so as to be sure it is large enough. Fold the pattern lengthwise to be sure the left and right sides match. Bind the canvas. Pin the pattern to the canvas, making sure the lengthwise fold is lined up with the canvas threads. Draw an outline of the pattern, add the design, and work the embroidery. Then block.

Cut off the binding and all but 1 inch of the excess canvas. Face the curved openings. (See "Finishing Canvas on a Curve.") Turn under the rest of the excess canvas, mitering the lower corners (Fig. 2). Hem the ends of the facings over the excess canvas.

FIG. 1

RECTANGULAR CANVAS

Cut out the lining, using the pattern, and allowing ¾ inch seam allowance. Make pockets in the lining, if desired (Fig. 3). (See Style A, Handbags.) Hem the lining to the bag all around. Fold it over, right side out, and seam the sides and bottom (Fig. 4). (See "Joining Pieces of Canvas—Seaming.")

Finish the edges of the openings with a decorative stitch pattern, such as Binding stitch, Buttonhole, or Fringe (Fig. 5).

Style B. Soft, all canvas, 1 piece, boxed bottom

Materials needed

Same as for Style A with additional length to accommodate the boxed bottom (Fig. 6).

Line A to B must equal A to C. Part of the upper edge will be used to complete the boxing (Fig. 6).

Make the bottom a little wider than in Style A. Face the curves, and hem and miter the rest of the excess canvas (Fig. 7). (See "Finishing Canvas on a Curve.")

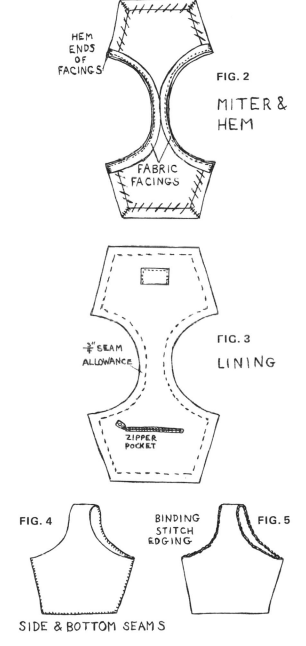

HEM ENDS OF FACINGS

FIG. 2

MITER & HEM

FABRIC FACINGS

¾" SEAM ALLOWANCE

FIG. 3

LINING

ZIPPER POCKET

FIG. 4

FIG. 5

BINDING STITCH EDGING

SIDE & BOTTOM SEAMS

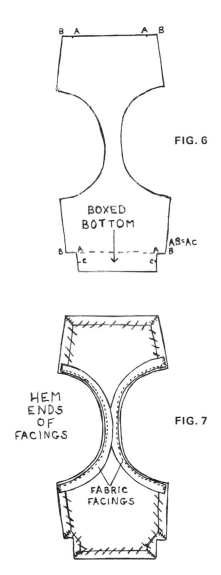

B A   A B

FIG. 6

BOXED BOTTOM

B   A
  C   C
AB=AC

HEM ENDS OF FACINGS

FIG. 7

FABRIC FACINGS

Prepare the lining with pockets (Fig. 8) and hem all around to the canvas and the facings. Sew up the sides and the seams along the boxing (Fig. 9). (See "Joining Pieces of Canvas—Seaming.") Finish the opening with a decorative edging (Fig. 10).

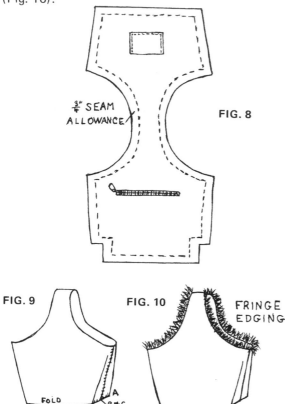

¾" SEAM ALLOWANCE

FIG. 8

FIG. 9

FOLD

A
B+C

FIG. 10

FRINGE EDGING

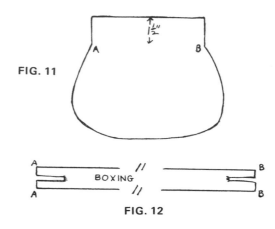

FIG. 11

1½"

A   B

A   B
BOXING
A   B

FIG. 12

Bind the canvas, and work the embroidery for the front and back. Follow the directions for the boxing in style C, Handbags, p. 122.

Make pockets in the lining, if you wish. (See Style A, Handbags, p. 122.) Line the pieces and seam them on the right side. (See "Joining Pieces of Canvas—Seaming."). Turn down and hem the casing for the dowels. Turn the ends of the boxing in, and sew them along the hem for the casings (Fig. 13, 14). Make the handles all of canvas, or line them with ribbon. Attach the handles to the ends of the casings, insert the dowels, and add the ball finials (Fig. 15).

Style C. Soft, wooden dowel and balls, 3 pieces and handle

Materials needed

Canvas: See Style B, Handbag, for pattern for the canvas, but add 1½ inches extension at the top, plus enough for 2 handles (see Style F)

Lining material for the above, plus extra for pockets, if desired (see Style A, Handbags, for pocket patterns)

2½ inch dowels and ball finials

The bottom part of this bag is made in the conventional bag shape, with a straight-sided extension 1½ inches wide at the top (Fig. 11). The boxing is made like the one for Style C, Handbags, except that it does not extend up into the top part. It extends from one end of the hem line, A around to B (Figs. 11, 12).

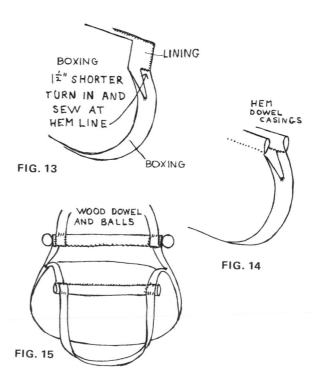

BOXING
1½" SHORTER
TURN IN AND
SEW AT
HEM LINE

LINING

BOXING

FIG. 13

HEM DOWEL CASINGS

FIG. 14

WOOD DOWEL AND BALLS

FIG. 15

Style D. Soft, knitting bag handles, 3 pieces

Materials needed

Same as for Style C, but with knitting-bag handles

Make the top edge to fit through the slot in the knitting bag handles (Fig. 16).

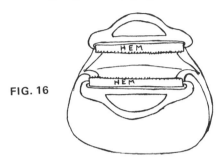

FIG. 16

Style E. Soft, 12 inch rulers or wooden pieces, 3 pieces and handles

This bag is made in the same way as C and D except that 12 inch rulers, or flat pieces of wood, 1 inch by ⅛ inch by 12 inches, are put in the casings at the top. Close the ends of the casings, and make canvas handles (Fig. 17).

Bags C, D, and E can be made using the pattern for Style B, Handbags. Use the alternate curved end pieces.

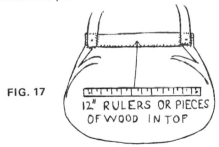

FIG. 17

12" RULERS OR PIECES OF WOOD IN TOP

Style F. Stiffened, flat, 1-piece, and handles

Materials needed

Canvas: A long strip equal in width to the depth of the bag, and the length equal to twice the width of the bag plus 1¼ inches excess canvas all around. A piece about 4½ by 14½ inches for the handles. (If both handles are worked on one piece, be sure to leave 2 inches excess canvas between them.)

Interlining material 1 inch shorter each way than the worked area of the main part

Lining material for the bag, plus seam allowance, plus extra for pockets

1 yd. dark-colored ribbon to line the handles

2 corset stays, or pieces of plastic from a bottle, ½ inch shorter than the depth of the bag, and tape to enclose one of them

Make a long strip equal in width to the depth of the bag. Make the length twice the width of the bag. Make the handles about 12 inches long (Fig. 18).

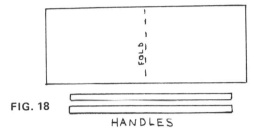

FOLD

FIG. 18

HANDLES

Get your lining, ribbon, and stiffeners before planning the bag, so that colors can be matched, and the depth of the bag made to fit the stays or plastic pieces.

If you have the patience, you can plan a geometric design to exactly fit the thread count of the bag so it can be matched across the side seam, making the seam almost invisible. You will need to plan your design on graph paper before beginning the needlework. Leave 1 stitch of the design out along the seam. After the edges are joined, this one row can be added over the seam. (See "Joining Pieces of Canvas—Seaming.")

Bind the canvas, work the embroidery, and block. Sew the piece of tape for one stay where the fold will be, and insert the stay. Hem and miter the excess canvas, enclosing the other stay in the hem at one end (Fig. 19). Cut the binding off

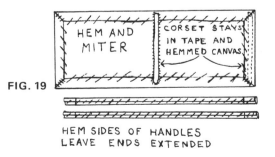

FIG. 19

HEM AND MITER

CORSET STAYS IN TAPE AND HEMMED CANVAS

HEM SIDES OF HANDLES
LEAVE ENDS EXTENDED

the handles, turn in, and hem the excess canvas along the sides. Leave the excess canvas on the ends extended. Overcast the ends. Cut the interlining for the main part to fit up to the turned back canvas, and hem in place. Line the handles with ribbon, leaving the ends unfinished. Securely sew the handles to the interlining and the top edge of the canvas, flattening them as much as possible (Fig. 20).

Prepare the lining with pockets, if desired (Fig. 21). (See pocket instructions for Handbag Style A, page 122.) Hem the lining in place all around.

Fold the canvas in half, and, on the right side, seam the side and bottom with strong thread. Go over the seam with matching yarn. (See "Joining Pieces of Canvas—Seaming.") The top edge and the edges of the handles can be covered with Binding stitch (Fig. 22).

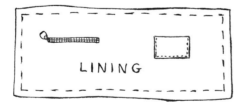

FIG. 20

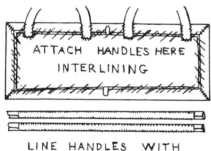

FIG. 21

FIG. 22

Style G. Stiffened, boxed bottom, 1-piece and handles

Materials needed

Same as for style F, with added depth for the boxing
Piece of heavy cardboard to put in the bottom

You can make curves along the top edge, with points where the handles are attached (Fig. 23).

Bind the canvas, work the embroidery, and block. Hem and miter the excess canvas, adding corset stays, if you have them. Face the top if you have curved edges (Fig. 24). Line a heavy piece of cardboard, and sew it to the wrong side of the boxing. Make the handles as for F, and sew them to the interlining, and the excess canvas, or facing at the top edge.

Prepare the lining with pockets, if desired. Hem it all around the edges of the canvas. Fold the bag parts together, matching As and Bs and seam on the right side. Cover the seam with matching yarn (Fig. 25). (See "Joining Pieces of Canvas—Seaming").

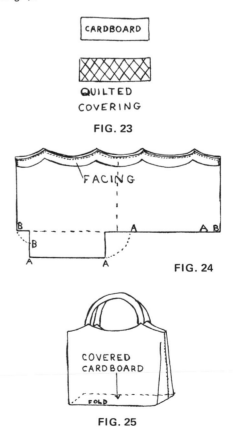

FIG. 23

FIG. 24

FIG. 25

Style H. Stiffened, separate boxed bottom, 2 pieces and handles, metal studs for feet (optional)

Materials needed

Canvas: Same as for Style F, with an added separate piece for the base
Heavy cardboard for the base
Outing flannel to quilt the lining of the base
Little stud feet to put on the bottom of the base, if desired

You can round the ends, if you wish. Just be sure the perimeter of the boxed bottom equals the length of the bottom of the bag (Fig. 26).

Embroider the bottom canvas separately. Cut the cardboard a little smaller than the canvas so the worked canvas will cover the edges. If you have rounded the ends, see "Finishing Canvas on a Curve." Draw up the gathers and lace the excess canvas over the cardboard. Insert stud feet, if you want to use them. Now make a padded lining and hem it all around the edges (Fig. 27). Prepare the bag handles as in Style F. If you have a curved top

edge see "Finishing Canvas on a Curve" for instructions for facing directions. Add the interlining, and attach the handles as in Style F. Sew up the side seam, covering the seam with matching yarn. See "Joining Pieces of Canvas—Seaming.") With the help of safety pins, overcast, then sew the base in place, using heavy thread (Fig. 28). Cover the bottom and top seams with Binding stitch.

Style I. Soft, 1 piece, shoulder strap handle

Materials needed

Piece of canvas to accommodate 2 sides of the bag, with a fold at the bottom, plus 1¼ inches excess canvas all around
Lining material equal to the worked area, plus ½ inch seam allowance all around
Allow extra material for pockets if desired (see Style A, Clutch Bags, page 113, for pockets)
Yarn of your choice, plus enough uncut yarn to make a cord shoulder handle

This is a very simple bag made in 1 piece, folded at the bottom with seams at the sides. Be sure to reverse the design of the lower part (Fig. 29). If you want pockets in the lining, make one of them upside down (Fig. 30).

Bind the canvas, work the embroidery, and block. Cut off the binding, and hem back the excess canvas, mitering the corners. Prepare the lining with pockets, and hem it to the canvas on all 4 sides. Cover the top and bottom edged with Binding stitch. Fold the piece in the middle, and,

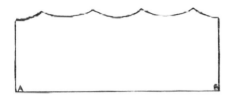

SEPARATE BASE WITH CURVED ENDS. PERIMETER EQUALS BAG BOTTOM.

FIG. 26

QUILTED COVERING INSIDE. EM-BROIDERED CANVAS OUTSIDE

FIG. 27

FIG. 28

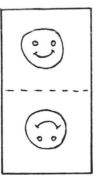

FIG. 29

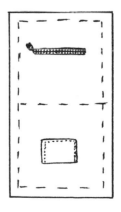

FIG. 30

starting at the top edge, sew the side seams on the outside. Use heavy thread (Fig. 31).

You will need uncut yarn for the shoulder strap handle. Make a long heavy cord, and put a tassel at each end. Sew the ends of the cord to the sides of the bag, as invisibly as possible. Sew securely, as these stitches will take the weight of the bag (Fig. 32).

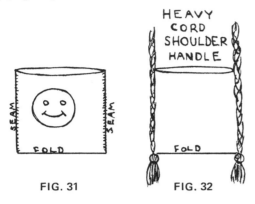

FIG. 31 FIG. 32

Style J. Stiffened, 1 piece (flap), shoulder strap handle

Materials needed

See Style A, Clutch Bags, flat style
Yarn of your choice, plus enough uncut yarn to make a cord shoulder handle

Follow the directions for Style A Clutch Bags, the flat style. You can make the bag deeper, if you wish. Just add the long cord shoulder strap (Fig. 33).

A sort of saddle bag can be made like the flat clutch bag with the side pieces. For a chain handle, have grommets put in, 2 at the top corners of the flap, and 2 more beneath them in the back.

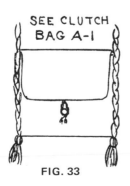

FIG. 33

The end links of the chain will allow you to lift the flap. Weights in the corners of the flap can be used instead of the corset stay or strip of stiff plastic (Fig. 34).

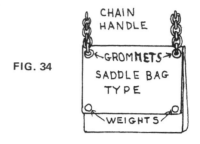

FIG. 34

Style K. Stiffened, 1 piece, plastic, or embroidery hoop handles, metal studs for feet

Materials needed

Corset stays or strips of stiff plastic, see below
5 inches circular plastic handles or embroidery hoops
Canvas twice the depth of the bag, plus 2 inches boxing, plus 1½ inches excess canvas all around (work with a rectangular piece of canvas)
Lining material equal to the worked area, plus some for the facings on the curves, plus enough for pockets (see Style A, Clutch Bags, page 113, or Style A, Handbags, page 122)

This bag is made in 1 piece, seamed down the sides, with boxing in the bottom. Plastic rings or embroidery hoop handles make it easy to carry (Fig. 35). If you wish your bag to stand, corset

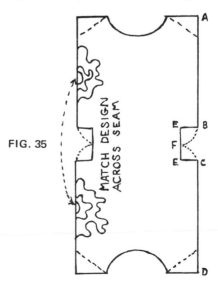

FIG. 35

stays, or strips of stiff plastic are placed from the corners to the top at the ends of the curves. Another pair can be crossed in the boxed bottom to keep it flat (Fig. 35). Metal studs can be placed near the corners on the bottom. If you can find the corset stays, get them first, before planning the bag. They should be about ½ inch shorter than the depth of the bag. The sides A to B and C to D must be exactly equal in length. Count the threads, if you have the patience. Also B to E and C to E must equal E to F for perfect fitting (Figs. 32, 35). Reverse the design on the lower half of the canvas. If you have an allover design, match the parts at the edges so they will come together when you sew up the sides. The ends of the top edge can be square or sloping (Fig. 36).

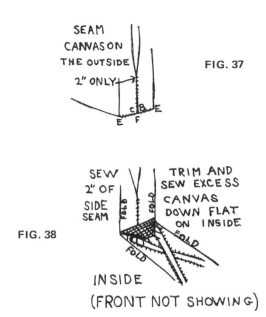

FIG. 37

FIG. 38

INSIDE
(FRONT NOT SHOWING)

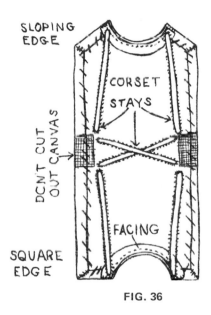

FIG. 36

Bind the canvas, work the embroidery, and block. Cut off the binding, cutting straight across the indentation for the boxing. Hem the excess canvas, mitering the top and bottom corners. (See "Finishing Canvas on a Curve" for directions for finishing the top and bottom curves.) If you don't use corset stays, add interlining up to the turned back canvas. Fold the bottoms of the sides to meet the ends of the boxing, seam across and up the sides about 2 inches (Fig. 37). On the inside, trim away some of the excess canvas, and fold the rest flat on the bottom. Sew it in place (Fig. 38).

Prepare the lining with pockets, if desired (Fig. 39). (See Style A, Handbags, page 122.) Seam the boxing of the lining, and about 2 inches up the sides (Fig. 40). Fit the lining into the corners, and

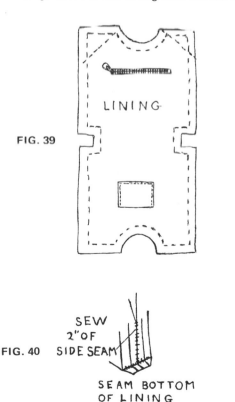

FIG. 39

FIG. 40

SEAM BOTTOM
OF LINING

pin it in place with safety pins on the outside (Fig. 41). Smooth lining up and hem the rest to the front and back of the bag (Fig. 42). Finish the side seams (Fig. 43). (See "Joining Pieces of Canvas—Seaming.")

If you are using embroidery hoops for handles, cover them with yarn or ribbon (Fig. 44).

Don't use velvet; it doesn't wear well. Sew one side to the curve of the bag top (Fig. 45). Plastic rings can be attached with yarn wrapped around, or fine cording tacked to the curves (Fig. 46).

Short cords can be attached to one side of the top, brought over, and looped over a button on the other side (Fig. 47). You can use them for any bag without a flap—C, D, F, H, I, or K.

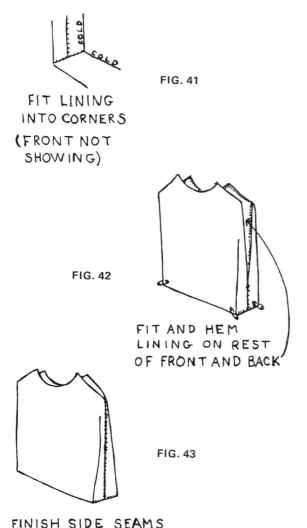

FIG. 41

FIT LINING INTO CORNERS (FRONT NOT SHOWING)

FIG. 42

FIT AND HEM LINING ON REST OF FRONT AND BACK

FIG. 43

FINISH SIDE SEAMS

5" PLASTIC RING HANDLE

WRAPPED EMBROIDERY HOOP HANDLE

FIG. 44

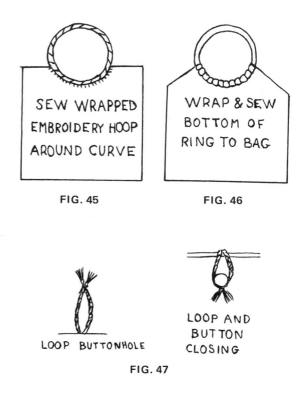

SEW WRAPPED EMBROIDERY HOOP AROUND CURVE

FIG. 45

WRAP & SEW BOTTOM OF RING TO BAG

FIG. 46

LOOP BUTTONHOLE

LOOP AND BUTTON CLOSING

FIG. 47

Style L.
Semi-stiff—needlework tote bag

This is the handiest bag for carrying your "piece" around with you. Everything you'll use has a place, even the different colors or kinds of yarn are separated and right at hand. No more tangled mass of threads in the bottom of your bag. The bag opens flat so you can lay it on a table, or you can just open the top so you can pick out whatever piece of yarn you need at the moment. You can make the bag any size, but the measurements illustrated will accommodate even a large piece (Fig. 48).

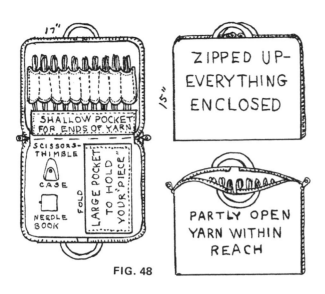

FIG. 48

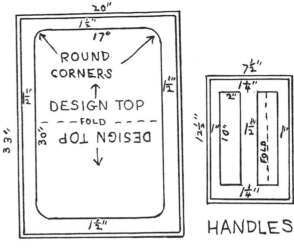

HANDLES

FIG. 49

Materials needed

One piece of canvas twice the depth desired by the width
you want, plus 1½ inches excess canvas all around
(33 inches by 20 inches); you can make the handles
of a double thickness of canvas; allow 1 inch all
around, and 1½ inches between the pieces (12½
inches by 7½ inches) (Fig. 49)

Lining to cover the inside, plus enough for 2 pockets, and
the fluted tubes for the yarn (you can make the
scissors, thimble case, and the needle book of lining
material, too. Adapt the "Travel Sewing Kit," p.
108, and "Needle Book," p. 106. The large pocket is
double thickness. 1¼ yd. of material will accommodate all the pieces [Fig. 50]. Use something with
enough body to hold its shape.)

2 zippers equal to the depth of the bag, plus ½ the width,
minus ½ inch (It would be a good idea to get these
long zippers first, as it may be hard to find the right
length, (23 inches), in the color you want. You
might have to alter the measurements of the bag to
suit the length of the zippers. You could tuck an
extra inch under the lining on the fold, however)

Interlining A piece of waterproof interlining to fit between the edges of the turned back canvas (Fig. 52)

You could make cord handles of yarn but they would get
pretty fuzzy with use; so if you'd like cord handles
instead of canvas ones, try making them out of
matching macramé cord (See "Cords and Braids,"
p. 213)

Yarn of your choice

Bind the canvas, work the embroidery, and
block. Cut off the binding, turn in the excess
canvas and hem, making little folds at the rounded
corners (Fig. 51). Sew in the interlining (Fig. 52).

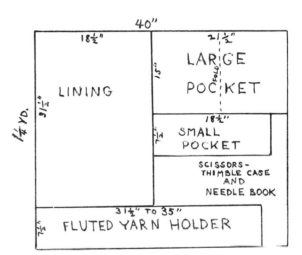

LINING PATTERN LAYOUT

FIG. 50

FIG. 51

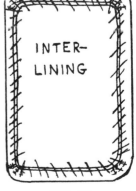

FIG. 52

For canvas handles, cut off the binding and cut the handles apart. The pieces will have ¾ inch at each side and 1 inch at each end. Overcast the ends to prevent fraying. Turn in the excess canvas along the sides, and folding the canvas in half, seam the handles on the right side, leaving the canvas on the ends extended. Seam this, too (Fig. 53). Sew the extended ends of the handles securely to the ends of the main part (Fig. 54).

Open the zippers all the way, and starting in the middle of each side with the joined end, sew the 2 halves to the edges of the bag. Leave an inch at the top. It would be a good idea to baste with large hemming stitches first. Getting the zippers in right is important (Fig. 55).

Using the pattern layout (Figs. 56 and 55), prepare the pockets, needle book, scissors, thimble case, and the fluted tubes for the yarn. Hem the pieces as indicated in Figure 56 so there will be no raw edges to fray. The long piece for the fluted yarn holder can be arranged any way you like. They can be all the same size, or one or two can be larger to hold larger quantities of yarn, such as background yarn. A good average size is a 2 inch loop sewed to a 1⅛ inch width of lining. Arrange

them with pins and then baste. Last, sew them on the machine. Don't make any loops too small, it would be hard to get a loop of yarn through, and a too large loop wouldn't keep the yarn in (Fig. 56). Sew the needle book, and the scissors—thimble case in place. .Now sew the prepared lining to the edges of the zipper tapes. Skip over the ends of the zippers in the middle (Fig. 57).

Note: An easy way to get the yarn through the fluted tubes is with a table fork. Loop the yarn through the tines and, starting at the bottom, push the fork through until you can catch hold of the yarn. Then back the fork out the bottom again.

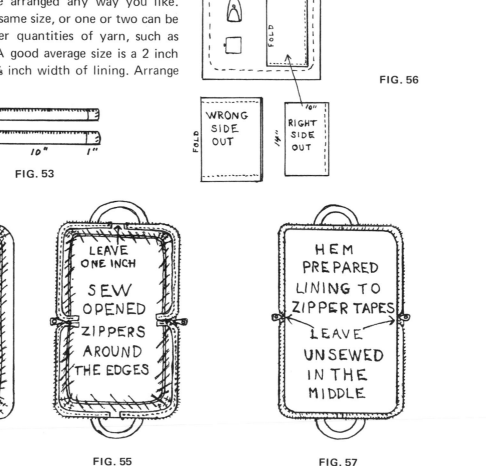

FIG. 53

FIG. 56

FIG. 54

FIG. 55

FIG. 57

Golf Club and Putter Covers

Golf Club Covers

Materials needed for a set of 3 woods

Canvas enough for 3 central pieces and 6 side pieces (Canvas for 1 cover will fit on a piece 11 inches by 23 inches. See measurements in Figure 1. Be sure to have 1½ inches excess canvas around the edges, and at least 2 inches between pieces. Line A to B must equal line C to D [Fig. 1])
Sturdy lining material for all 9 pieces
3 zippers 8 inches long, closed at one end
Yarn of your choice

Make a set of paper patterns by following the measurements in Figure 1. It is drawn to scale. Bind the canvas first, then lay out your patterns. Be sure the central pieces are lined up with the canvas threads, and that there are at least 2 inches between pieces. Draw lines around the pieces.

Work the embroidery, and block, using the patterns as a guide. It is a good idea to choose stitch patterns that don't warp the canvas. Then the covers can be washed and won't get out of shape.

Cut off the binding and all but 1 inch of the excess canvas. Hem and miter the excess canvas of the central part. Leave the ends of the side pieces unfinished until you have fitted them to the central part in case of slight inaccuracies. You may need to adjust their length to exactly meet the ends of the central part (Fig. 2). (See "Finishing Canvas on a Curve.") Use the patterns to cut out

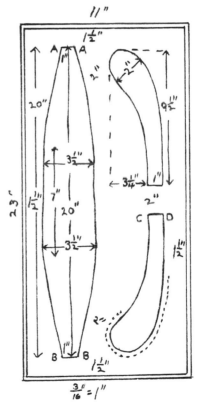

PATTERN LAYOUT

FIG. 1

the linings. Allow ¾ inch seam allowance around each piece. Line the side pieces, leaving the ends and 8 inches of the concave curved side of one piece unfinished. Line the center piece except for 8 inches to correspond with the unfinished edge of the side piece (Fig. 3). Using safety pins to help, fit the pieces together. Adjust the lengths of the side pieces, if necessary. Then finish them (Fig. 4).

Take out the pins so you can get at the zipper. Baste or pin the zipper in place. Hem the canvas to the tapes on the right side, and the lining to the tapes on the wrong side. Tuck the ends of the zipper tapes into the seams (Figs. 5, 6). Replace the pins, and then seam the pieces together. Work on the right side, using strong thread (Fig. 7).

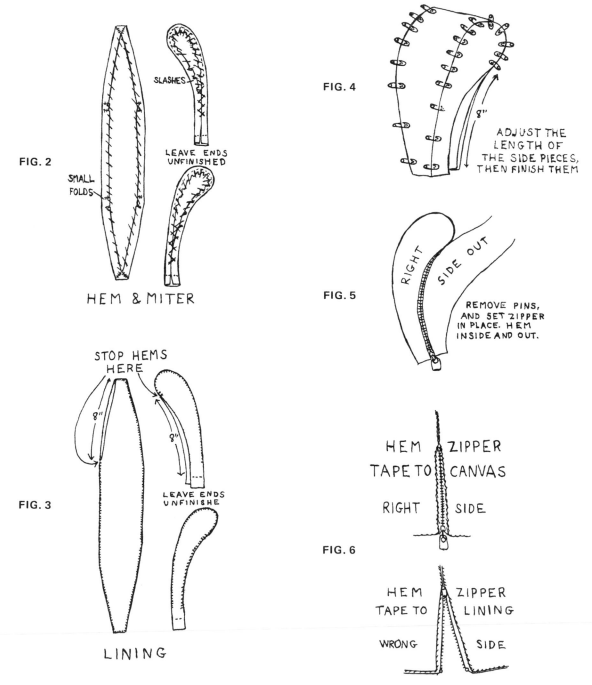

FIG. 2

SLASHES

LEAVE ENDS UNFINISHED

SMALL FOLDS

HEM & MITER

FIG. 3

STOP HEMS HERE

8"

8"

LEAVE ENDS UNFINISHE

LINING

FIG. 4

8"

ADJUST THE LENGTH OF THE SIDE PIECES, THEN FINISH THEM

FIG. 5

RIGHT

SIDE OUT

REMOVE PINS, AND SET ZIPPER IN PLACE. HEM INSIDE AND OUT.

HEM ZIPPER TAPE TO CANVAS

RIGHT SIDE

FIG. 6

HEM ZIPPER TAPE TO LINING

WRONG SIDE

Place a good sturdy loop, well anchored, on the top of the curve of the center part for a connecting cord. Go over the seams with Binding stitch (Fig. 8).

Note: Fringe edging would look very attractive as a finish, but you couldn't put it along the zipper edge. It would get tangled in the zipper.

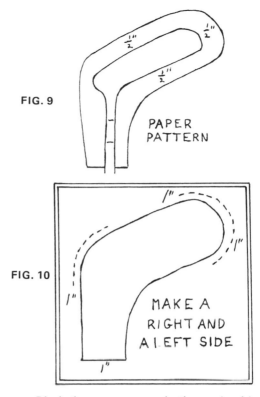

FIG. 9

PAPER PATTERN

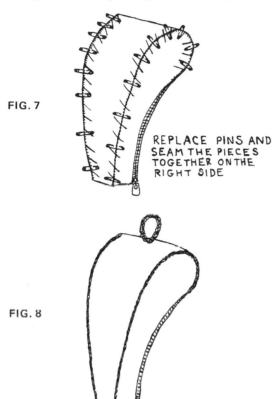

FIG. 7

REPLACE PINS AND SEAM THE PIECES TOGETHER ON THE RIGHT SIDE

FIG. 10

MAKE A RIGHT AND A LEFT SIDE

FIG. 8

Bind the canvas, work the embroidery, and block. Make 2 rows of machine stitching, one on top of the other, around the convex curves. Then run gathering threads through the stitching (broken lines in Fig. 10).

Baste the lining to the canvas, right sides together. Turn over to the canvas side, and stitch as close to the embroidery as possible around the *concave* curve. Trim off the binding and all but ¾ inch of the excess canvas. Slash the excess canvas and the seam allowance of the lining in the curve (Fig. 11). Holding the canvas up out of the way,

Putter Covers

Draw a paper pattern, allowing about ½ inch extra width on all sides (Fig. 9). Make 2 pieces, one for each side, allowing 1 inch excess canvas around each piece (Fig. 10). If both sides are to be worked on one piece of canvas, be sure to leave at least 2 inches excess canvas between the pieces.

Materials needed

Canvas as above; fairly fine canvas will reduce the bulk, and make the mounting much easier
2 pieces of lining material; use the pattern, allowing about ⅝ inch seam allowance
A matching zipper about 4 inches long
Yarn of your choice

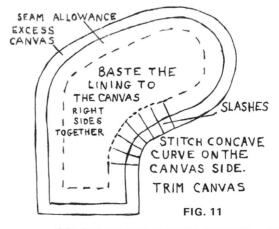

SEAM ALLOWANCE
EXCESS CANVAS

BASTE THE LINING TO THE CANVAS RIGHT SIDES TOGETHER

SLASHES

STITCH CONCAVE CURVE ON THE CANVAS SIDE.
TRIM CANVAS

FIG. 11

lay the lining flat. Spread the slashes apart, and sew again about ⅛ inch out from the first line of stitching, anchoring the slashed edge to the lining (Fig. 12). (See "Finishing Canvas on a Curve.") Now fold the lining back and hem and miter the excess canvas (Fig. 13). (See "Finishing Canvas on a Curve.") Smooth the lining out, and hem to the rest of the edge. Leave a small opening at the back of the bottom so you can tuck the ends of the zipper into it (Fig. 14).

Pin the pieces together and seam them on the right side. Leave the length of the zipper unsewed on the outside edge (Fig. 15).

Sew in the zipper, tucking the ends of the tapes into the openings you left between the canvas and the lining (Fig. 16).

Add a decorative edging. Don't use fringe. It would get tangled in the zipper (Fig. 17).

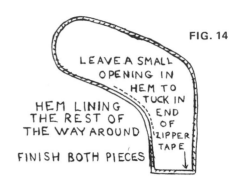

FIG. 14

LEAVE A SMALL OPENING IN HEM TO TUCK IN END OF ZIPPER TAPE

HEM LINING THE REST OF THE WAY AROUND

FINISH BOTH PIECES

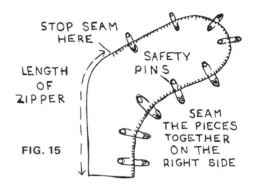

STOP SEAM HERE

LENGTH OF ZIPPER

SAFETY PINS

SEAM THE PIECES TOGETHER ON THE RIGHT SIDE

FIG. 15

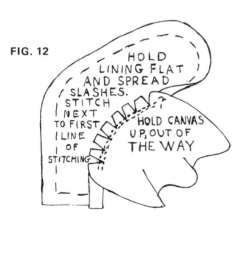

FIG. 12

HOLD LINING FLAT AND SPREAD SLASHES. STITCH NEXT TO FIRST LINE OF STITCHING

HOLD CANVAS UP, OUT OF THE WAY

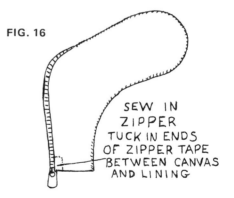

FIG. 16

SEW IN ZIPPER TUCK IN ENDS OF ZIPPER TAPE BETWEEN CANVAS AND LINING

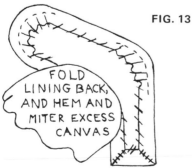

FIG. 13

FOLD LINING BACK, AND HEM AND MITER EXCESS CANVAS

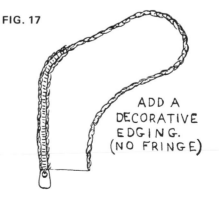

FIG. 17

ADD A DECORATIVE EDGING. (NO FRINGE)

Tennis Racket Cover

Materials needed

1 or 2 pieces of canvas 3 inches wider and 3 inches longer than the top part of the racket

10 inch zipper, closed at one end

Sturdy lining material for both sides, and an extra piece for backing if only one side is embroidered

Yarn of your choice

Lay the racket on a piece of paper, and draw a pattern about 1 inch larger all around than the racket. Fold the pattern in half to be sure the curves of the 2 sides match (Fig. 1). Make the bottom opening small enough so no ties are needed. Double check by measuring the girth of the handle. Bind the canvas next. Lay the pattern on the canvas, lining up the center fold with the canvas threads. Draw a line around the edge of the pattern (Fig. 2). Work the embroidery and block, using the pattern as a guide.

FIG. 1

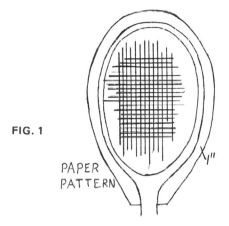

PAPER PATTERN

1"

Canvas, one side only

Lay the blocked piece on 1 piece of lining material, right sides together, and baste, leaving the bottom and 10 inches of one side open. Turn over to the canvas side, and machine stitch as close to the embroidery as possible (Fig. 3). (See "Finishing Canvas on a Curve.") Trim off the binding and all but 1 inch of the excess canvas. Pull up the gathering thread, and hem the excess canvas all

FIG. 2

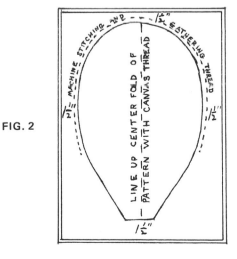

around, mitering the lower corners (Fig. 4). Turn right side out. Join the other 2 pieces of lining material, right sides together, all but the bottom and 10 inches of one side (Fig. 5).

Insert the lining into the outside piece, using the racket to make sure the lining is in all the way. Turn in, and baste the seam allowance along the bottom. Pin and baste the zipper in place in the side opening. Be sure all seam allowances, inside and out, are turned under. Tuck the ends of the zipper tapes into the ends of the bottom opening. Hand sew the bottom opening, and the edges of the material along the zipper, both inside and out (Fig. 6). The racket cover should just fit comfortably so the zipper works easily, and the cover doesn't slide around. Cover the curved edges, and the bottom opening with Binding stitch, worked with a sharp needle.

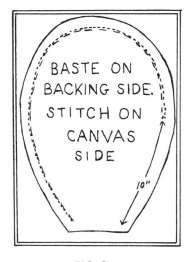

FIG. 3

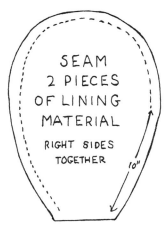

FIG. 5

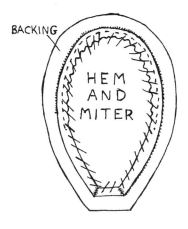

FIG. 4

FIG. 6

Canvas, both sides

Since the embroidery is the most enjoyable part of the project, why not make both sides of canvas? It will last longer, and will be a little easier to make up.

Make 2 pieces like Figure 2. (See "Finishing Canvas on a Curve.") Trim off the binding and all but 1 inch of the excess canvas. Draw up the gathering thread, and hem, mitering the lower corners of both pieces (Fig. 7). With strong thread, right sides out, join the 2 pieces, all but the bottom and 10 inches of one side (Fig. 8). (See "Joining Pieces of Canvas—Seaming.") Join the 2 pieces of the lining, right sides together, all but the bottom and 10 inches of one side (Fig. 5). Slide the lining in between the 2 pieces of canvas, using the racket to push the lining all the way in. Pin and baste the zipper in place, turning in all seam allowances along the zipper and the bottom edge. Tuck the ends of the zipper tapes into the ends of the bottom opening. Hem the edges all around (Fig. 6). Finish the curved edges and the bottom opening with Binding stitch, if you think it is needed.

FIG. 7

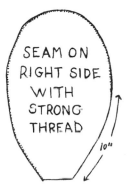

FIG. 8

Dolls

Attractive and original dolls can be created with canvas embroidery. If you plan to design your own, there are a few things to remember.

Use fine canvas, 14 threads to the inch or more; it is easier to handle, especially if the arms are to extend out, and the legs are to be separated. Make the doll fairly big, 12 inches to 15 inches tall. You can work both sides so as to have a front and a back. Avoid a narrow neck or the head will soon flop over, or give the doll a "backbone," using a stick or corset stay.

You can copy the clothes and hair style of a favorite child, or make the popular "Raggedy Ann" type, or perhaps a clown. Another type is the "Lady" doll with a long full skirt for which a circular piece is set in the base.

One important thing to remember is that the doll will be rounded. Each piece represents a front or back and half of the sides, so make the drawing very wide or the finished doll will be too narrow. Heads can be rounded by making darts along the seam. Leave the canvas unworked on the part to be covered with hair. The head can be covered with yarn hair in any style and color that suits you after the doll is stuffed.

Doll with extended arms and legs

Materials needed

2 rectangular pieces of canvas to accommodate your pattern, plus 1¼ inches excess canvas all around (Fig. 1)

Cotton or polyester fiber for stuffing
A narrow piece of stiff plastic, or a corset stay for a "backbone"
Yarn of your choice

Make the outline very simple, as narrow pieces for fingers, for example, would be impossible to turn right side out and stuff. You'll want the doll to be sturdy enough to be played with. Hands and feet can be just rounded. If you want the toes to tip forward slightly, pinch up a small dart of unworked canvas across the fronts of the ankles. Allow at least 6 threads of unworked canvas between the legs so there will be enough excess canvas on each side when you cut up between them (Fig. 1).

Make a paper pattern to use as a blocking guide. Bind rectangular pieces of canvas, work the embroidery, and block. Pin the pieces, right sides together, and sew around the edges, first by hand and then by machine, using small stitches. You'll need strong seams. Leave a good 3 inch opening at the top of the head (Fig. 2). Put extra machine stitching around the points where the canvas will be slashed, especially at the top of the legs and the insides of the arms (Xs in Fig. 2). Cut away all but ¾ inch of the excess canvas. Cut up between the legs, ending in a V up to the corners. Slash the canvas up to the seam at the neck, arms, and legs. Be careful not to cut the stitching of the seams. Overcast the opening at the top of the head to prevent fraying. Pinch and sew the ankle darts. Now carefully turn the doll right side out. Turning back and hemming the canvas is not necessary. Poke your fingers into the hands and feet.

Stuff the doll firmly, but don't strain the seams. Insert the "backbone," if you plan to use one. Cotton or polyester fiber pack well. Sew up the top of the head, push in, and sew the darts on the right side. Cover the seams with matching stitching if they show. (See "Joining Pieces of Canvas—Seaming.")

Last, cover the head with yarn hair. Tufting, made with fairly long loops, works well. Start across the back of the neck (Fig. 3).

FIG. 1

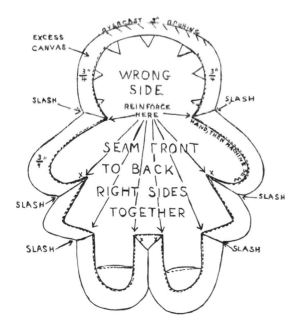

FIG. 2

FIG. 3

Lady Doll

This type of doll is essentially bell shaped. Arms are usually just worked on the front. By using a deep or high stitch pattern, they can be made to stand out from the dress. Be sure to make the pieces wide so the doll will be in good proportion when stuffed (Fig. 4). Make a round base, and put the soles of her feet on it (Fig. 5).

· Materials needed

Rectangular pieces to accommodate the front, back, and base

A narrow piece of stiff plastic or a corset stay for a "backbone"

Cotton or polyester fiber stuffing

A thin circular piece of wood to set in the base, if desired

Yarn of your choice

Bind rectangular pieces of canvas, work the embroidery, and block. Leave the part of the head to be covered with hair unworked. Pin the pieces,

FIG. 4

FIG. 5

right sides together, hand, and then machine sew around the edges, leaving the bottom open. Reinforce the seam where the slashes will come. Cut away all but ¾ inch of the excess canvas, and overcast the bottom opening to prevent fraying. Slash the excess canvas at the neck and waist (Fig. 6). Now carefully turn right side out.

Stuff the doll firmly, inserting the stick or corset stay, if you are using one for a "backbone." Be sure to push out and stuff firmly at the top of the head and shoulders. If you want the doll to stand, cover a circular piece of thin wood, and sew the circular base to it before attaching the base to the bottom of the skirt (Fig. 7). Yarn hair in any style is worked over the head last. Tufting, either cut or uncut, works well (Fig. 8). By omitting the circular base, and making a lining, this type of doll makes a very effective hand puppet (Fig. 9).

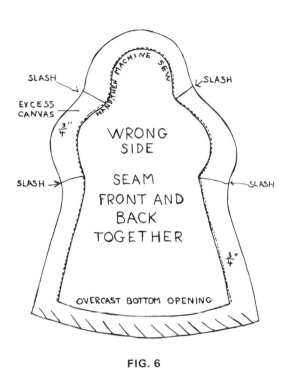

FIG. 6

FIG. 7

FIG. 8

FIG. 9

Clown

A clown doll can be made in a similar manner. Because of the full costume, it would be simpler and easier to make (Figs. 10, 11, 12). For materials needed and directions, see "Doll with Extended Arms and Legs." Pandas, dogs, teddy bears, etc. can be made the same way using commercial patterns.

FIG. 10

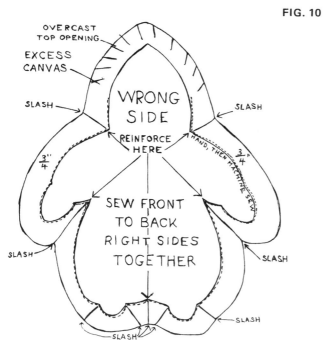

FIG. 11

FIG. 12

Cigarette Case

Materials needed

Fine canvas
Interlining
Lining
Yarn of your choice

Measure the height, width, and thickness of whatever size pack you wish to use. Add ⅛ inch to each measurement to allow for the thickness of the seams.

The case is made in 3 pieces. Piece 1 extends down the front, across the bottom, up the back, across the top, and 2/3 of the way down the front again for a flap (Fig. 1). The other 2 pieces are long, narrow rectangles that fit into the sides, the thickness and height of the cigarette pack. Use fairly fine canvas, and stitchery that is not too bulky. Be sure to leave at least 1 inch between the side pieces if they are to be worked on one piece of canvas (Fig. 2).

Bind the pieces of canvas, work the embroidery, and block. Cut off the binding, hem, and miter all square corners. Finish the curved end of the flap (Fig. 3). (See "Finishing Canvas on a Curve.") Cut the interlining to cover almost all of the hemmed back excess canvas of the side pieces for extra stiffness. Hem in place (Fig. 4). Cut the interlining for the large piece to almost cover the excess canvas on the bottom and sides, and about ½ inch short on the flap end. Hem the interlining

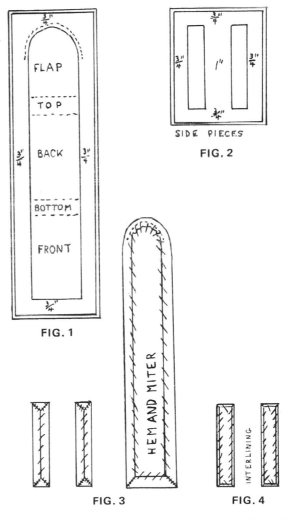

FIG. 1

SIDE PIECES

FIG. 2

FIG. 3

HEM AND MITER

INTERLINING

FIG. 4

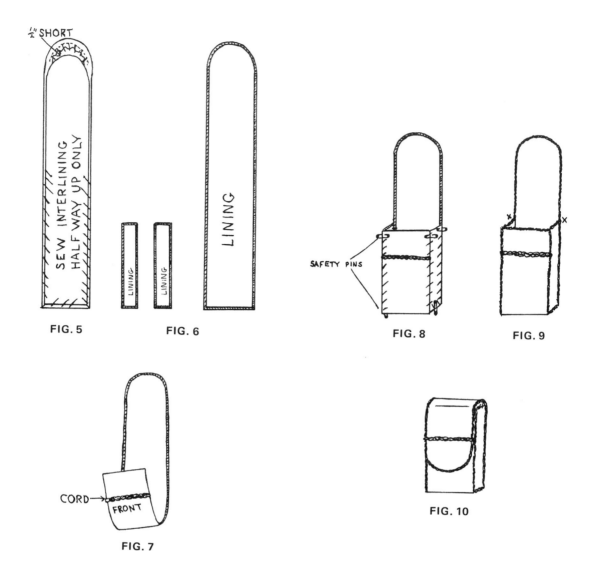

FIG. 5

FIG. 6

FIG. 7

FIG. 8

FIG. 9

FIG. 10

on the bottom and about half way up the sides (Fig. 5). Leave the rest loose so the interlining can slide when the flap is folded over. Line all 3 pieces (Fig. 6). Work a short cord that will stretch a little, and attach it at the ends halfway up the front section (Fig. 7).

Matching the corners of the front with the tops of the side pieces, overcast the side pieces in place. Use safety pins to hold the side pieces in place while you do the overcasting (Fig. 8). Work Binding stitch around the flap, and across the opening. Use it to join the side pieces to the main part, adding a few extra stitches at the points of strain (Xs in Fig. 9).

Insert the cigarette pack, fold the flap over, and slip it under the cord (Fig. 10).

Book Mark

Prepare a piece of canvas 2½ inches by 6 inches or 7 inches. Bind it and draw lines for the book mark measuring 1¼ inches by 5 inches or 6 inches (Fig. 1). Work the embroidery, and block. Cut off the binding, and hem the excess canvas to the back of the embroidery, mitering the corners (Fig. 2).

Line the piece with ribbon or a piece of thin lining material (Fig. 3). Make a small pompon or tassel and attach it to a cord about 2 inches long. Sew this to the top of the book mark so it will extend out between the pages to mark your place in the book (Fig. 4).

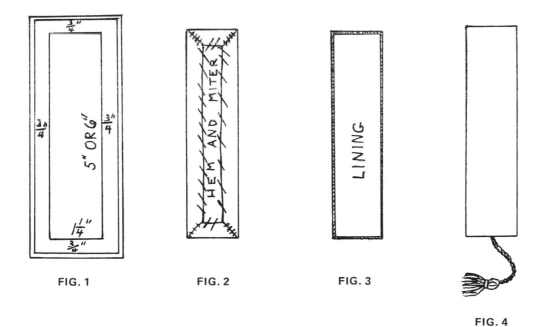

FIG. 1   FIG. 2   FIG. 3

FIG. 4

Head Bands

Head bands are worn 2 ways: across the top of the head and under the hair in back (Fig. 1), or Indian style, horizontally across the forehead and around the largest part of the head in back (Fig. 2).

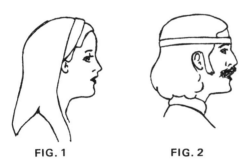

FIG. 1   FIG. 2

Prepare a piece of fairly fine canvas to accommodate the embroidered area about 1½ inches shorter than head size, with ¾ inch excess canvas all around (Fig. 3).

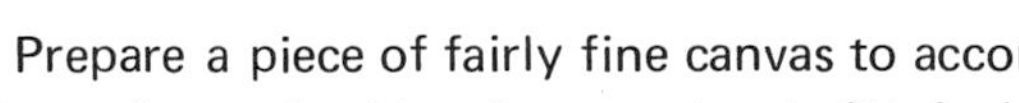

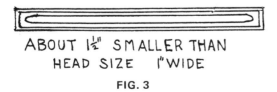

ABOUT 1½" SMALLER THAN HEAD SIZE 1"WIDE

FIG. 3

Materials needed

Canvas
Ribbon backing
Elastic or ties
Yarn of your choice; it is a good idea to buy the ribbon for backing and the ties (½ yd.) before selecting the yarn because of limited color choice

Bind the canvas, work the embroidery, and block. Cut off the binding and all but ½ inch of the excess canvas along the sides. Leave ¾ inch excess canvas around the ends. Hem the sides, and make a modified mitered corner at the ends (Fig. 4). Try the band on and measure the distance between the ends. Attach the elastic securely to one end. Make the elastic just long enough to be completely contracted and the band snug. Don't make the elastic so short that it will have to stretch. This would be uncomfortable around the head in style 2 and would slide back in style 1. Attach the elastic to the other side (Fig. 5).

If ties are used, attach ¼ yard to each end (Fig. 6).

Face the band with the matching ribbon, hem all around (Fig. 7).

Be sure to use washable materials throughout.

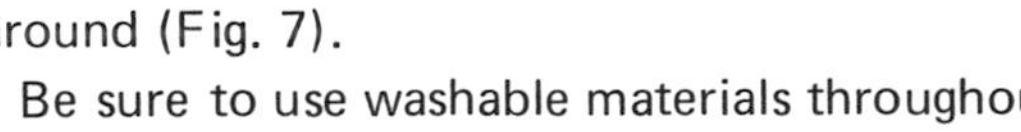

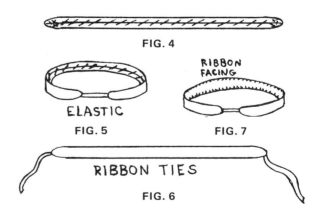

FIG. 4

RIBBON FACING

ELASTIC

FIG. 5   FIG. 7

RIBBON TIES

FIG. 6

Chokers

Materials needed

Canvas
Ribbon backing
Elastic or ties
Snap or hook and eye (if elastic is used)
Yarn of your choice

Have a piece of canvas large enough to accommodate an embroidered area ½ inch shorter than the neck size, with excess ½ inch along the sides, and ¾ inch at the ends (Fig 1)

Bind the canvas, embroider, and block.

Cut off the binding and enough excess canvas so it doesn't overlap in the back. Miter the corners (Fig. 2).

The choker can be joined with a short piece of elastic or ribbon ties. If elastic is used, make sure it is just long enough to fit fully contracted. If it has to stretch, it would be uncomfortable to wear. Hem one end of the elastic (Fig. 3). Sew half a snap or an eye for a hook to the hemmed end (Fig. 4). Sew the other end to one end of the band, and line the choker with matching ribbon

(Fig. 5). Make sure of the fit before putting the other half of the snap, or the hook on the other end of the choker (Fig. 6). If ribbon ties are used, attach one piece to each end. They can be long or short. Line the choker last. Long ties look attractive tied on the side (Fig. 7). Be sure all materials are washable.

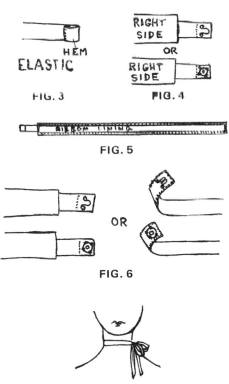

FIG. 3

FIG. 4

FIG. 5

FIG. 6

FIG. 7

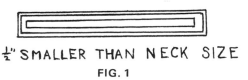

¼" SMALLER THAN NECK SIZE

FIG. 1

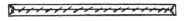

FIG. 2

Belts

Directions are given below for four styles of belts. In all cases, it is a good idea to buy your buckle and lining material before deciding on the width and main color of your belt, since choices of both are limited. Heavy grosgrain ribbon makes a good lining, as the edges don't have to be turned under.

Ribbon may have a tendency to pucker, however. A good solution to this problem is to use a piece of material cut on the bias. When it is sewed on, you pull it slightly lengthwise so it will stay smooth when the belt curves around your waist. This is especially needed if the belt is to be blocked with a slight curve. Don't use felt. It is bulky, not washable, and might not wear well.

Suede or suede cloth is fine but quite expensive.

A blocking tip. Because a belt tends to rest on the hips, rather than actually encircling the waist, it is a good idea to block it in a slight curve (Fig. 1). The belt is made on the straight of the canvas, but can be curved a little during the blocking. This eliminates gaping at the top of the back. This form of blocking will be especially needed if the belt is to be worn low on the hips. The lining can be eased around the curve.

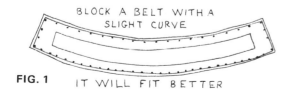

FIG. 1

BLOCK A BELT WITH A SLIGHT CURVE

IT WILL FIT BETTER

Style A. Overlapping with a buckle at one end

Materials needed

Canvas
Buckle
Backing
An eyelet kit
Yarn of your choice

Measure the waist size, add 4 inches for the overlap, and one more inch for excess canvas. At the other end add an extra 1½ inches for attaching the belt to the buckle (Fig. 2). Make the canvas 2 inches wider than the belt. Design the belt with a curved or pointed end.

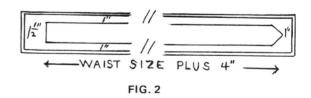

WAIST SIZE PLUS 4"

FIG. 2

Bind the canvas, work the embroidery and block. (See "blocking tip" above.) Cut away the binding and diagonal pieces of canvas on either side of the tip. Leave about ¾ inch on either side. Don't cut away the extra length of canvas at the buckle end, just the binding. Fold the excess canvas back, and hem it to the back of your needlework, mitering the tip. Leave the excess canvas on the buckle end extended. Overcast the edge to prevent fraying (Fig. 3).

Cover the back with the lining, but leave it loose at the buckle end (Fig. 4). Fold the buckle end back so about ½ inch of worked canvas is underneath. If your buckle has a prong, push it through the worked canvas on the fold. Take both ends of the belt down through the openings next to the center bar (Fig. 5). Sew the 1¼ inches of unworked canvas to the underside of the worked area (Fig. 6). This extra length will come in handy if the belt should ever need to be lengthened. Bring the lining material up, turn under the edge, and hem it to the end of the worked area (Fig. 7). Put the belt on and mark the spot where you want an eyelet for the prong. There are devices available in notion departments for making eyelets. Don't use the cutter, however. Instead use an awl or a punch to make a hole big enough for the eyelet. It will be stronger, with no danger of canvas or yarn pulling out (Fig. 8). Make 2 additional eyelets, one on either side of the one you intend to use.

For the type of buckle with only one side, a cord or braid will be needed to hold the belt tip. A 7-strand braid is good for this. Attach it before sewing the lining down. Buttonhole stitch can be used to cover a buckle form meant to be covered with fabric. Whip the edges with a contrasting color, if you like (Fig. 9).

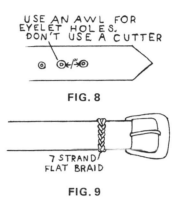

USE AN AWL FOR EYELET HOLES. DON'T USE A CUTTER

FIG. 8

7 STRAND FLAT BRAID

FIG. 9

Style B. Clasp type buckle that meets in the front

Materials needed

Canvas
Buckle
Backing
Yarn of your choice

Measure the waist size, and subtract the length of the closed buckle. Now add 1½ inches at each end. Since this belt is not adjustable, this allows 2 inches extra in case of future "expansion." Purchase your buckle and backing material before deciding on the width and main color of the belt. Allow 1 inch of excess canvas on each side (Fig. 10).

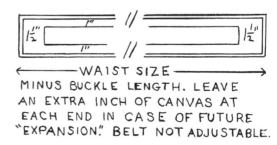

←————WAIST SIZE————→ MINUS BUCKLE LENGTH. LEAVE AN EXTRA INCH OF CANVAS AT EACH END IN CASE OF FUTURE "EXPANSION." BELT NOT ADJUSTABLE.

FIG. 10

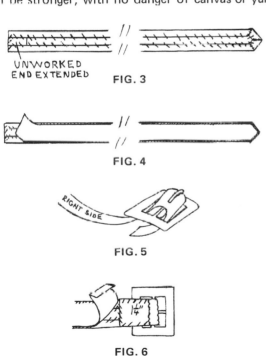

UNWORKED END EXTENDED   **FIG. 3**

FIG. 4

RIGHT SIDE

FIG. 5

FIG. 6

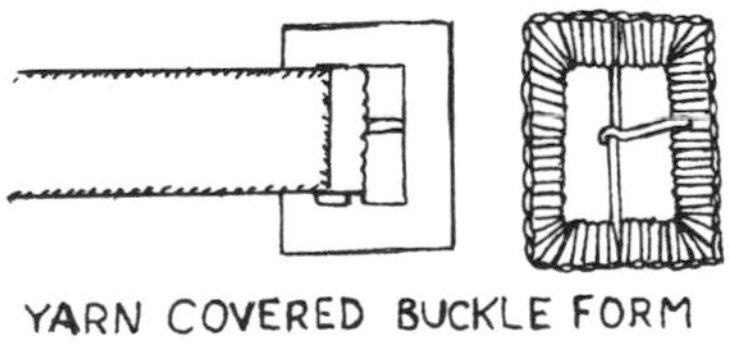

YARN COVERED BUCKLE FORM

FIG. 7

Bind the canvas, work the embroidery, and block. (See "blocking tip," p. 164.) Cut away the binding and hem back the excess canvas on the sides. Leave the excess canvas extended on the ends (Fig. 11). Overcast the ends to prevent fraying. Measure the lining material, allowing an extra inch at each end, too. Hem it to the back of the belt, leaving the ends open (Fig. 12). Bring the belt ends through the slots in the buckle, and fold it back, with about ½ inch of worked canvas on the wrong side. Check the length again, and then sew the ends securely. Bring the lining up over the ends, folding the extra inch of lining under. Hem along the fold (Fig. 13).

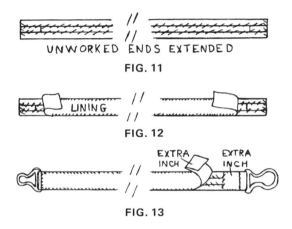

UNWORKED ENDS EXTENDED

FIG. 11

LINING

FIG. 12

EXTRA INCH EXTRA INCH

FIG. 13

Style C. Single tie type

Materials needed

Canvas
Backing
Material for a tie. If you plan to make a yarn tie, you will need uncut yarn, as the yarn can't be pieced in a cord. (See "Cords," p. 213.) The grommets for the tie must be made by a professional. See suggestions below
Yarn of your choice

The worked area should equal the exact waist size. Allow an inch of excess canvas all around for finishing (Fig. 14). Round the ends of the worked area.

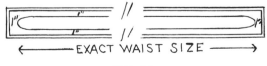

EXACT WAIST SIZE

FIG. 14

Bind the canvas, work the embroidery, and block. (See "blocking tip" above.) Cut away the binding, following the curve of the ends about ¾ inch out. Hem back the excess canvas, folding it at the ends to follow the curves. Sew the folds securely (Fig. 15). Cover the entire back with lining material (Fig. 16). You will need large eyelets or grommets near the ends. If you can't put them in yourself, a leather worker, or awning maker can do it for you. Tell him to just snip a couple of threads in the center of each hole, and enlarge the hole with an awl. This will prevent any canvas or embroidery threads from working loose (Fig. 17).

The cord tie can be a leather thong, or any of the round yarn cords. Finish the latter with a small tassel at each end (Fig. 18).

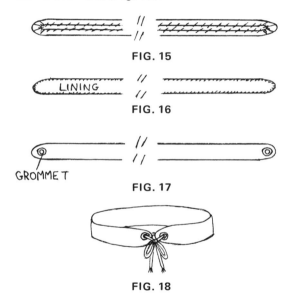

FIG. 15

LINING

FIG. 16

GROMMET

FIG. 17

FIG. 18

Style D. Laced front

Materials needed

Canvas
Backing
An eyelet kit
2 short stays, or strips of stiff plastic the width of the belt at the front opening
Material for lacing. If you plan to make a cord lacing of yarn, you will need uncut yarn, as cords can't be pieced. (See "Cords," p. 213.)
Yarn of your choice

This type can be all the same width, or, as illustrated, wider in the front. You will need at least 2 short stays, one on either side of the front opening. Strips of stiff plastic cut from bleach or milk bottles will work well. Make them double thickness if the plastic is thin. They go next to the lacing to keep it smooth. You might be able to find short stays, made to support strapless gowns in the notion or sewing departments of the stores. Don't use anything that would rust. Measure the waist size and subtract 1 inch. Allow an extra inch all around for finishing (Fig. 19).

Bind the canvas, work the embroidery, and block. (See "blocking tip" above.) Cut away the binding and hem back the excess canvas, mitering the corners. The belt with the narrow back will have to have a few slashes in the excess canvas on the curves. Insert the stays inside the hems on the ends (Fig. 20). Hem the lining to the entire back (Fig. 21).

Make 3 or 4 eyelets on each side of the front opening, just back of the stays. Use an awl or a punch to make the holes for the metal eyelets. Don't use a cutter. This will prevent any yarn or canvas threads from working loose (Fig. 22). The lacing can be a fine leather thong, or you can make a cord of matching yarn. Finger cord is fine for this. Add a small tassel at each end for a final touch (Fig. 23).

Note: A man's cummerbund, p. 175, could be adpated for wear by a woman.

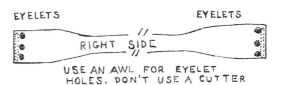

USE AN AWL FOR EYELET HOLES. DON'T USE A CUTTER

FIG. 22

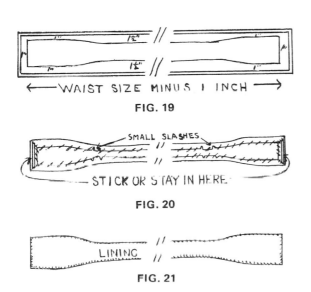

←—WAIST SIZE MINUS 1 INCH—→

FIG. 19

FIG. 20

FIG. 21

FIG. 23

Scuffs

Take apart an old pair of scuffs, ones with fairly soft soles, so you can get a needle through them. Undo the stitching, and remove the top part that goes over the foot, and use it for a pattern. Make the opening in the front fairly large. Be careful not to make the pattern too small; you'll need room for padding. Make 2 pieces, a left and a right. If both pieces are on one piece of canvas, leave 2 inches excess canvas between them (Fig. 1).

FIG. 1

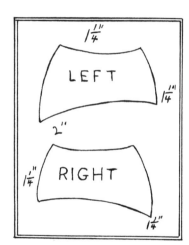

Materials needed

A pair of soft soles in fairly good condition
Canvas for 2 pieces as above, with 1¼ inches excess canvas all around
Outing flannel of terry cloth for padding for tops and soles
Lining material for tops and soles, plus enough to face curved edges (Fig. 5)
Sheet rubber for the bottoms of the soles, if needed
Heavy thread, curved needle, and an awl, if needed
Yarn of your choice

Bind the canvas, work the embroidery, and block, using your pattern as a guide. Cut off the binding and all but 1 inch of the excess canvas. Overcast the canvas along the sides. Face and turn under the front and back edges. (See "Finishing Canvas on a Curve.") Leave the canvas on the sides extended (Fig. 2). Pad the wrong side with the outing flannel or terry cloth (Fig. 3). Pad the soles too, leaving the sides open where the edges of the top will be inserted. Put an extra piece of padding in the middle to equalize the thickness of the

FIG. 2

FACE FRONT AND BACK EDGES. OVERCAST EXTENDED CANVAS ON THE SIDES

FIG. 3

PADDING

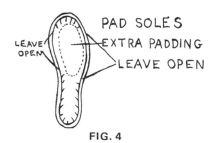

PAD SOLES
LEAVE OPEN
EXTRA PADDING
LEAVE OPEN

FIG. 4

PULL BACK LINING

TUCK IN ON "LITTLE TOE" SIDE. SEW THROUGH SOLE

FIG. 7

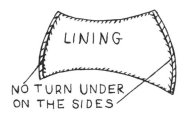

LINING
NO TURN UNDER ON THE SIDES

FIG. 5

HEM LINING

FIG. 8

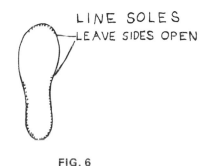

LINE SOLES
LEAVE SIDES OPEN

FIG. 6

PULL OVER

TUCK IN "BIG TOE" SIDE. REACH IN TO SEW TO SOLE.

FIG. 9

COVER BOTTOM OF SOLES

FIG. 10

canvas (Fig. 4). Line the tops and the soles, again leaving the sides of the soles unsewed. Be sure the lining covers all of the canvas, as the rough canvas could irritate your foot (Fig. 6).

Now push the canvas smoothly into the opening on the little toe side, and, with strong thread, sew all the way through the canvas and the sole. Use an awl to make the holes, if this is hard to do. Pull the lining out of the way (Fig. 7). Sew securely without knots. Hem the lining of the sole to the top (Fig. 8). The other side, the big toe side, is going to be a little hard to get at. A curved needle will help you reach the seam area. You will have to sew through the lining too, as you won't be able to get at it to hem it as you did the other side. Make the stitches as smooth as possible (Fig. 9).

If it is necessary, glue pieces of sheet rubber to the bottoms of the soles, using waterproof glue (Fig. 10). The scuffs will be hand washable.

Note: For closed toe slippers, you can cover the upper parts with embroidered canvas, but don't try to replace them. You would never be able to get the inside smooth enough for comfortable wearing. The rounded toe and heel need special tools. This is beyond most home sewers' abilities. And having slippers professionally made up is quite expensive.

Baby Shoes

First, don't use persian or other embroidery yarn. They are too scratchy. Soft wool or synthetic yarn, such as is used for knitting baby garments, can be used for canvas embroidery. It will be a little harder to handle, but the results will look fine. Use Diagonal Tent stitch, and unsized canvas, if you can find it. The large patterns are actual size suitable for a tiny baby's foot, but it is wise to measure a baby shoe that you know will fit. Make the pattern fairly large. Babies grow so fast, and you will want room for lining and soft padding. Remember, baby feet are fat, and the toes must have room to wiggle. The line from A to B must be ½ inch longer than the perimeter of the sole (Fig. 1).

Materials needed

2 pieces of canvas large enough to accommodate the pattern, with 1¼ inches excess canvas around the edges, and at least 1½ inches between parts (Fig. 2)
Outing flannel for the padding, and fine cotton cloth for the lining
Waterproof interlining for the sole
½ yd. of ribbon for ties
Yarn of your choice

Bind the canvas, work the embroidery, and block. Put in the machine stitching and gathering threads around the curves. (See "Finishing Canvas on a Curve.") Cut off the binding and all but ¾ inch of the excess canvas. Face the concave curve at the instep with a piece of muslin. Turn under

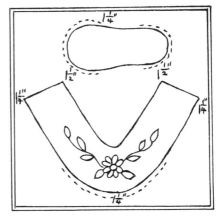

FIG. 2

FIG. 3

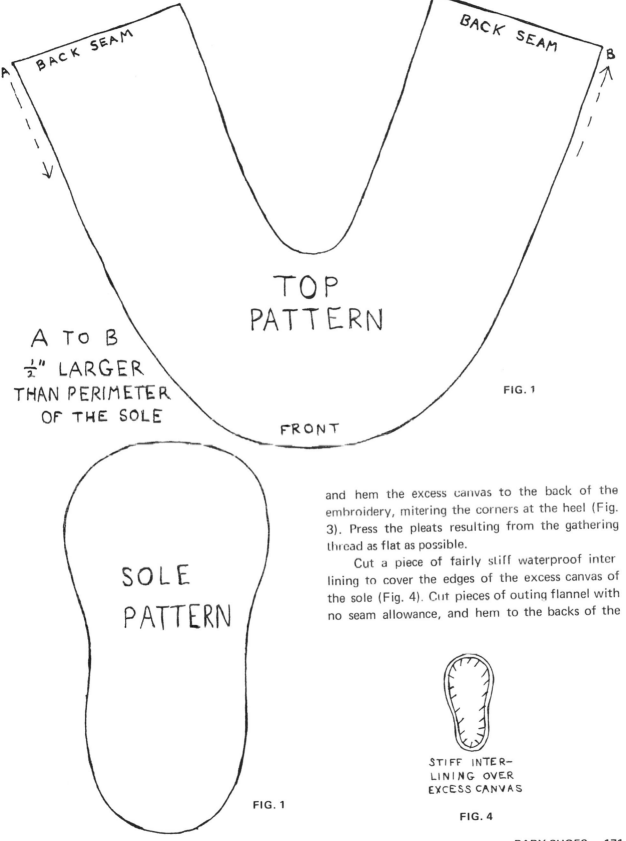

BACK SEAM

A

BACK SEAM

B

TOP
PATTERN

A TO B
½" LARGER
THAN PERIMETER
OF THE SOLE

FRONT

FIG. 1

SOLE
PATTERN

FIG. 1

and hem the excess canvas to the back of the embroidery, mitering the corners at the heel (Fig. 3). Press the pleats resulting from the gathering thread as flat as possible.

Cut a piece of fairly stiff waterproof inter lining to cover the edges of the excess canvas of the sole (Fig. 4). Cut pieces of outing flannel with no seam allowance, and hem to the backs of the

STIFF INTER-
LINING OVER
EXCESS CANVAS

FIG. 4

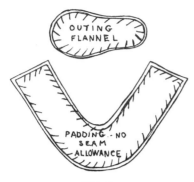

FIG. 5

OUTING FLANNEL

PADDING - NO SEAM ALLOWANCE

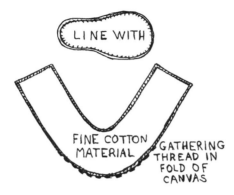

FIG. 6

LINE WITH

FINE COTTON MATERIAL

GATHERING THREAD IN FOLD OF CANVAS

DRAW UP GATHERING THREAD TO ROUND TOE, MAKING IT FIT SOLE.

STEAM TOE, STUFF WITH TISSUE, AND LET DRY

FIG. 7

ATTACH TIES TO BACK AT TOP OF HEEL SEAM

FIG. 8

pieces (Fig. 5). Line the pieces with fine cotton cloth, such as batiste. Run another gathering thread in the fold of the canvas around the toe (Fig. 6). Seam the heel. Pin and hem the back and sides of the top to the sole. Draw up the gathering thread to round the toe, and fit it to the end of the sole. (Fig. 7).

Finish the seam. Go over the seam with a fine Binding or Feather stitch. You can use silk or cotton embroidery floss for this. An edging of

Buttonhole stitch could be placed around the opening. Make ties of ribbon or yarn cord. Add tiny pompons to the cord ends, if you like. Attach the tie to the back at the top of the seam (Fig. 8). Last, steam the toe of the shoe and stuff it with tissue. Allow it to dry thoroughly. This will smooth out the easing of the toe of the shoe.

The entire shoe will be washable. Wash gently by hand, and stuff with tissue, patting and pulling the shoe into its original shape.

Guitar Straps

A canvas guitar strap will not be adjustable, so make it to the exact length needed. If you are making the strap for a boy or girl, allow 1½ inches at each end of the canvas so the strap can be lengthened later, if necessary (Fig. 1).

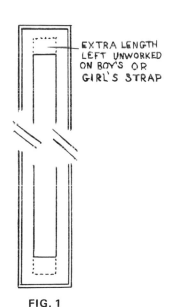

FIG. 1

Materials needed

Canvas of the desired length and width, plus 1¼ inches excess canvas all around; add 3 inches extra for a boy or girl to allow for growth

Leather ends

Lining material, 3 inches extra length for a boy or girl

Yarn of your choice

Bind the canvas, work the embroidery, and block. Cut off the binding and, for a strap for an adult, hem all around, mitering the corners (Fig. 2). Hem the sides only for a boy's or girl's strap, leaving the ends extended (A in Fig. 3). Fold the extra length under and hem (B in Fig. 3). If you have taken the ends off an old strap, use the holes

END OF
MAN'S STRAP
HEM & MITER

FIG. 2

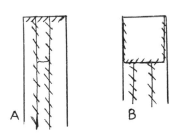

END OF BOY'S OR GIRL'S
A-END LEFT EXTENDED
B-END FOLDED UNDER

FIG. 3

already in them. If you have to buy new leather for the ends, a shoe repair shop should be able to supply you with the heavy leather needed to support a guitar. Cut the leather with heavy shears. Use an awl to make the sewing holes, and a knife or razor blade to cut the "buttonhole" (Fig. 4).

You will have to sew all the way through the canvas, embroidery and all, to make the leather end really secure, so use a thread that will harmonize with your color scheme. Try to sew evenly so the stitches will seem to be part of your design (Fig. 5).

Hem the lining for the strap along the sides, since you can't sew across the ends into the leather. Hem the bottom edge of the adult's strap lining before finishing the sides. One turn under is enough (Fig. 6).

Turn the extra length of lining under on a boy's or girl's strap. It will not be necessary to hem it in place because of the extra length. Hem the sides to the canvas (Fig. 7).

A removable shoulder pad can be covered with lining material, and fastened in place with regular snaps.

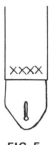

FIG. 5

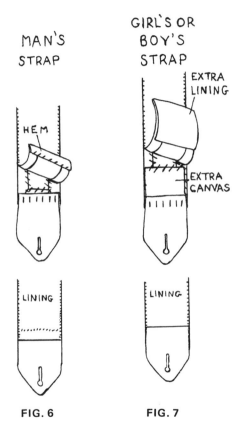

MAN'S STRAP

GIRL'S OR BOY'S STRAP

FIG. 6   FIG. 7

LEATHER END WITH HOLES FOR SEWING

FIG. 4

Man's Cummerbund

Measure the waist size of the gentleman involved. The canvas part of the cummerbund should extend part way around to the back, all but about 1/3 of the waist size. Make the canvas about 5 inches wide in the center, tapering to about 1¼ inches at the ends. Make a pattern. For the design, a diagonal plaid would be effective, and Alternating Tent stitch a good one to use.

Materials needed

Canvas to accommodate the above, plus 1¼ inches excess canvas all around (Fig. 1)
Elastic for a little more than 1/3 the waist size
Lining material, and a link hook
Yarn of your choice

Bind the canvas, work the embroidery, and block. Cut off the binding and all but 1 inch of the excess canvas. Hem and miter the corners (Fig. 2). Hold up to the man's waist and measure the distance across his back between the ends. Divide this number in half, and add 2 inches to each half. Cut the pieces of elastic to this length. Securely sew 1 inch of the elastic to the back of the ends of the cummerbund (Fig. 3). Sew in the lining (Fig. 4). Try the cummerbund on again and stretch the elastic just enough to make the cummerbund fit snugly. Mark the lengths with pins. Hem the end of one piece. Slip the end of the other piece through the slot in the link hook. Check the fit for the last time, and hem the elastic (Fig. 5).

Note: Cummerbunds can be adapted for women's wear.

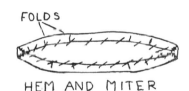

FIG. 1

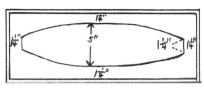

HEM AND MITER

FIG. 2

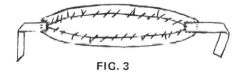

FIG. 3

FIG. 4

FIG. 5

Necktie

The necktie illustrated can be really tied. Use fine canvas and small stitch patterns to reduce bulk to a minimum. Canvas is used for the front only. A piece of firm material is inserted at the back of the neck to eliminate a bulge under the collar (Figs. 1, 3). Use a regular tie as a pattern (Fig. 1).

Materials needed

Fine canvas as in Figure 2
Piece of heavy material 9 inches by 2¾ inches for the back of the neck
Lining for the entire length (an old necktie will do, see below)
Yarn of your choice

Designs can be conservative, such as diagonal stripes, or as ornate as you please. You could make an attractive monogram in the middle of the larger piece. Lay out the pattern as in Figure 2.

Bind the canvas, work the embroidery, and block, using your pattern as a guide. Cut off the binding and all but ¾ inch excess canvas. Seam the canvas pieces to the back of the neck piece. If the canvas isn't too bulky, fold the excess canvas and the seam allowance away from the seam, or if this would make a thick place, bring the ends of the canvas over the ends of the piece of material (Fig. 4).

Turn in the excess canvas, hem, and miter so that the worked area is curved over to the back. Cut away additional excess canvas if necessary so

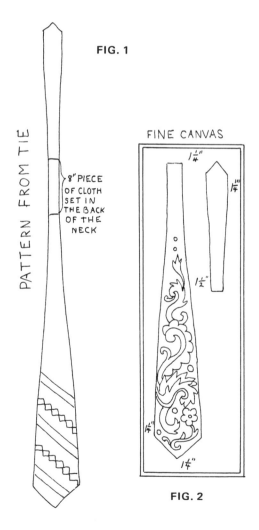

FIG. 1

PATTERN FROM TIE

8" PIECE OF CLOTH SET IN THE BACK OF THE NECK

FINE CANVAS

1¼"

1¼"

1½"

¼"

1¼"

FIG. 2

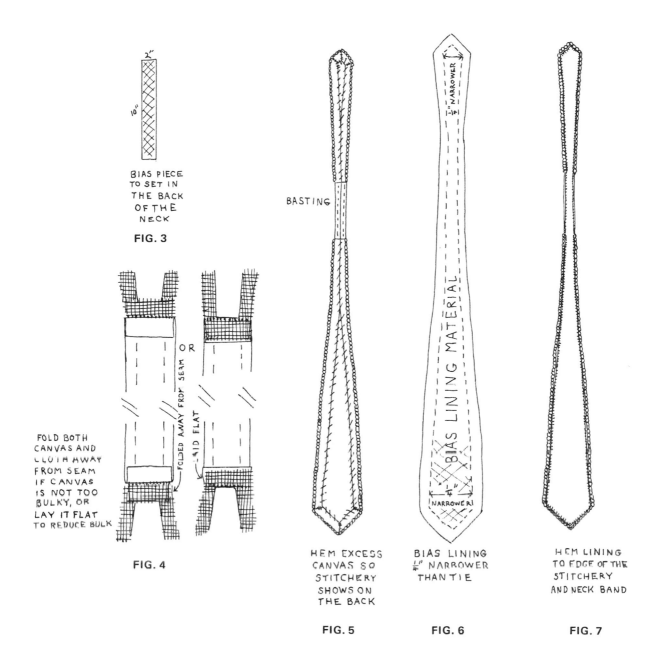

2"

10"

BIAS PIECE
TO SET IN
THE BACK
OF THE
NECK

FIG. 3

FOLD BOTH
CANVAS AND
CLOTH AWAY
FROM SEAM
IF CANVAS
IS NOT TOO
BULKY, OR
LAY IT FLAT
TO REDUCE BULK

OR

FOLDED AWAY FROM SEAM

LAID FLAT

FIG. 4

BASTING

HEM EXCESS
CANVAS SO
STITCHERY
SHOWS ON
THE BACK

FIG. 5

NARROWER

1¾"

BIAS LINING MATERIAL

¼"

NARROWER

BIAS LINING
¼" NARROWER
THAN TIE

FIG. 6

HEM LINING
TO EDGE OF THE
STITCHERY
AND NECK BAND

FIG. 7

the edges don't overlap where the tie is narrow. Baste the seam allowance of the strip of material (Fig. 5).

The material for the lining should be cut on the bias. If you don't want to have to buy a large piece of material for this, you could use an old necktie. Open it up, wash, and press it. Using your original pattern, and allowing for seams, cut out the lining for the tie. Make it ¼ inch narrower than the canvas measurements, except for the part at the back of the neck (Fig. 6). Baste and press the seam allowance before sewing the lining in place. This will make it much easier to handle.

Hem the lining to the back of the canvas, and the back of the neck strip (Fig. 7). Because the lining is slightly narrower than the worked canvas, the canvas will roll at the edges, making soft folds along the sides.

When it is knotted you will have a fashionable wide tie with a large knot.

NECKTIE 177

Bow Tie

You can't make a bow tie that actually ties unless you make both sides of canvas, and that is too bulky. Make one piece for the loops and a separate piece for the ends, plus the cross piece for the "knot" (Fig. 1). Narrow the canvas where the piece for the knot will go across, but make it wide enough so there will be a small fold in the middle (Fig. 12). You'll need a piece of stiff plastic or metal inside the back of the loops to keep the tie flat against the collar (Fig. 2), lining for the two larger pieces, and about ½ yd. of ½ inch elastic. Fine canvas is essential, about 18 threads to the inch. Use small-scale stitch patterns. These two qualifications will prevent bulkiness.

Materials needed

Canvas to accommodate all 3 pieces (See Fig. 1)
Lining for the 2 larger pieces
Piece of plastic or metal 2½ inches by ½ inch at the ends, and ¼ inch in the middle for stiffening (see Fig. 2)
½ yd. of ½ inch elastic

Bind the canvas, work the embroidery, and block. Hem and miter the excess canvas so the stitchery can be seen from the back. Slash and pleat where necessary. Leave ½ inch excess canvas on one end of the knot piece extended. Overcast the raw edge to prevent fraying. If necessary, trim the excess canvas on the larger pieces so it doesn't overlap on the back (Fig. 3).

The lining should be of thin but fairly firm material that will cling to the back of the needle-

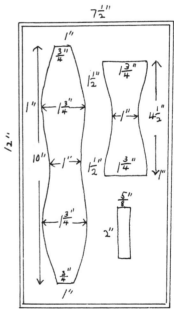

FINE CANVAS

FIG. 1

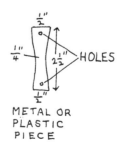

METAL OR PLASTIC PIECE

FIG. 2

work. Make it slightly narrower than the canvas measurements (Fig. 4). Baste and press the seam allowance before sewing it in place. This will make it much easier to handle. Line the piece for the ends completely. Don't put any lining in the piece for the knot. Sew the lining to the piece for the loops, all but about 1½ inches at each end (Fig. 5).

The piece of plastic or metal should be about 2½ inches long, ½ inch wide at the ends, and ¼ inch wide in the middle. There must be a hole at each end (Fig. 2). The plastic from which many bottles are made can be cut with strong scissors if it is heated thoroughly in hot water. An easy way to make a hole in plastic is with a nail. Hold a small nail near the head with a pair of pliers, and heat it quite hot over a gas range burner or with a cigarette lighter. Then press the point against the plastic. It will melt its way right through. Center the stiff piece on one end of the piece for the loops, and sew through the hole to the back of the embroidery (Fig. 6). Sew the ends of the piece together, forming a big loop, and then sew the other end of the stiff piece to the other side (Fig. 7). Complete the sewing of the lining (Fig. 8).

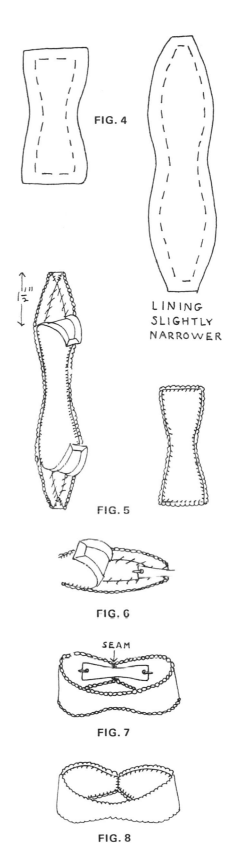

FIG. 4

LINING
SLIGHTLY
NARROWER

FIG. 5

FIG. 6

SEAM

FIG. 7

FIG. 8

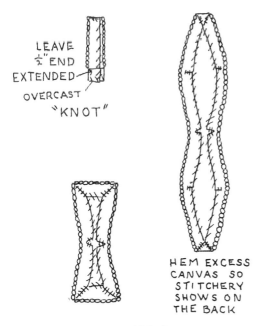

LEAVE
½" END
EXTENDED
OVERCAST
"KNOT"

HEM EXCESS
CANVAS SO
STITCHERY
SHOWS ON
THE BACK

FIG. 3

Tack the 2 pieces of the tie together (Fig. 9).
Measure the distance around the inside of the shirt
collar, that is, between the folds, when it is but-
toned. Allowing for small hems at each end, cut
the elastic to fit snugly, just a little stretch, but
not enough to pucker the collar. Hem the ends of
the elastic and attach a hook and eye or a snap as a
closure. Three inches from the right end, sew the
elastic to the back of the tie, sewing all the way
through to the back of the looped piece so as to
keep it down tight. Make the stitched area about 1
inch long to help keep the tie from tipping
crooked. You might have to make this a little
shorter. It depends on the amount of space between the edges of the collar points (Fig. 10, 11).

Last, place the extended end of the knot
piece against the back near the top. Bring the piece
down and up over the front, and down in the back to
cover the extended canvas. Sew securely across the
end. Adjust the loops to make the small folds
(Fig. 12).

The proportions illustrated are for a moderate
size tie. For large bow ties, you can increase all the
measurements. An attractive set would be a tie and
cummerbund that match. (See "Man's Cummerbund," p. 175.)

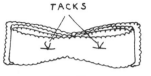

FIG. 9

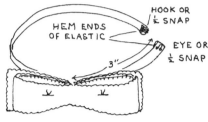

FIG. 10

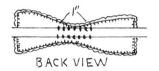

FIG. 11

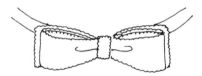

FIG. 12

Suspenders—Men's, Women's and Girls'

Men's

If you can get an old pair of suspenders, you can use the hardware and leather parts. Also the old pair will serve as a pattern. If you don't have an old pair, elastic loop buttonholes will do. Canvas suspenders won't stretch, so be sure they fit. Make long strips to cross in the back, and reach the top of the pants, or the top of the V shaped leather piece in the front. Don't try to make them too long, and lap the ends up to an adjusting buckle. Canvas work is too bulky for this. They look best if they are straight, one piece on each side. You will need long strips of canvas. Don't try to piece them; the piecing would show.

Materials needed

Long strips of canvas the required length to fit the individual man, plus 1¼ inches excess canvas all around (if both strips are to be worked on one piece of canvas, be sure to allow at least 2 inches excess canvas between them [Fig. 1])

Cloth lining material or grosgrain ribbon to line both pieces

Hardware and leather parts, if you have them, or 20 inches of ¼ inch elastic

Bind the canvas, work the embroidery, and block. Cut away the binding and enough excess canvas so the edges just meet when they are turned under. If you have metal or leather parts, turn under and hem the sides of the canvas only. Leave the canvas extended on the ends, and overcast the ends to prevent fraying (Fig. 2). Pass the ends of the excess canvas through the slots in the metal

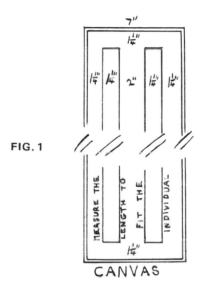

FIG. 1

CANVAS

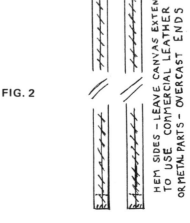

FIG. 2

parts. Turn it back so the edge of the embroidery shows on the back a little. Sew the excess canvas securely in place (Fig. 3). If you are going to use elastic loops, hem and miter the ends (Fig. 4).

If you use elastic loop buttonholes, fold a 5 inch piece of ¼ inch elastic in the middle so the sides are beside each other, and there is a triangle at the bottom. Sew the top of the triangle securely (Fig. 5). Make 4 of these. Cross the ends, and sew them securely to the back of the canvas (Fig. 6).

Line the suspenders with lining material or ribbon (Fig. 7).

Have the man for whom you are making the suspenders fasten the loops or leather pieces to the front buttons. Pass the suspenders over his shoulders, and fasten the ends to the buttons in back, after crossing the strips in the middle of his back. Pin together the diamond-shaped place where the strips cross, and sew them together securely (Fig. 8).

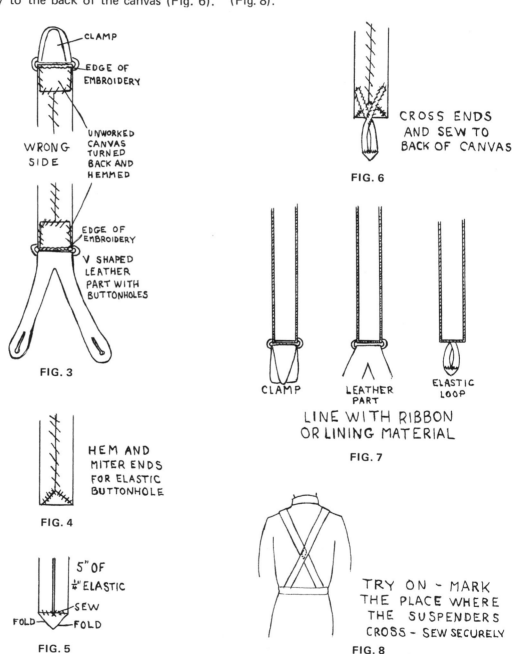

CLAMP

EDGE OF EMBROIDERY

UNWORKED CANVAS TURNED BACK AND HEMMED

WRONG SIDE

EDGE OF EMBROIDERY

V SHAPED LEATHER PART WITH BUTTONHOLES

FIG. 3

HEM AND MITER ENDS FOR ELASTIC BUTTONHOLE

FIG. 4

5" OF ¼" ELASTIC

FOLD   SEW   FOLD

FIG. 5

CROSS ENDS AND SEW TO BACK OF CANVAS

FIG. 6

CLAMP   LEATHER PART   ELASTIC LOOP

LINE WITH RIBBON OR LINING MATERIAL

FIG. 7

TRY ON - MARK THE PLACE WHERE THE SUSPENDERS CROSS - SEW SECURELY

FIG. 8

Women's and Girls'

Feminine suspenders can be wider and more decorative than the male variety. Little girls look very appealing in the Tyrolean style over a blouse and with a pleated skirt. Big girls like them, too. If you are making a pair for a child, you will want some spare canvas and lining material on the ends, so the suspenders can be let out, and won't be outgrown so quickly. You can open the ends, embroider the inch or inch and a half that was turned under, so they will fit a while longer.

Materials needed

Canvas strips equal to the measurements from spots about 2 inches or 3 inches on either side of the middle of the back, crossing, and passing over the shoulders, then straight down to the waistband of the skirt (In Tyrolean suspenders there is an additional piece across the chest. [Fig. 13]). Allow 2 inches to 4 inches extra length in the long strips for a girl's suspenders. Canvas enough for an added strip across the chest, and 1¼ inches excess canvas all around. If all 3 pieces are to be worked on 1 piece of canvas be sure to leave at least 2 inches excess canvas between them. Make the strips 1¼ inches to 1½ inches wide [Fig. 9])

Matching lining material (Grosgrain ribbon works well. Allow the extra length in the lining, too, for a girl's suspenders. It is a good idea to buy the lining before selecting the yarn because of the limited color and width choice)

20 inches of ¼ inch elastic for the buttonholes

Yarn of your choice

Bind the canvas, work the embroidery, and block. Cut off the binding and enough of the excess canvas so the edges just meet when they are turned under. For girl's suspenders, turn under and hem the sides, leaving the ends extended. Overcast the ends. For a woman's suspenders, hem and miter the ends (Fig. 10). Hem and miter the front piece for both types. For a girl's suspenders, turn up and hem the extra length of canvas, folding it so a little of the embroidery shows on the back (Fig. 11). Make elastic buttonholes. (See directions for Men's Suspenders.) Line all 3 pieces, turning under the extra length of lining in the girl's suspenders (Fig. 12). Try on the suspenders to place

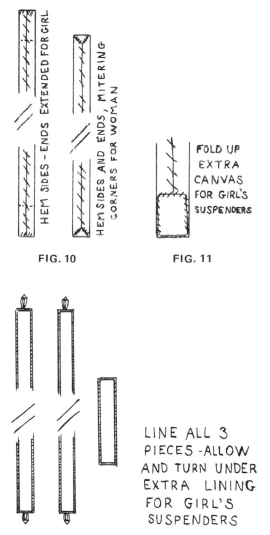

FIG. 10   **FIG. 11**

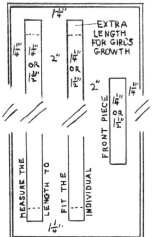

CANVAS
ALLOW AN EXTRA 1" TO
1½" AT EACH END FOR
GIRL'S GROWTH
LEAVE EXTRA LENGTH
UNWORKED

FIG. 9

LINE ALL 3
PIECES - ALLOW
AND TURN UNDER
EXTRA LINING
FOR GIRL'S
SUSPENDERS

FIG. 12

TRY ON AND PLACE
FRONT PIECE - SEAM
TO SIDE PIECES
ADD A DECORATIVE
EDGING IF DESIRED

FIG. 13

MARK THE PLACE
WHERE SUSPENDERS
CROSS - SEW SECURELY

FIG. 14

the front piece. Sew it to the edges of the side pieces (Fig. 13). Work a decorative edging along the edges, if you wish. Cross the suspenders in the back and button to the skirt. Pin them where they cross, then sew them securely together (Fig 14).

Vests and Bolero Jacket

Don't attempt to make these unless you're pretty good at sewing. They can be made up professionally, but it's rather expensive. Be sure the pattern fits, as there is no give or drape to canvas. You can use a regular pattern for the shape, but not the sewing directions. Canvas must be handled in a different way. Use fine canvas to reduce the bulk. Don't put pockets in the canvas. You can put pockets in the lining, if you like.

Man's vest—fabric back

Materials needed

Pattern, a fairly simple one
Canvas to fit the pattern pieces, minus the seam allowance, plus 1¼ inches excess canvas around each piece
Material for the back of the vest, and a buckled half belt, if you want it
Interfacing for the front edges
Lining material for all 3 pieces, plus enough to face the arm holes and the back of the neck, and enough to make a set in pocket or two
Buttons
Yarn of your choice

Cut out the lining and the back from the pattern as it comes (Fig. 1). Cut the seam allowance off the pattern. Bind the canvas, and pin the pattern to it, being careful to line up the arrows on the pattern with the canvas threads. Allow 1¼ inches excess canvas on all sides. Work with rectan-

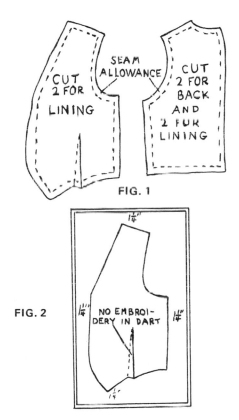

FIG. 1

FIG. 2

gular pieces of canvas (Fig. 2). Draw lines around the edges, marking the darts clearly. These areas will be left unworked.

Work the embroidery, and block, using the pattern as a guide. If no facing pattern comes in the pattern package, you can make your own, using the main pattern pieces. On a piece of paper draw the outlines of the edges, and then another line about 2 inches in from the first. Pin the darts in the pattern together before drawing your lines. The front facing won't need seam allowance, but the outer edges of the armhole and back of the neck facings will (Fig. 3).

Trim off the binding and all but 1 inch of the excess canvas. Overcast the edges to prevent fraying. Sew up the darts on the right side. Cover the seams with yarn if the canvas shows. Press lightly. Sew the interfacings for the fronts to the back of the embroidery only (Fig. 4).

If the back comes in two pieces, sew them together. Make and attach the back belt. Then sew the shoulder seams, leaving the excess canvas and the seam allowance of the back unsewed at the neck ends (Fig. 5). Don't fold the excess canvas toward the front. Sew the shoulder seams of the armhole facings (Fig. 6). Face the armholes. (See

"Finishing Canvas on a Curve.") Hem the front of the armhole facings only (Fig. 7). Sew the halves of the back lining together, and baste the back of the neck facing to the lining on the wrong side (Fig. 8). Sew up the darts, and add pockets to the lining fronts (Fig. 9). (See Style A, "Handbags," p. 122.) Sew the lining shoulder seams, leaving the seam allowance unsewed at the neck ends. Baste the lining to the vest, matching shoulder seams, right sides together.

Turn over to the canvas side. Starting at the bottom of a side, stitch across the bottom of a front, up and around the back of the neck, and down and across to the other side. Stitch as close to the embroidery as possible (Fig. 10). Turn the excess canvas in and hem it to the interfacing. Miter the front corners, and slash along the curves at the bottoms of the fronts. Slash the seam allowance of the lining too. Slash the seam allowance at the back of the neck (Fig. 11). Then turn the vest

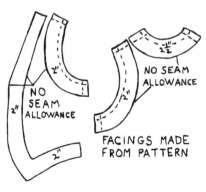

FIG. 3

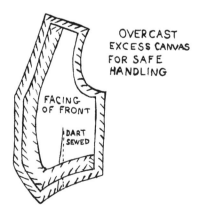

FIG. 4

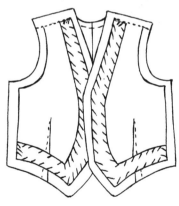

SEAM BACK AND SHOULDERS

FIG. 5

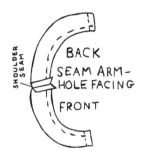

FIG. 6

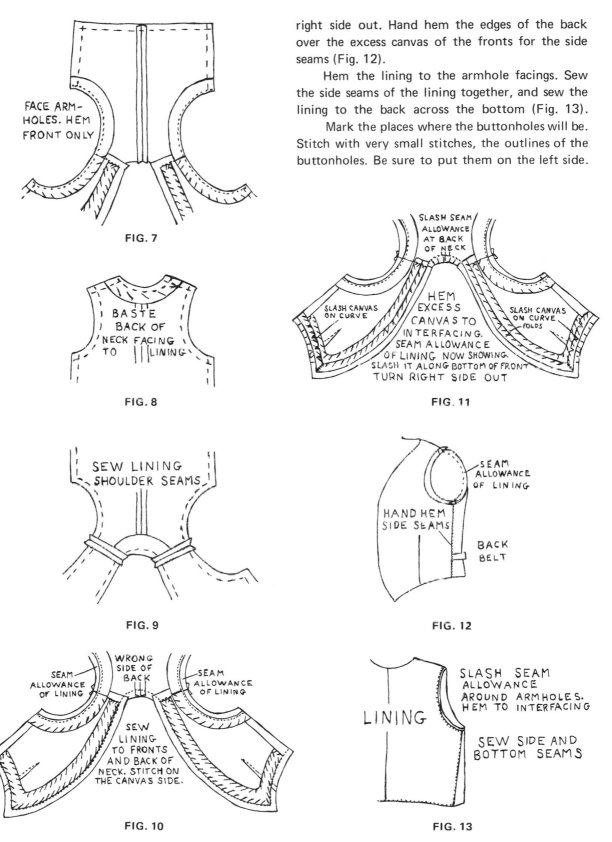

FACE ARM-
HOLES. HEM
FRONT ONLY

FIG. 7

right side out. Hand hem the edges of the back over the excess canvas of the fronts for the side seams (Fig. 12).

Hem the lining to the armhole facings. Sew the side seams of the lining together, and sew the lining to the back across the bottom (Fig. 13).

Mark the places where the buttonholes will be. Stitch with very small stitches, the outlines of the buttonholes. Be sure to put them on the left side.

BASTE
BACK OF
NECK FACING
TO LINING

FIG. 8

SLASH SEAM
ALLOWANCE
AT BACK
OF NECK

SLASH CANVAS
ON CURVE

HEM
EXCESS
CANVAS TO
INTERFACING.
SEAM ALLOWANCE
OF LINING NOW SHOWING.
SLASH IT ALONG BOTTOM OF FRONT
TURN RIGHT SIDE OUT

SLASH CANVAS
ON CURVE
FOLDS

FIG. 11

SEW LINING
SHOULDER SEAMS

FIG. 9

SEAM
ALLOWANCE
OF LINING

HAND HEM
SIDE SEAMS

BACK
BELT

FIG. 12

SEAM
ALLOWANCE
OF LINING

WRONG
SIDE OF
BACK

SEAM
ALLOWANCE
OF LINING

SEW
LINING
TO FRONTS
AND BACK OF
NECK. STITCH ON
THE CANVAS SIDE.

FIG. 10

LINING

SLASH SEAM
ALLOWANCE
AROUND ARMHOLES.
HEM TO INTERFACING

SEW SIDE AND
BOTTOM SEAMS

FIG. 13

VESTS AND BOLERO JACKET   187

This will anchor the yarn and canvas threads that will be cut (Fig. 14). Then take the vest to a tailor, and have him make professional tailor's buttonholes, such as you would see on a man's suit or coat. They will be firm, good looking, and will wear well. Sew on the buttons, allowing for the thickness of the canvas.

Note: It may be necessary to stitch all around the edges to produce a sharp edge. Work carefully, and use a large machine needle to sew through the thickness of the canvas and the embroidery.

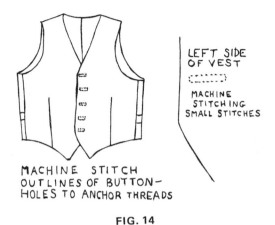

MACHINE STITCH OUTLINES OF BUTTONHOLES TO ANCHOR THREADS

FIG. 14

Woman's vest—fabric back

Follow the same procedure as for a man's vest, modifying the directions to suit a woman's pattern. Eliminate the back belt.

Woman's vest—all canvas

Materials needed

Pattern, a fairly simple one, the fewer darts and seams, the better
Canvas for 2 fronts and a back, minus seam allowance, plus 1¼ inches excess canvas around each piece
Interfacing for the front and lower back edges
Lining for all 3 pieces, plus enough to face the armholes, and the back of the neck, plus enough to make a set in pocket or two
Buttons
Yarn of your choice

Cut out the lining and the facings from the pattern as it comes in the package (Fig. 15). Bind the canvas. Cut the seam allowance off the front

and back pattern pieces, and draw their outlines on the canvas, being careful to line up the arrows on the pattern with the canvas threads. Mark all darts clearly. They will be left unworked (Fig. 16).

Work the embroidery and block, using the pattern as a guide. If no facing patterns come in the pattern package, you can make your own, using the main pattern pieces. On a piece of paper, draw the outlines of the edges of the fronts and the bottom of the back. Then draw another line 2 inches in from the first. Pin the darts of the pattern together before drawing your lines. Add 1 inch seam allowance at the ends of the back of the neck facing (Fig. 17).

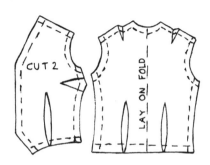

CUT LINING FROM PATTERN

FIG. 15

DRAW CANVAS PATTERNS WITHOUT SEAM ALLOWANCE. LEAVE DARTS UNWORKED

FIG. 16

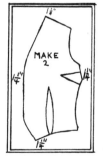
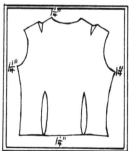

FACINGS

FIG. 17

Cut off the binding and all but 1 inch of the excess canvas. Overcast the edges to prevent fraying. Sew up the darts on the right side, going over the seams with yarn if the canvas shows. Press lightly (Fig. 18). Sew the interfacings to the edges of the fronts, and the bottom of the back, sewing into the back of the embroidery only (Fig. 19). Sew shoulder seams, leaving the excess canvas at the neck ends unsewed (Fig. 20). Fold back the excess canvas. On the right side, sew the neck facing from one shoulder to the other (Fig. 21). Slash the seam allowance and the excess canvas to this line of stitching. Turn the facing to the wrong side and sew again. (See "Finishing Canvas on a Curve.") Hem down the excess canvas of the shoulder seams (Fig. 22). Tuck the corners of the excess canvas of the fronts under the neck facing, and hem the edges of the facing (Fig. 23). Sew the side seams and hem back the excess canvas. Turn in the excess canvas along the outside edges, and hem to the facing. Miter the front corners, and slash the edges of the canvas at the bottoms of the fronts, if there are concave curves there. Make little folds where necessary (Fig. 24).

SEW DARTS-OVERCAST EXCESS CANVAS FOR SAFE HANDLING

FIG. 18

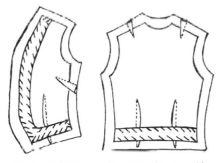

SEW FRONT AND LOWER BACK FACINGS TO EMBROIDERY ONLY

FIG. 19

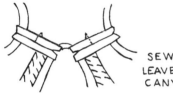

SEW SHOULDER SEAMS LEAVE NECK EXCESS CANVAS UNSEWED

FIG. 20

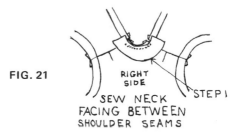

FIG. 21   RIGHT SIDE   STEP I

SEW NECK FACING BETWEEN SHOULDER SEAMS

FINISHING CANVAS ON A CURVE

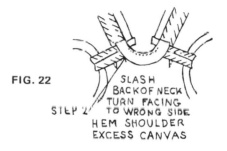

FIG. 22   SLASH BACK OF NECK TURN FACING STEP 2   TO WRONG SIDE HEM SHOULDER EXCESS CANVAS

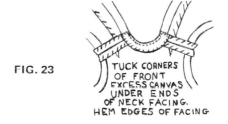

FIG. 23   TUCK CORNERS OF FRONT EXCESS CANVAS UNDER ENDS OF NECK FACING. HEM EDGES OF FACING

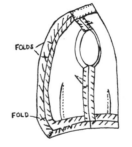

FOLDS

FOLD

SEW SIDE SEAMS AND HEM CANVAS. TURN BACK EXCESS CANVAS OF FRONT AND BOTTOM BACK. HEM TO FACINGS. MITER FRONT CORNERS.

FIG. 24

VESTS AND BOLERO JACKET   189

Sew the seams of the armhole facings (Fig. 25), and face the armholes (Fig. 26). (See "Finishing Canvas on a Curve.")

Sew the darts in the lining pieces. Add an inset pocket or 2, if you like (Fig. 27). Sew the shoulder and side seams (Fig. 28).

Fit the lining into the vest, and hand hem around all edges. Outline the buttonholes on the right side (not the left) with machine stitching (Fig. 29). (See directions for "Man's Vest," pp. 187-188.) After the buttonholes are made, sew on the buttons, allowing for the thickness of the canvas and the embroidery.

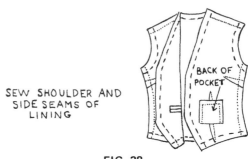

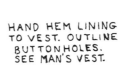

SEW SHOULDER AND SIDE SEAMS OF LINING

FIG. 28

HAND HEM LINING TO VEST. OUTLINE BUTTONHOLES. SEE MAN'S VEST.

FIG. 29

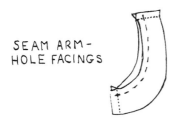

SEAM ARM-HOLE FACINGS

FIG. 25

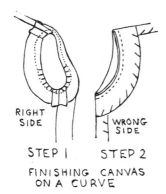

RIGHT SIDE   WRONG SIDE

STEP 1   STEP 2

FINISHING CANVAS ON A CURVE

FIG. 26

Woman's bolero jacket

Follow the same procedure as for a woman's all canvas vest, modified to suit a bolero jacket (Figs. 30, 31). To make the curved front edge, see "Finishing Canvas on a Curve."

SET-IN POCKET IN LINING

SEW DARTS

FIG. 27

COORDINATE FRONT AND BACK OF DESIGN

FIG. 30

BOXED JACKET VERSION

FIG. 31

Use the diagrams and directions in the all-canvas vest, pp. 188-190, where indicated below. Continue with Figures 32-36, 20-23 (in the all-canvas vest), 37, 25-27 (in the all-canvas vest), 38, and 39.

Design Suggestions. Bolero jackets can be quite gay. Coordinate the design of the back over the shoulder and side seams. If you like you can work surface stitchery over the canvas work. Use beads or sequins and make a decorative edging. If you want to embroider over the canvas work, do so just before you put in the lining.

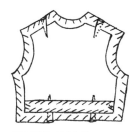

OVERCAST EDGES TO PREVENT FRAYING

SEW FRONT AND LOWER BACK FACINGS TO EMBROIDERY ONLY

FIG. 35   **FIG. 36**

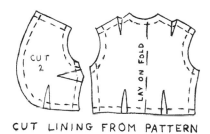

CUT LINING FROM PATTERN

FIG. 32

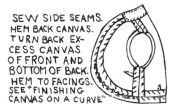

SEW SIDE SEAMS. HEM BACK CANVAS. TURN BACK EXCESS CANVAS OF FRONT AND BOTTOM OF BACK. HEM TO FACINGS. SEE "FINISHING CANVAS ON A CURVE"

FIG. 37

MAKE 2

LEAVE DARTS UNWORKED

PATTERNS WITHOUT SEAM ALLOWANCE

FIG. 33

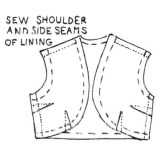

SEW SHOULDER AND SIDE SEAMS OF LINING

FIG. 38

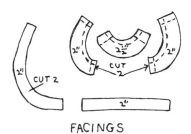

2"   CUT 2

2"   CUT 2   2½"   2"

2"

FACINGS

FIG. 34

HAND HEM LINING TO JACKET

FIG. 39

Man's vest—all canvas

Follow the same procedure as for a woman's all canvas vest, modified to suit a man's pattern. Eliminate the back belt.

Man's Halter Neck Vest

Don't attempt this unless you're pretty skilled at sewing. The vest can be made up by a tailor, but it's rather expensive.

Buy a pattern for a halter neck vest, a simple one with no lapels. Make sure the pattern fits, as there is no give or drape to canvas.

Materials needed

Canvas for the 2 pieces, minus the seam allowance, plus 1¼ inches excess canvas all around (if both pieces are to be worked on one piece of canvas, make sure there is 2 inches excess canvas between them)

Interfacing for all edges

Lining material for both pieces

¼ yd. of ¾-inch elastic for the neck, and half of the waist size of ½ inch elastic

1 link hook

4 buttons

Yarn of your choice

Using the pattern as it comes, cut 2 pieces of lining material (Fig. 1). Trim the seam allowance off the pattern, and make a duplicate for the left side if you are going to work both pieces on one piece of canvas. Arrange the pieces on the canvas and draw their outlines, lining up the arrows on the pattern with the canvas threads (Fig. 2). If no interfacing pattern is included in the pattern package, you can make your own. Use the pattern with no seam allowance. On a piece of paper draw along the curved arm side, adding seam allowance. Draw another line about 2 inches in from the first (Fig.

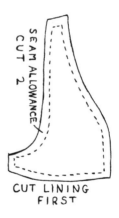

FIG. 1

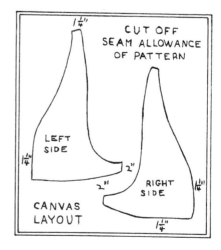

FIG. 2

3). Draw a line around the outside edges of the pattern and down to where the side facing will come. Curve the line across toward the front, and around to the side again. Make this part about 2 inches wide (Fig. 3). Cut 2 pieces of each.

Bind the canvas, work the embroidery, and block, using the pattern as a guide. Sew the large pieces of interfacing to the back of the embroidery. Trim off the binding, and all but 1 inch of the excess canvas (Fig. 4). Face the arm side curve. (See "Finishing Canvas on a Curve.") Turn the rest of the excess canvas in and hem it to the interfacing. Miter the front corners, but not the top or side ends. Just turn them under. You can trim some more canvas away at the top, so the edges just meet to reduce bulk. Slash the slight concave curves along the front edges (Fig. 5).

Overlap the pieces in the front and pin them together. Hold the vest up to the man, and measure the distance across the back of the neck, and the back of the waist. Cut a piece of the narrower elastic for the back of the neck, allowing an extra inch on each side to sew to the canvas. Sew the elastic to the top ends of the vest a little shorter than the measurement so the elastic will stretch slightly (Fig. 6). Cut 2 pieces for the waist, each one 2 inches longer than ½ the waist back measurement. Attach 1 inch on each end to the side ends of the vest. Try the vest on again, and bring the pieces together, stretching the elastic enough

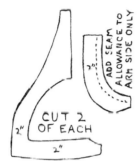

INTERFACING PATTERNS
MADE FROM MAIN PATTERN
NO SEAM ALLOWANCE
ON MAIN PIECE

FIG. 3

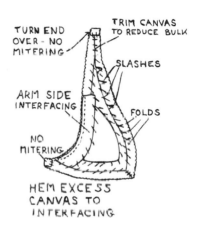

HEM EXCESS
CANVAS TO
INTERFACING

FIG. 5

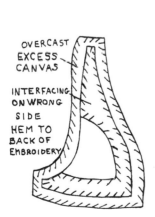

FIG. 4

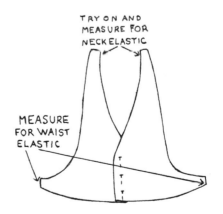

FIG. 6

to make the vest fit snugly. Fold under one end of the elastic about 1 inch, and hem. Slip the end of the other side through the slot in the link hook. Check the length again, and hem the elastic (Fig. 7).

Line the vest (Fig. 8).

Lap the left side over the right and pin. Sew the buttons through both thicknesses of the vest front (Fig. 9).

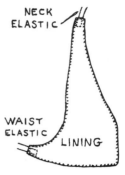

FIG. 8

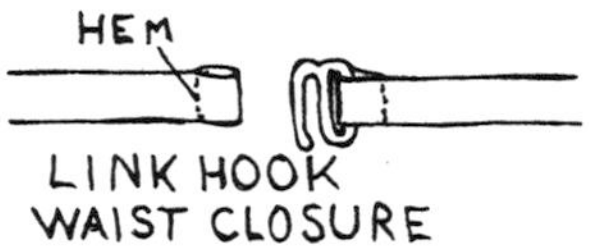

FIG. 9

HEM

LINK HOOK
WAIST CLOSURE

FIG. 7

Patches, Pockets, and Key Chain Charm

Patches

People are making canvas patches for so many things—to glue or sew on the side of a straw bag, or on a bicycle basket, or on clothing (Fig. 1). The latter is a form of applique. You will find fine canvas much easier to handle. Cut off all but ¾ inch to 1 inch excess canvas, depending on the size of the patch. Turn under and hem the edges to the back of the embroidery, mitering the corners where needed (Fig. 2). (See "Finishing Canvas on a Curve" for curved edges.) Then sew or glue it in place. Sometimes it is hard to hide the edges of the canvas on the fold. The Binding stitch works well to cover these edges (Fig. 3).

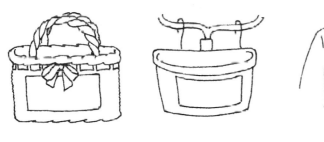

FIG. 1

HEM AND MITER

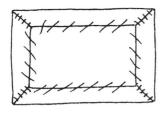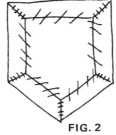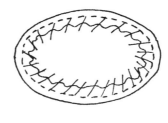

BINDING STITCH EDGING

FIG. 2

FIG. 3

Pockets

If you would like a canvas pocket, follow the above procedure, then line the pocket with material to match the garment (Fig. 4).

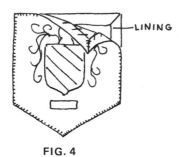

FIG. 4

There are other ways to make a pocket that are a little different. If it is to go on a garment that you are making, you can use some of the material to make a fabric frame, either following the shape of the pocket, or in any shape you wish. A monogram worked on fine canvas can be framed and mounted on a jacket to give it a personal touch. Or you could use this method for a patch pocket in a handbag (Fig. 5). Cut out the pocket in the regular way. Omit the hem at the top, just have seam allowance all around. Cut a piece of lining to match. Work the canvas inset that is the same size as the pocket but without seam allowance (Fig. 6). Cut a hole in the center of the pocket front in a shape to match the worked area of the canvas, but with ⅜ inch seam allowance. Slash the corners of a rectangular hole, and at intervals all the way around in a circular hole so when you turn under the seam allowance the hole will exactly match the worked area of the canvas (Fig. 7). Pin the frame firmly in place. Now tuck the edges under and sew them down with a Buttonhole stitch (Fig. 7).

FABRIC FRAMES

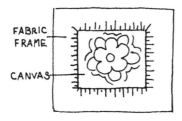

FABRIC
FRAME
CANVAS

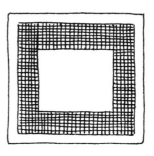

FIG. 6

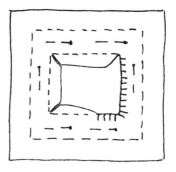

FIG. 7

FIG. 5

Place the pocket on the lining, right sides together, and machine sew the top and sides next to the edges of the canvas (Fig. 8). Carefully turn the pocket right side out, making sure the edges of the canvas are straight and smooth. Now seam the fourth side (Fig. 9). The canvas will provide a little stiffening, and the pocket is completely finished, inside and out.

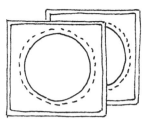

FIG. 10

FIG. 8

FIG. 11

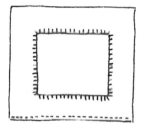

FIG. 9

FIG. 12

Key chain charm

Make 2 patches, any size. Mount one on each side of a piece of stiff cardboard. Put Binding stitch around the edges, and make a loop for the key chain (Figs. 10, 11, 12, 13).

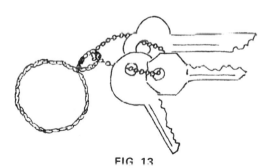

FIG. 13

Tobacco Pouch

Make a rectangular piece to be folded twice, forming 3 sections. (See style A, "Clutch Bags," p. 113.) Make a small pouch about 5 inches by 3 inches (Fig. 1). Allow 1¼ inches all around on the canvas (Fig. 2).

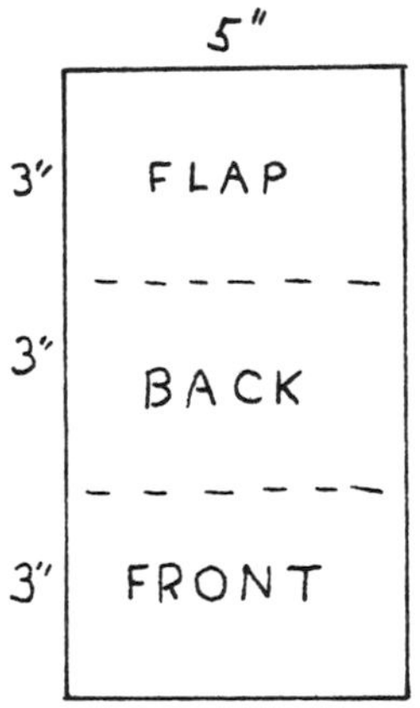

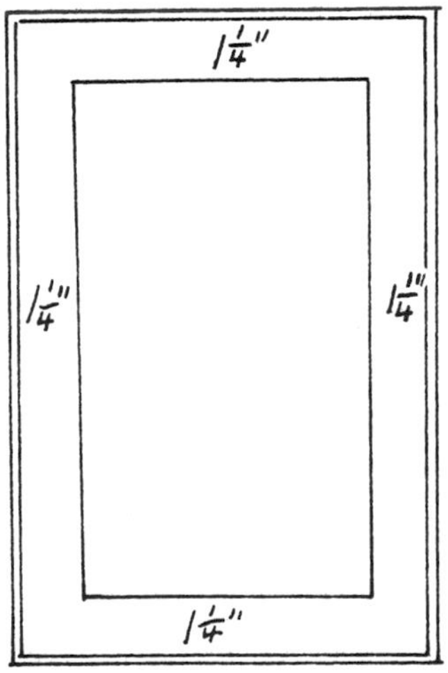

Materials needed

Piece of canvas 7 inches by 11 inches
Lining material to cover the worked area (5 inches by 9 inches), plus seam allowance
Heavy Pliofilm 5 inches by 6 inches
5 inch zipper
Yarn of your choice

Bind the canvas, work the embroidery, and block. Cut off all but about ¾ inch excess canvas, and hem, mitering the corners (Fig. 3). Make a flat braid, and anchor it on both sides of the front portion about 1½ inches up from the bottom (Fig. 4). Line the piece with a dark material, leaving small spaces unhemmed so you can tuck the ends of the zipper tapes into them (Fig. 5). Sew a piece

5"

3" FLAP

3" BACK   FIG. 1

3" FRONT

1¼"

1¼"   1¼"

FIG. 2

1¼"

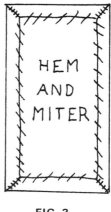

HEM AND MITER

FIG. 3

of fairly heavy Pliofilm over the front and back portions (Fig. 6). Open the zipper and sew one side to the top edge of the front, and the other side on the fold between the back and the flap, tucking the ends of the tapes into the holes you left between the lining and the canvas; then close the openings (Fig. 7). Sew up the side seams, putting a few reinforcing stitches at X in Figure 8. Cover the seams and the edges of the flap with Binding stitch, and tuck the flap under the cord (Fig. 9).

FIG. 6

FIG. 4

FIG. 7

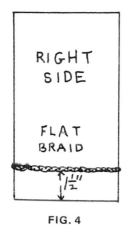

FIG. 5

FIG. 8

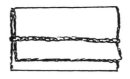

FIG. 9

Barrette

Materials needed

Piece of canvas to accommodate the main part of the barrette about 3½ inches by 2¼ inches, plus 1¼ inches excess canvas all around
Interlining to fit the worked area
Lining to fit the worked area, plus seam allowance
Smooth stick about 4 inches long to use as a pin

Work a design on a piece of canvas in the shape you want, usually an oval (Fig. 1, 2). Block if necessary. Cut off all but ¾ inch of the excess canvas, and hem the edges (Fig. 3). (See "Finishing Canvas on a Curve" for rounded edges.) Add a piece of stiff interlining (Fig. 4) and line the piece (Fig. 5). Mark the spots for the holes for the pin. Nick the lining and the interlining with scissors, and make the holes with an awl. Don't cut the canvas. Whip yarn around the edges of the holes (Fig. 6).

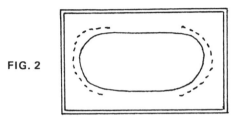

FIG. 2

FIG. 3

FIG. 4

FIG. 5

FIG. 6

NICK THE LINING AND INTERLINING. THEN MAKE THE HOLES WITH AN AWL

FIG. 1

Hats, Bonnets, Caps, and Hat Bands

There is lots of room for imagination in planning the design for hats and caps. Many stitch patterns can be used to give a 3-dimensional effect. Pompons, tassels, fringes, either cut or left in loop form, can be used to decorate the finished canvas. Surface stitchery or crewel designs can be worked over the canvas work. Beads, sequins, metal threads, felt, bits of fur, all manner of things can be used to produce unusual effects and give individual touches. It is best to work with a cap or hat form, or a pattern that has been professionally made. The canvas pieces are worked and joined, and the whole is lined. Keep in mind that canvas is not stretchy, like knitting or crocheting.

To use a pattern meant for fabric, first cut out the lining from the pattern as it comes. Then cut off the seam allowance, and arrange the pattern pieces on the canvas, allowing 1 inch to 1¼ inches excess canvas around each part. If 2 or more parts are to be worked on 1 piece of canvas, be sure to leave at least 2 inches of excess canvas between them. You won't be able to follow the sewing directions, as canvas must be handled in a different manner.

Note: The patterns shown are not authentic. Buy a professional pattern or see a milliner.

Hats

Pillbox. This is best made over a stiff form. A millinery shop would probably carry the forms for this type of hat. A pattern can be used if no form is available. Make a pattern from a form. Using tissue paper or cloth, carefully make pattern pieces, that, when joined, will cover the form exactly. Make them a little large so as to allow for the thickness of the embroidery, and the bulk of the turned under canvas. Be sure that the circumference of the crown equals the inside curve of the side piece (A to B in Fig. 1). Plan the design so it will match across the seam in the back.

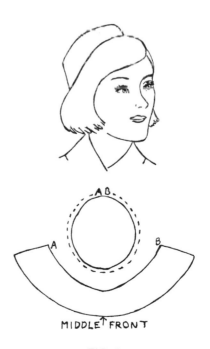

MIDDLE FRONT

FIG. 1

Bind the canvas, work the embroidery, and block, using your pattern as a guide. Cut off the binding and all but ¾ inch of the excess canvas. Turn under and hem the pieces, mitering the back corners. (See "Finishing Canvas on a Curve.") If no form is used, interline the pieces so they will keep their shape. Seam the back and join the pieces on the right side. Work a decorative edging over the seam between the crown and the side piece, if you like.

Make the lining from the pieces you have cut. Insert the lining into the hat, and hem around the edges. Cover this edge with decorative stitching, too.

Bonnets

Bonnet, 2 pieces. You might be able to find a pattern for this type of bonnet in a book of patterns for felt articles. Like canvas, felt is also unyielding and bulky, so a pattern for this material would work very well. If a pattern for fabric is used, remember to cut the lining first, then cut off the seam allowance before tracing the outlines on the canvas. Make the edges A to B in Figure 2 equal in length. Leave the area in all darts unworked.

The bonnet could be lined with a quilted material for extra warmth and softness. Be sure to make the bonnet a little large to allow for the extra bulk of a quilted lining. Fringes, tufting, felt applique, or buttons can be added to create a charming bonnet. A tie under the chin makes it complete.

Caps

Cap, 3 pieces. This could be made for a little girl, or a big one. It would be becoming to an older girl to complement the present plain hair styles. An under-the-chin-strap or ties is optional. Teenagers will have lots of ideas for designs. Line the cap with wool or quilted material for extra warmth. Leave the dart areas unworked (Fig. 3).

Beanie, or Juliet cap. You might be able to make your own pattern for the 6 pie-shaped pieces, or an old beanie could serve to give you the proper proportions and measurements (Fig. 4). Line up the bottom edges of the pieces with the canvas threads. If more than one piece is to be worked on one piece of canvas, remember to leave at least 2 inches of excess canvas between the parts. Finish the pieces separately, making modified mitered corners at the top. Make them as flat as possible. The matching lining pieces must have about ¾ inch seam allowance. You can decorate the cap lavishly. A large pompon on top might be appropriate.

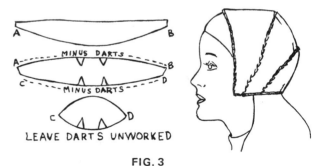

LEAVE DARTS UNWORKED

FIG. 3

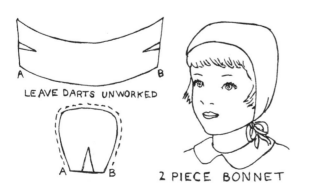

LEAVE DARTS UNWORKED

2 PIECE BONNET

FIG. 2

FIG. 4

Scotch cap. If you plan to make a plaid or Scotch tartan for this cap, using Alternating Tent stitch you will have to place the side pieces on the straight of the canvas, and the top piece on the bias (Fig. 5). If you are using a professional pattern, cut the lining first, then cut off the seam allowance of the pattern. It will be easier to arrange the pieces on the canvas if you cut a duplicate pattern for the second side. Arrange the pieces on the canvas, allowing 1¼ inches excess canvas around each piece.

Bind the canvas, work the embroidery, and block, using the pattern as a guide. Cut off the binding and all but 1 inch of the excess canvas. (See "Finishing Canvas on a Curve.") Make modified mitered corners at the points. You can add interlining to the sides, if you wish. Join the 3 pieces, seaming them on the right side. (See "Joining Pieces of Canvas—Seaming.") Make and insert the lining, hemming it around the edges. Finish the edge with a piece of matching grosgrain ribbon. Arrange a flat bow and a couple of short streamers in the back.

FIG. 6

Note: Because canvas is so unyielding, you may have to steam and press the cap or bonnet after it is completed to make it conform to the contour of the head. A wig form would be ideal for this purpose. If the form is made of Styrofoam, be sure to cover it with several layers of cloth, or a towel before using a steam iron. The Styrofoam might melt if it gets too hot. Press very lightly, letting the steam do the work. You can pat the canvas into proper shape with your fingers.

With slight modifications, these directions can be used for embroidered fabric hats or caps.

Hat bands

These could be used on hats with wide floppy brims. They are popular with sportsmen when decorated with fishing flies, game birds, etc. Be sure to use quite fine canvas, as the narrow width will limit the design. The seam where the ends are joined can be covered in lots of ways. If you would like to give the appearance of a buckle closing, finish one end with a point. Slip a flat buckle over this end, and tack it over the square end as flat as possible. No lining is needed (Fig. 7).

FIG. 5

Band on beret. Make or buy the beret first. Be sure it fits well. When planning the band, make sure it fits exactly, as there is no stretch to canvas. Cut a long strip of canvas, allowing 1 inch of excess canvas all around (Fig. 6).

Bind the canvas, work the embroidery, and block, checking the measurement again. Cut off the binding and join the ends. Turn in the excess canvas and hem. A piece of interlining will help to keep the band from crushing. Then line the band. A piece of grosgrain ribbon is good for this. Last, sew the band on the beret.

BUCKLE-FAKE CLOSING   NO LINING NEEDED

FIG. 7

Dog Collar

If you have an old collar, it can serve as a guide to making a pattern. You can also use the buckle and the ring for the dog's license and leash. Make a pattern a little wider to one side of the center than at the ends. The wide part should be nearer the buckle end of the collar than the end with the holes. Draw an outline of the pattern on a piece of canvas, allowing 1¼ inches excess canvas at the sides and 1½ inches at the ends (Fig. 1).

FIG. 1

Materials needed

Canvas to accommodate the pattern, plus 1 inch at the sides and 1½ inches at the ends (for a pattern see below)
Interlining for the wider part
Buckle and ring
Eyelets
Yarn of your choice

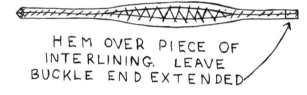

HEM OVER PIECE OF INTERLINING. LEAVE BUCKLE END EXTENDED

FIG. 2

Bind the canvas, work the embroidery, and block. Cut a piece of interlining to fit into the wide part of the collar, cut off the binding and hem the excess canvas, sewing over the interlining. Leave the canvas on the buckle end extended (Fig. 2). Using the pattern, cut a lining of a sturdy but not too thick material, with ½ inch seam allowance. Sew the lining to the tip and part way down the sides (Fig. 3). Sew the ring securely to the back of the canvas about 1 inch to 1½ inches from the buckle end (Fig. 4). Sew the lining a little farther along, over the back of the ring. Pass the end of the collar up one side of the buckle. Use an

FIG. 3

RING FOR LEASH AND LICENSE

FIG. 4

INSERT PRONG OF
BUCKLE AND HEM

FIG. 5

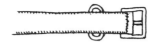

FINISH HEMMING
LINING

FIG. 6

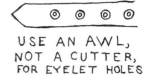

USE AN AWL,
NOT A CUTTER,
FOR EYELET HOLES

FIG. 7

awl to make a hole for the buckle prong. Push it through, then pass the end of the collar down the other side of the buckle (Fig. 5). Fold the piece of unworked canvas back against the back of the collar and sew securely in place. Bring the end of the lining over the end of the canvas and finish hemming it (Fig. 6).

Using the old collar as a guide, mark the spots where the eyelets should be. Kits for making eyelets can be bought in notion or sewing aid departments. Make the holes for the eyelets with an awl, not the cutter that comes with the kit. Then insert the eyelets and clamp in place with the tool provided in the kit (Fig. 7).

Bicycle Seat Cover

Bicycle seats vary in size and shape, so it is best to make a cover for a specific seat. If there is an opening at the front of the seat, cover it when you make your pattern. The cover will stay in place better.

Make a cloth pattern to completely cover the seat, placing darts where necessary to fit the cloth to the sides of the seat. Make the folds of the darts perpendicular to the edge. The line of stitching can curve, if necessary (Fig. 1). Allow about 1½ inches of excess canvas around the edges (Fig. 2).

Materials needed
Canvas to accommodate the cloth pattern and 1½ inches excess canvas
Fairly heavy tape to put around the edges for a casing
About ½ yard strong elastic
Strong thread or string to fasten the cover to prevent slipping
Yarn of your choice

Bind the canvas, work the embroidery, leaving the dart areas unworked, and block, using your pattern as a guide. Cut away the binding and all but about 1 inch of the excess canvas. Sew the darts together on the right side, sewing down into the excess canvas. Overcast the edges to prevent fraying (Fig. 3). Try the cover on the seat and see how much room there is between the seat and the underlying metal parts. It will probably be small near the front and wider near the back. You may have to trim the canvas down to ½ inch near the

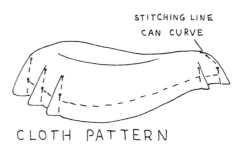

CLOTH PATTERN

FIG. 1

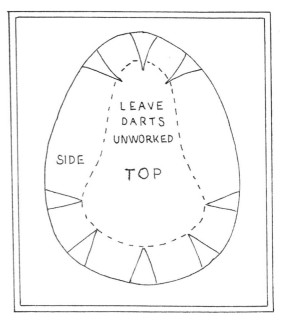

FIG. 2

front. Using heavy tape, make a casing all around over the edges of the excess canvas (Fig. 4). Put strong elastic in the casing. Try the cover on the seat again, and pull up the elastic quite tight (Fig. 5).

The cover must be held quite firmly. It may be necessary to lace back and forth under the seat with string (Fig. 5). Or you could attach ties. These could be tied to some of the metal parts so the cover couldn't slide around (Fig. 6).

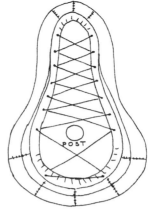

ELASTIC IN CASING
STRING LACING

FIG. 5

EXCESS CANVAS TRIMMED
EDGE OVERCAST- DARTS SEWED
ON THE RIGHT SIDE

FIG. 3

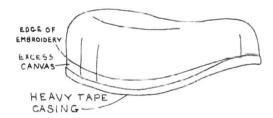

EDGE OF
EMBROIDERY

EXCESS
CANVAS

HEAVY TAPE
CASING

FIG. 4

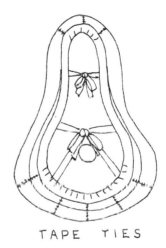

TAPE TIES

FIG. 6

Indian Hair Decoration

Materials needed

Canvas to accommodate 2 pieces, plus about 1 inch excess canvas around the edges (if both pieces are to be worked on 1 piece of canvas, be sure to allow 1½ inches between them so there will be enough excess canvas for each when they are cut apart)

Interlining and lining equal to the worked area; the latter must have about ½ inch seam allowance around each piece

About 12 inches of ¼ inch elastic or 2 elastic loops used to hold ponytails

The circular pieces worn over the ears to hold the hair can be made any size. Allow about ¾ inch excess canvas between the circles and the edges of the canvas (Fig. 1). (See "Finishing Canvas on a

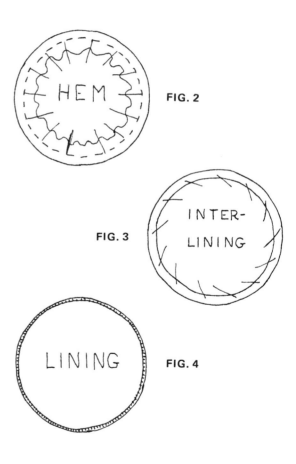

FIG. 2

FIG. 3

FIG. 4

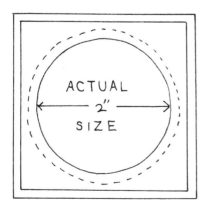

FIG. 1

Curve.") For the size illustrated, trim the excess canvas down to about ⅜ inch, draw up the gathering thread, and hem the excess canvas to the back of the embroidery (Fig. 2). Sew in a piece of stiff interlining and line the piece (Figs. 3, 4). Make a loop of ¼ inch elastic, and sew this to the back a little above the center or attach the ponytail elastic loops. Sew through to the interlining. The loop should be large enough to double over the hair (Fig. 5). These discs can be elaborately decorated with beads or sequins. For an authentic Indian touch, attach a cord to the center of the disc on which you have put some beads (Fig. 6).

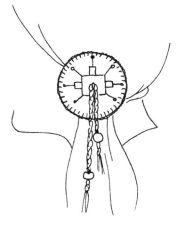

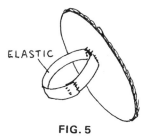

ELASTIC

FIG. 5

FIG. 6

Shoe Buckles

There is lots of room for originality in planning shoe buckles. Use buttons, beads, sequins, fur—anything you like. They could be rectangular, oval, or circular.

Materials needed

Canvas to accommodate 2 buckles, plus ¾ inch excess canvas all around (if both buckles are to be worked on 1 piece of canvas, be sure to leave about 1¼ inches excess canvas between them so there will be enough to turn under on each piece when they are cut apart)

Interlining to match the worked area, plus 2 pieces of 1½ inch square to fasten to the shoe

Lining material for the buckles with seam allowance, and 2 pieces about 2 inches square to match the shoes

Work the canvas forms, hem, and miter any corners (Figs. 1, 2). Add a piece of stiff interlining, and line with some sturdy material (Figs. 3, 4). Now cover a double piece of interlining about ¾ inch by 1½ inches with material to match the shoes (Fig. 5). Sew this securely to the back of the buckle in a rectangle about ¾ inch square (Fig. 6). Sew the under piece to the shoe. You will need heavy thread and a strong needle. A curved needle, which should be available at a sewing aid counter, might help. Hold the end of the buckle up out of the way, but don't bend it back too far or it won't stay flat afterwards (Fig. 7). You might take the buckles to a leather shop and have them attached with rivets.

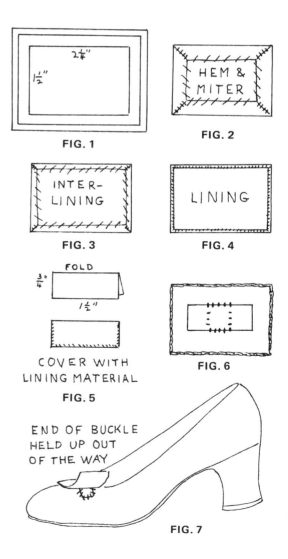

FIG. 1

HEM & MITER
FIG. 2

INTER-LINING
FIG. 3

LINING
FIG. 4

FOLD
COVER WITH LINING MATERIAL
FIG. 5

FIG. 6

END OF BUCKLE HELD UP OUT OF THE WAY
FIG. 7

FINISHING TOUCHES

Cords and Braids

Cords and braids add much to an attractive finish. They can be used for the cords to hang hangings, to fasten hangings to rods, as edgings for pillows, coasters, etc. They are excellent for hiding seams, and can be used instead of cloth covered cords on pillows. They make fine loops for button closures, and as ties for almost anything. Finished with decorative tassels, they add an elegant touch to many things that will lift your work out of the ordinary. They can be made in many ways. Here are a few.

Cord A

Untwisted cord. Either use 1 piece twice the required length or use 2 pieces knotted together. If one strand is used, mark the center with a plain knot (Fig. 1). Anchor one end to something stationary. Now pull the other end until the strand is very tight. Start to untwist the strand. Continue until the plies are straight and parallel. Continue to twist the yarn the "wrong" way until it is twisted quite tight. Keep the strand taut. Don't allow any slack or it will kink.

Now hold the end in one hand, and grasp the center knot in the other. Bring the outside end up to the anchored end. Gradually release the cord at the middle knot, and it will retwist itself into a cord twice the thickness of the original strand. This method produces a soft, loosely twisted cord (Fig. 2).

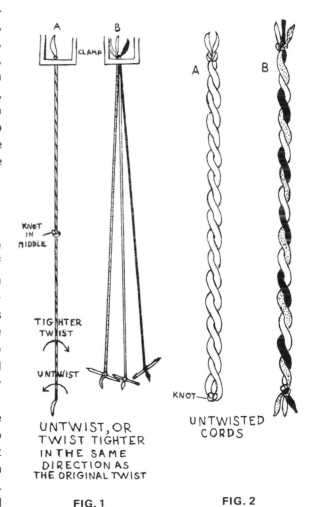

UNTWIST, OR
TWIST TIGHTER
IN THE SAME
DIRECTION AS
THE ORIGINAL TWIST

FIG. 1

UNTWISTED
CORDS

FIG. 2

Tighter twisted cord. Use the same arrangement as for the untwisted cord, but, instead of untwisting the strand, twist it tighter in the same direction as the original twist. When the ends are brought together, and the loop is released, you will get a tighter, firmer cord (Fig. 3).

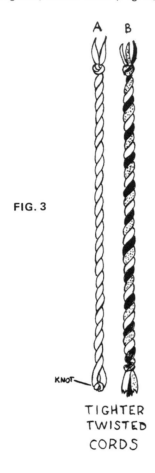

FIG. 3

TIGHTER
TWISTED
CORDS

Cord B

Untwisted cord. If several strands, perhaps of different colors or materials, are to be twisted together, they will have to be untwisted separately. Use strands about ¼ longer than the length desired for the finished cord. Knot the ends together and anchor them to something stationary. Tie a pencil, or anything easy to grasp to the other end of each strand (Fig. 1). Untwist the first strand until the plies are parallel, then keep twisting the "wrong" way, counting the number of turns past the parallel point. Keeping the strand

taut, fasten or weight it so it can't retwist. Do the same with the other strands, counting the same number of turns past the parallel point (Fig. 1).

Bring the strands together, side by side, and gradually release them. They will retwist themselves into a fairly loose cord. Knot the open end (Fig. 2). This process is a lot easier if someone helps you by holding the strands as you get them ready for retwisting.

Tighter twisted cord. Use the same arrangement as for the untwisted cord, only instead of untwisting the strands, twist them tighter in the same direction as the original twist. Count the same number of twists for each strand. You will get a tight firm cord (Fig. 3).

Finger or hand-looped cord

In reality this is a double chain stitch, made without a crochet hook. Use 2 strands 4 to 8 times as long as the desired cord length, depending on the thickness of the cord. It is best to test before cutting the yarn. Don't try to piece the yarn, there's no place to hide a knot.

Knot the 2 ends together. Hold the knot between the thumb and middle finger of your right hand. Pass one end up and over your raised index finger, and down to the knot again. Push the other strand around the loop to the right, and bring it around to the left (Fig. 4). Holding the strand with the ring and little finger of your left hand, pass the index finger, nail up, through the loop from front to back, bend the knuckle, and dip up the left-hand strand (Fig. 5). Hold the right strand with the ring and little finger of your right hand. Now pass the knotted end to the thumb and middle finger of your left hand. Take the finger of your right hand out of the loop, and pull down on the right end (Fig. 6). You will now have a loop over your left index finger, and the start of the cord between the thumb and middle finger of your left hand. Keep the ends held with the ring and little fingers of your 2 hands fairly tight.

Pass the index finger of your right hand, nail up, through the loop from front to back, bend the knuckle, and dip up the right-hand strand (Fig. 7). Pass the knotted end over to the thumb and mid-

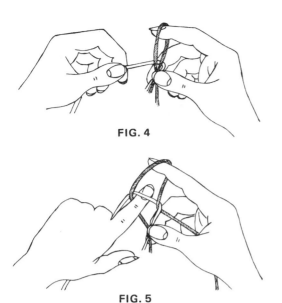

FIG. 4

FIG. 5

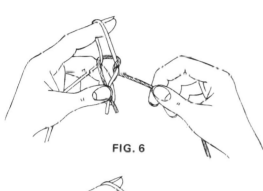

FIG. 6

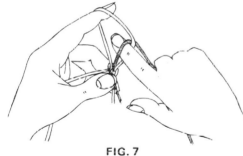

FIG. 7

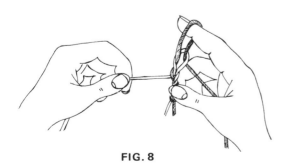

FIG. 8

dle finger of your right hand, and pull down on the left strand (Fig. 8). Repeat these motions, passing the growing cord back and forth between your hands. Finish by pulling one of the ends through the last loop (Fig. 9).

This cord can be made with 1 or 2 colors. For practice, use 2 colors at first. It can be made with fine thread or heavy yarn. If thread other than wool yarn is used, pull the loops quite tight. Wool yarn should be snug but not too tight.

FIG. 9

Rounded-plaited cords

4 Strand plait. The strands should be 1½ times required finished length. For practice, use 2 dark and 2 light strands. Knot all 4 strands together. Anchor the knotted end to something stationary. Have 2 dark strands on one side and 2 light strands on the other. Pass the outside left strand under 2 strands and back over 1. Then the outside right strand under 2 and back over 1. Repeat these 2 motions, first one side then the other. This looks much like Finger cord but is not so heavy (Fig. 10).

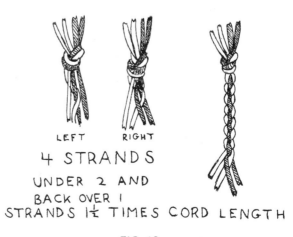

LEFT   RIGHT

4 STRANDS
UNDER 2 AND
BACK OVER 1
STRANDS 1½ TIMES CORD LENGTH

FIG. 10

LEFT   RIGHT   LEFT   RIGHT

6 STRANDS
UNDER 3 AND BACK OVER 1
STRANDS 1½ TIMES CORD LENGTH

FIG. 11

6-Strand plait. Use the same principle as for the 4-strand cord, only pass the outside strands under 3 and back over 1 (Fig. 11).

8-Strand plait. Use the same principle as for 6-strand and 4-strand plaits, only pass the outside strands under 4 and over 1 (Fig. 12). You will know you are working these cords properly if all the ends of one color stay on one side, and all the second ends stay on the other, divided down the middle. The larger ones are rounded on the front and flat on the back.

Woven braids

In order to keep the width of these woven braids the same throughout, don't pull the yarn tight. You can pin the edges to a piece of tape or ribbon as you go along, if you wish. This type of braid is usually mounted on a firm backing. Use 1½ to 2 times the required length. You can lengthen or shorten the woven braids by narrowing or widening them. For a repeated color rotation, be careful not to mix the sequence of the strands.

LEFT   RIGHT   LEFT   RIGHT

8 STRANDS
UNDER 4 AND BACK OVER 1
STRANDS 1½ TIMES CORD LENGTH

FIG. 12

4-Strand woven braid. Knot the 4 strands together, and anchor the knot to something stationary. Arrange the strands beside each other. Pass the left outside strand over 1, under 1, and over 1. Repeat from the left each time (Fig. 13).

6-Strand woven braid. This is made the same way, passing the left outside strand over 1, under 1, over 1, under 1, over 1 (Fig. 15).

6 STRAND

FIG. 15

4 STRAND

FIG. 13

5-Strand woven braid. Knot the 5 strands together and anchor to something stationary. Arrange the strands beside each other. Pass the left outside strand over 1, under 1, over 1, and under 1. Repeat from the left side each time (Fig. 14)

Flat braids

3-strand braid. This is the common braid, known to practically everybody. Knot the strands together and anchor them to something stationary for all of these. Take the outside left strand over 1, and then the outside right strand over 1. Repeat, alternating left and right (Fig. 16).

5 STRAND

FIG. 14

3 STRAND (COMMON)

FIG. 16

5-Strand braid. This is worked much like the 3 strand, only the outside strand is taken over 2 each time, instead of 1 (Fig. 17).

5 STRAND BRAID

FIG. 17

7-Strand braid. Work like the 5-strand, only take the outside strand over 3 each time. If you use different colors for practice, it is easier to keep the sequence of colors in the proper order. A pleasing chevron effect is obtained by using 4 light on one side and 3 dark on the other (Fig. 18).

CHEVRON
DESIGN

7 STRAND BRAID

FIG. 18

Cords with cores

These cords look best when made with string, macramé, threads, or anything with little or no "give" to it. The center core can be any desired thickness, usually 2 to 4 threads. Both ends of the core must be fastened so it is held straight and tight. You can anchor both ends to stationary things, or one end to something stationary, and tie a weight to the other end. Watch that it doesn't twist while you are working.

Solomon's knot. The core threads should be a little longer than the desired finished length. Use 2 threads in a contrasting color 4 times the finished length. Attach these 2 threads, one on each side of the top of the core. Bring the left strand down, and then horizontally over the core (Fig. 19). Bring the right thread down, over the end of the left thread, under the core, and out through the loop formed where the left strand bends. Pull the threads tight (Fig. 20). Repeat, using the right thread first (Fig. 21). Don't allow the core threads to twist.

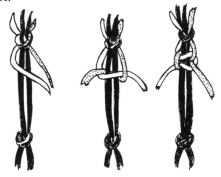

SOLOMON'S KNOT

FIG. 19   **FIG. 20**

FIG. 21

REVERSE
SIDE

Spiral Solomon's knot. Use the same amount of thread as for Solomon's knot. Tie the top end to a piece of string, and anchor the string to something stationary, because this cord will twist. Make the first knot as in plain Solomon's knot. Don't alternate left and right, but make each knot from the left. This will make the cord twist in a spiral (Fig. 22).

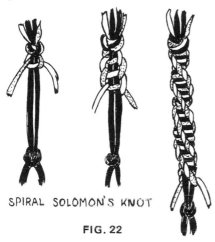

SPIRAL SOLOMON'S KNOT

FIG. 22

Double buttonhole. Make the core of 2, 3 or 4 threads slightly longer than the required length. The covering threads should be 4 times the length of the core. Attach one on each side of the anchored core. Bring the left thread down, and then under the core horizontally. Take it back over the core, and through the loop at the left (Fig. 23). Pull tight. Do the same with the right thread (Fig. 24). Continue, left and right. Don't allow the core to twist (Fig. 25).

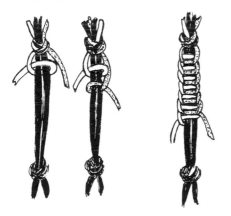

DOUBLE BUTTONHOLE

FIG. 23   FIG. 24   FIG. 25

Spiral buttonhole. The core of 3 or 4 threads is slightly longer than the desired length. Attach a string to the top knot, and anchor the string so the cord can twist. The single covering thread should be 10 times the length of the core. Bring the covering thread down the left side, under the core, back over the core and through the loop. Take it under the core, back over, and through the second loop (Fig. 26). Continue in this manner. The core will round itself, and twist so the buttonhole covering thread will form a spiral ridge (Fig. 27).

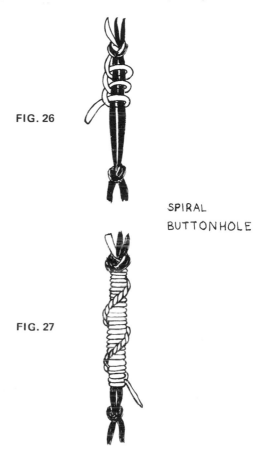

FIG. 26

SPIRAL

BUTTONHOLE

FIG. 27

False cording on embroidered boxing. There is a way to make a cording at the edge of a boxing that really isn't a cording at all. Work an extra inch on either side of the boxing, and fold it in half. Sew through the edge of the extra inch and the outside edge. The bulk of the needlework will give the appearance of a needlework-covered cording. Then, sewing through the same place, attach the boxing to your piece, using strong matching thread. (See Figs. 24 and 25, p. 57.)

Fringes

Commercial fringes are quite varied and decorative, but there are times when you'd like to make your own. Fringes are usually made with a long thread, looped through an edge or over a seam. They can be cut or left uncut. Here are a few varieties.

PLAIN FRINGE

STICK OR CARD

Plain fringe

To make the simplest fringe, pass the needle through an edge, leaving a large loop. Then make a small fastening stitch to hold it in place. Wrap the loops around a card or smooth stick to make them all the same size (Fig. 1). If you are going to leave the loops uncut, end the threads and start new ones at the top, hiding the ends. If you plan to cut the loops, do so before removing the card or stick. Trim the edge if it isn't quite even.

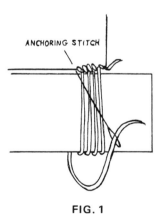

ANCHORING STITCH

FIG. 1

Knotted fringe 1

The plain fringe can be knotted, using a given number of strands in each knot (Fig. 2).

KNOTTED FRINGE I

FIG. 2

Knotted fringe 2

The strands of the fringe can be crossed, and alternating groups knotted (Fig. 3).

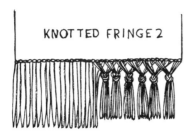

FIG. 3

Tasseled fringe

The strands of fringe can be divided into large groups, and wrapped in 2 places, forming tassels. Longer fringe will be needed for this. The ends will have to be trimmed to make them even after the tassels are made (Fig. 4).

FIG. 4

Looped fringe

Cut pieces of thread a little more than double the length needed for the fringe. Either use a crochet hook or thread each piece in a needle (Fig. 5).

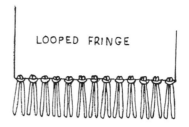

FIG. 5

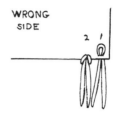

FIG. 6

Make a loop on the wrong side, with 2 even ends on the right side (1 in Fig. 6). Fold the loop down and pass the 2 ends through it (2 in Fig. 6).

Twisted fringe

Because it can't fray, twisted fringe is practical if a piece is to be laundered or will get a lot of wear. Attach a long strand at the right end of the edge. Measure double the length you want the fringe to be along the thread. Grasp it firmly, and untwist the thread until the plies are straight and parallel. Pull tight (Fig. 7). Place the forefinger of

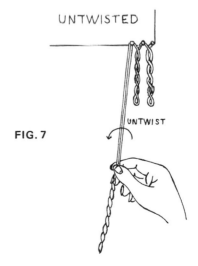

FIG. 7

your left hand across the strand, and bring your right hand up to the top (Fig. 8). Hold the strand in place while you remove your finger from the loop. It will retwist. Fasten the top of the twisted loop to the edge with a needle and thread. Repeat along the edge. Be careful to make all the loops the same size, as they can't be trimmed. If any adjustment is necessary, make it at the top. If you want a tighter twist in the loops, keep turning past the parallel point. Count the number of extra turns so all the loops will have the same number. You can also twist the yarn in the direction of the original twist. This makes very tightly twisted loops (Figs. 9, 10).

Sometimes fringes are left uncut. You can leave Plain Fringe, Knotted Fringe 1, and Tasseled Fringe uncut. If you want an uncut, looped fringe, you will have to pass the yarn around a card or smooth stick so all the loops will be the same size.

Don't limit yourself to wool yarn. Other materials make lovely fringes.

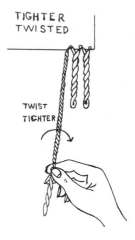

FIG. 9

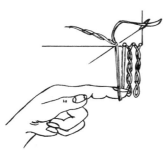

FIG. 8

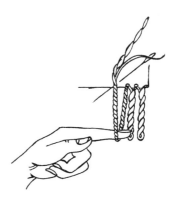

FIG. 10

Tassels and Pompons

Tassels

The conventional tassel can be made by wrapping a length of yarn around a smooth stick or a card (Fig. 1). Gather the loops together and fasten them with strong thread, either the main tassel thread or some other thread. Wrap the thread around tightly, and sew securely by passing the needle through the fastening (Fig. 2). Bring the needle out through the loops part way down from the top fastening (Fig. 3). Wrap and sew again, and bring the needle out through the top again so the end can be used to attach the tassel to your piece (Fig. 4). Cut the bottom of the loops, evening the ends, if necessary (Fig. 5). Tassels can be fastened

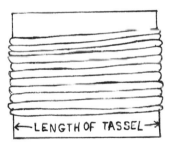

FIG. 1

NEEDLE OUT HERE

FIG. 3

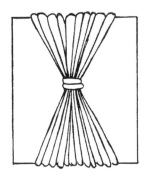

FIG. 2

FIG. 4   FIG. 5

close to the piece, or a short cord can be added so the tassel will hang down (Fig. 6).

A more decorative tassel can be made by using Pearl cotton, or other glossy yarn for the whole tassel, or just for the fastening wrappings. An additional touch of elegance can be achieved by covering the top, round part of the tassel with Buttonhole stitch (Fig. 7).

Pompons

Pompons are round fluffy tassels. Use yarn that fluffs well when cut. They can be made with a device available in art needlework departments (Fig. 8). To make a pompon with home materials, cut a "doughnut" of heavy cardboard (Fig. 9). Wrap yarn round and round, through the hole (Fig. 10). You can piece the yarn by tying on a new strand at the outside edge. Allow about 8 inches for the tie. Thread this into a needle, and pass the needle, eye first, around inside the loops,

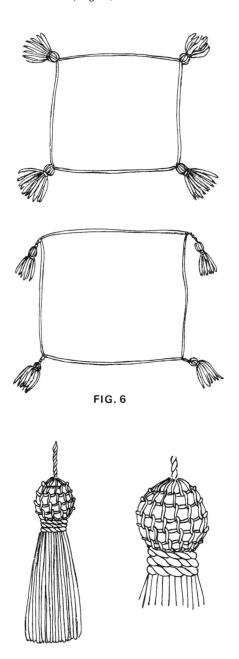

FIG. 6

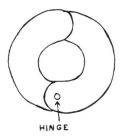

HINGE

FIG. 8

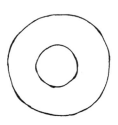

FIG. 9

FIG. 7

FIG. 10

next to the cardboard. Try not to pierce the loops (Fig. 10). Pull the loops together as tight as you can (Fig. 11). Hold the center firmly in one hand, and carefully cut all the loops (Fig. 12). Be careful not to cut the tying strand. Either cut the cardboard form away, or push the pompon through the hole. Pull the center tie tight. Sew back and forth through the center several times to anchor all the cut ends. Bring the end of the sewing tying strand to the outside to be used for fastening. Fluff the strands out by shaking and beating it against your hand. You may have to trim some of the ends to make the pompon round (Fig. 13).

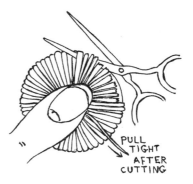

FIG. 12

FIG 11

FIG. 13

Buttons

To make your own buttons, get plastic rings. They come in several sizes. Or cut them out of a plastic milk or bleach bottle (Fig. 1). Make the hole at least ⅝ inch in diameter. An outside measurement of 1¼ inches should be maximum. Anything larger would be hard to handle. Thread the needle with enough yarn to complete the button.

Small. Wrap the ring closely with yarn, packing it firmly (Fig. 2). Sew back and forth across the hole (Fig. 3). You can fill in the space solidly, or just make spokes, like a wheel. Anchor the place where the spokes cross with a French Knot (Fig. 4). Use the end of the yarn to sew the button to your embroidery. When sewing the button to your piece, put a stitch or 2 into the back of the button so as not to depend on one strand of yarn to hold the button on.

Large. For a larger button, wrap as you did for the small one (Fig. 5). Thread the yarn into a sharp needle, and make 6 or 8 evenly placed spokes (Fig. 6). Then work a Spider Web stitch over them (Fig. 7). This makes a nice finish. After completing the Spider Web, make a stitch to get the yarn back in the center of the back of the button. When sewing the button to your piece, put a stitch or 2 into the back of the button so as not to depend on one strand of yarn to hold your button on.

If very fine canvas is used, covers can be made for fairly large button forms that have a metal

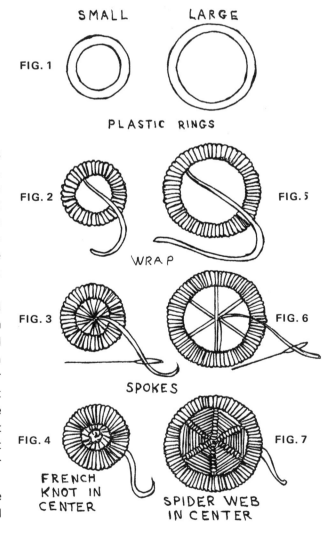

SMALL   LARGE

FIG. 1

PLASTIC RINGS

FIG. 2   FIG. 5

WRAP

FIG. 3   FIG. 6

SPOKES

FIG. 4   FIG. 7

FRENCH KNOT IN CENTER

SPIDER WEB IN CENTER

piece that clamps in the back. These are available where sewing aids are sold. They come in two types. For a button that is to be used as a closure, use the type with a shank that passes through a hole in the clamping device (Fig. 8). If the button is to be used for decoration only, the clamping part is attached to a half snap. The other half of the snap is sewed to the garment (Fig. 9).

Be sure the worked area of the canvas is large enough to come over the edges of the form, up to where the clamp is inserted, but not under the clamp (Fig. 10). Allow enough canvas so you can put 2 rows of machine stitching, one on top of the other, about ⅛ inch out in the excess canvas. Run a gathering thread through the stitching. Cut off the binding and all but ¼ inch of the excess canvas, and overcast the edges (Fig. 11). Place the form against the wrong side of the canvas, and pull up the gathering thread. You might need to sew back and forth across the back to hold the canvas in place (Fig. 12). Then follow the directions that come with the button forms.

HALF SNAP ATTACHED TO THE CLAMP

ATTACH TO GARMENT

FIG. 9

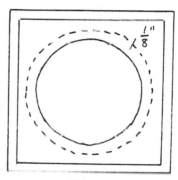

FIG. 10

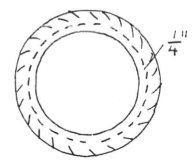

FIG. 11

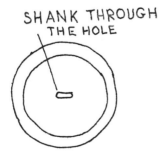

HOLE

SHANK THROUGH THE HOLE

FIG. 8

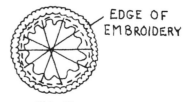

EDGE OF EMBROIDERY

FIG. 12

Loop Buttonholes

Regular Buttonhole stitch can't be used to make loop buttonholes because it would make the loop twist. This is overcome by using *Modified Buttonhole stitch.* It is made in 2 steps.

Step 1. Attach the yarn at the left end of the loop. Bring the yarn through the loop, and pass the needle under the working strand from *back* to *front* before pulling the strand tight (Fig. 1).

Step 2. Pass the needle through the loop again. This time pass the needle under the working strand from *front* to *back* (Fig. 2), and then pull it tight. Repeat these 2 motions. This produces an edge that will not twist (Fig. 3).

To make loop buttonholes, make a loop of thread, either 2 or 3 threads thick as a core. Begin and end the loop at one point. Work Modified Buttonhole stitch around the loop with the ridged edge toward the outside (Figs. 4, 5). Sometimes a small tassel is added at the outside end of the loop to make it easy to grasp.

Don't make a flat curved loop that is attached at 2 places. Any slack will allow the button to slip out (Fig. 6).

Note: Use a button and loop buttonhole instead of a snap for a closure. Home-sewed snaps look amateurish, and the gripper type can pull out. Besides, constant use can soil and wear out the lining material around the snap. A decorative button and an embroidered loop buttonhole can look quite nice.

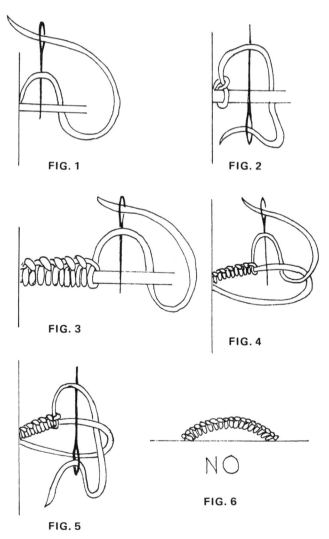

FIG. 1

FIG. 2

FIG. 3

FIG. 4

FIG. 5

FIG. 6

NO

Binding Stitch

The Binding stitch can be used to make a strong decorative edge on a rug, mat, coaster, etc. It can be used as a seam to join 2 finished pieces; for example, halves of eyeglass cases. It covers well and goes around corners readily.

The diagrams do not show the 3 dimensional quality. The needle is held in a horizontal position, pointing straight toward you, and the folded canvas is held vertically. The needle passes from back to front for all stitches.

Small size. Bring the needle out from inside the fold at 1. Pass the needle under 2 threads on the fold at 3. Back to 2, then to 4, back to 3, then to 5, etc. The sequence is 1-3, 2-4, 3-5, 4-6, 5-7, etc. (Fig. 1).

Larger size. The procedure is the same as for the small size, but the stitches are longer. The sequence is 1-4, 2-5, 3-6, 4-7, 5-8, etc. (Fig. 2).

Work out any sequence you wish to suit the weight of the yarn and the purpose of the stitch.

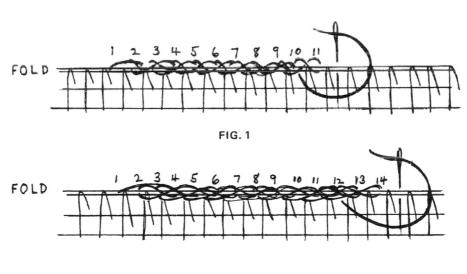

FIG. 1

FIG. 2

INDEX